THE SCIENCE OF LOGIC

THE SCIENCE OF LOGIC

EDITED BY
JOHN H. PIET
AND
AYODHYA PRASAD

COSMO PUBLICATIONS
2000 INDIA

THE SCIENCE OF LOGIC

First COSMO Print 2000

ISBN 81-7755-008-x

This indipendent and complete volume has been derived from the set -
Encyclopaedia of ETHICS AND LOGIC

Published by
MRS. RANI KAPOOR
for COSMO PUBLICATIONS Div. of
GENESIS PUBLISHING PVT. LTD.
24-B, Ansari Road,
Darya Ganj,
New Delhi-110 002, INDIA

Composed at
Cosmo Publications

Printed at
Mehra Offset Press

CONTENTS

1. The Science of Logic 1
- — The Science of Logic: its Perspective and Human Value
- — Preliminary work done in a course on Formal Logic

2. A Definition of Logic 9
- — Introduction
- — Logic as a Depth Grammar of Human Rationality
- — Logic as an Ontology of the Possible
- — Logic as the Science of Formal Truth

3. The Nature of Logical Space, of the Proposition and of Logical Operators 31
- — The Nature of Logical Space
- — The Nature of the Proposition
- — The Nature of Logical Operators

4. Logic and Subjectivity 49
- — Introduction
- — Aristotle and Leibniz
- — Wittgenstein
- — Structuralism
- — Husserl
- — Subjectivity in Contemporary Philosphy
- — Conclusion

5. Validity 71

— What about Truth Tables?
— Deductions
— A notation for Predicate Rules
— Universal Quantifier Rules
— Universal Quantifier Introduction
— Existential Quantifier Rules
— Operating with the Rules
— Logical Truth and Vanishing Premises
— Predicate, Rules and Algorithms

6. Logic and the Ideal Rational Life 107

— Introduction
— Formalization is Inherent to Rational Living
— The Limitations of Formalization
— Metaformalism as an Ideal for Rational Living
— Metaformalism and the new Logic of Framework Transpositions within Science
— General Conclusion

7. Logical Forms in the Empirical Sciences 127

— Introduction
— An historical survey of the development, structurally, of physical science and of scientific method generally
— Structure and method in the Biological and human Sciences
— The Logical forms and logical processes within empirical science

8. The Scope of Applied Logic 151

— Introduction
— Limits in the purpose and functioning of Applied Logic
— The specific contents of applied logic

9. Logical Problems in Empirical Science 161

— Introduction

— The general problem of contextual reasoning
— The problem of varification
— Probility values and truth values
— The Problem of Induction
— A general conclusion

10. Theoretical thought outside the Empirical Sciences 189

— Introduction
— Theoretical reasoning that is not subject to control and evaluation by either observation or experiment
— The Logical structure of philosophy and of philosophizing
— The use of logical techniques in formal analyses

11. Formal Detachment: Ideal or Myth? 213

— Introduction
— Michacl Polanyi
— John Henry Newman (1801-90)
— Conclusion

12. Computatinal Process Theories 233

— Definition of Process Equivalences
Finite trace equivalence
Full trace equivalence
Bisimulation
Generated graph Isomorphism
— Aximatization of Process Equivalences
— Infinitary Theory of Transition Systems
Definability of process equivalences
Scott Isomorphism Theorem
Invariance under Bisimulation
System for Bisimulation
— Special Transition systems
Finite models
Further classes of transition systems
— Process Algebra

Algebraic operations and term models
The finite graph model
From Algebras to labeled transition systems

— Safety for Process Constructions
Varieties of safety
Analyzing specific constructions
Respect for sequence extensions

— Appendix I: Modal Logic of Constructions
A modal calculus
Frame correspondences
Extended modal logic

— Appendix II: Concurrent Dynamic Logic

13. The Phenomenon of Meaning 267

— Human thought as a Fabric of Meaning and a context for phenomena of meaning
— Language as a Fabric of Meaning and a contxt for Logical Phenomena
— The structuring of meaning
— A dualism within Meaning: sense and reference
— More complex Meaning: propositional meaning
— The complexity of signification in Predicative sentences: some elemntary features
— Value as a phenomenon within Meaning
— Simple relationships between Predicative propositions

14. The Phenomenon of Implication 291

— Inference and implication
— Implications within the square of opposition
— Simple operations on predicative propositions which disclose implications: conversion, obversion, contraposition and inversion
— The crux of Inversion
Inverting an A proposition
Inverting an E Proposition

— Other simple Implications
— Complex Implications: the simple categorical syllogism
— Some exercises on the rules of the simple categorical syllogism
— Is there any real inference in the simple categorical syllogism?
— Syllogisms other than the simple categorical type
— Validity and truth in argument
— Rules of Inference
— How to analyse an argument

Chapter-1

The Science of Logic

Chapter 1

1. THE SCIENCE OF LOGIC: ITS PERSPECTIVE AND HUMAN VALUE

We are symbol-using beings. It Is this basic human fact which has created the opportunity and need for Logic. We talk and think about reality symbolically and we pore over our symbol-products in the libraries, law-courts, offices and homes of our planet. It is a common experience to scrutinize pages of printed symbols, commenting on them as a fabric of meaning in their clarity, their richness, their truth, the weight of the evidence in them, the validity of con-clusions drawn. Indeed perhaps we do not advert sufficiently to the amount of life time spent in this second-order world created by language.

This is the world in which Logic moves and such observations and discoveries as it makes are immediately concerned with the purport of symbols and symbolic expressions rather than with the physical, living human world which is first-order reality. It is not dealing with objects which *are* this or that. but with signs which *mean* or *disclose* this or that to a mind. For this reason the specific technical language of Logic is not a first-order language (an object language) referring to the world in which we live. But a second-order language which describes, and refers to, our own human symbolic talking and thinking. Of course when the logician becomes reflective about his own work (as he does in Metalogic or the Philosophy of Logic) he poses the question as to whether discoveries about the inner nature and laws of meaningful speech and thought may not be discoveries also of necessities inherent in any intelligible physical world. It is obviously possible, for instance. that in discerning what is logically contradictory we are also discerning what is physically impossible.

There are many sciences working in the world of symbols

as there are many natural sciences for first-order reality. Besides Logic there are e.g. Semiotics, Semantics, Linguistics, Grammar, Psychology. What is the specific interest and perspective of Logic? Without attempting a definition at this time (indeed this is a central question for Metalogic) we can say broadly that Logic is concerned with the most basic facts about the structuring of meaning and with necessities inherent in thought and speech which arise from the very nature of meaning Above all, the logician is concerned with the phenomenon of implication: like the physicist who is interested in gravitation and radio-activity. the logician is interested in the fact that evidence has force, gravitating our intelligence to a conclusion. that a conclusion is folded up in evidence *(plex*, a fold; hence 'implied') and falls out when we scrutinize the evidence sufficiently. Historically, this phenomenon has, one way or another, occupied a central position in Logic and it would not be a bad introductory description to say that Logic is concerned Principally, with observing and analysing varieties of implication and with formulating a theory of implication that will elucidate the phenomenon in general and will provide a logical foundation for reasoned conclusions in every area of life and science. 'There are . . . other elements in the tradition of logical teaching, but the greatest logicians of modern times have taken this as the central theme, and it seems reasonable to say that everything else in the corpus has its place there because of its connection with the main enterprise of classifying and articulating the principles of formally valid inference.' (W. and M. Kneale. *The Derdopment of Logic.* p 739).

What is the practical value of a course on Formal Logic? Intellectually in life we find ourselves doing two different things (I) employing symbols and orientating ourselves to symbolic expressions—to words, propositions. speech, print; (2) orientating ourselves—to real people and physical things. Human life requires us to combine both orientations, to respond to symbols as well as to physical nature. (using the terminology of Newman) to reach notional as well as real assents. One can say firstly, that Logic's contribution is to the symbolic side of human life, the area of notional beliefs. Indeed it used to be common to define Logic in terms of the use that could be made of it in our own personal thinking. Sample 'definitions' were: 'Logic is the science which directs the operations of the mind in the attainment of truth'. 'Logic is the science which studies the principles which should regulate human thinking', 'Logic is the science which deals with the cognitive operations of the understanding which are subservient to the estimation of evidence'. It is important to see, however. that one is not really defining or describing *the science* when one mentions secondary gains from it.

Secondly, in this age of minute analysis and of duplicating human brain work. the capacity to objectify meaning and to study in detail its structure and dynamics has become of great practical importance. Such a capacity is developed and constantly exercised, in a very generalized way. in Formal Logic. Whatever view one may have. humanly of thc type of thinking that will characterize a highly analytic computer age it is clear that the technique of analysis will draw heavily on the science of Logic.

Finally, Logic has become intimately linked with Mathematics and in this way is exercising an important influence in modern theoretical science. In the form of modern Mathematical Logic it has established its right to a position in university faculties of Science.

2. PRELIMINARY WORK DONE IN A COURSE ON FORMAL LOGIC

The science of logic began as an X-ray discipline. Its founder, Aristotle, discovered a way to display and study the basic forms of statements and arguments. Basically. his technique was to invent a simple language (or set of symbols) consisting of variables and constants: when properly translated or transformed into this symbolism a vernacular statement such as *All men are mortal* is drained of all its reference to the objective world of men and graves; only basic structural meaning appears on the X-ray plate which reads *SaP*. The metaphor of X-ray photography used in medicine and empirical science is modern, but it conveys Aristotle's insight and excitement when he realized he was the founder of a new science. Working in this X-ray, abstractive way, he was able to display and study forms more basic than those presented in the grammar of Greek speech, and he achieved powerful analyses of Greek forms of argumentation and proof.

It is the primary purpose of a preparatory section on logic (I) to make us sensitive and appreciative of the wonderful varied world of meaning that is brought into existence by human speech and thought; and (2) to cover the early X-ray work done by Aristotle in this world. The X-ray apparatus may, by modern standards, be crude; the areas of meaning X-rayed may be very simple, but they constitute the origins of the science and enable us to understand its modern format and development. Indeed Aristotle's influence on the whole history of logic has been decisive.

However, one distinctive aspect of modern logic should be noted. Logical language or symbolism was used abstractively by Aristotle to X-ray *existential* speech and argument. In modern logic this X-ray function disappears (except in Applied Logic): one designs a symbolism and then uses it constructively to make (logical) statements which can be tested and organized into systems of established logical truth. Thus while the value of logical language was displayed in the original abstractive X-ray approach of Aristotle, such a language functions now not primarily as an X-ray apparatus but primarily as a medium for *making* statements. In moving from the preparatory section to the section on formal logic in this book, one will be moving from the ancient abstractive use of a simple logical language to the modern constructive use of a more complex one.

The preliminaries of the course are concerned with bringing the student to the point where he can work with ease in a purely symbol-world, where he is alive to the varying shapes and structures of meaning and to its dynamic character. Any science that is directly concerned with symbols may provide helpful observations and topics for the student during this preliminary stage. It Is customary not only to anticipate some elementary facts and X-ray operations of Formal Logic itself but also to draw on Semantics, Linguistics, Grammar and Psychology. The objective is that phenomena of meaning will be *experienced* as observable and complex facts in life deserving technical, scientific study.

Formal Logic itself will then begin with a presentation of the special Ian guage (or symbolism) that is used today.

Chapter-2

A Definition of Logic

Chapter-2.

I. INTRODUCTION

Ultimately, what is the concern of logic? How does one define it? What precisely is its position in the corpus of human sciences? The present chapter presents two complementary descriptions ('logic is the depth grammar of human rationality'; 'logic is the ontology of the possible) as developing naturally from any substantial experience of formal logic and metalogic, and a third description ('logic is the science of formal truth') which integrates the first two in a single viewpoint.

II. LOGIC AS A DEPTH GRAMMAR OF HUMAN RATIONALITY

The metaphorical phrase, *depth grammar,* being spatial and linguistic in its root force, requires an interpretation that is exactly suited to the context of logic.

The image of a grammar and of rules can be a significant model for many contexts. We can conceive processes as regular, as actively conforming to rules in the fullest sense of this word, and can endeavour to formulate a set of rules with maximum explanatory power. This is true even of unconscious processes. In *Man* on *his Nature,* Sir Charles Sherrington writes on the development of a whole human body from a single cell and describes in some detail the coming into existence of a human eye:

> The eye's parts are familiar even apart from technical knowledge and have evident fitness for their special uses. The likeness to an optical camera is plain beyond seeking. If a craftsman sought to construct an optical camera let us say for photography, he would turn for his materials to wood and metal and glass. He would not expect to have to provide the actual motor power adjusting the focal length

> or the size of the aperture admitting light. He would leave the motor power out. If told to relinquish wood and metal and glass and use instead some albumen, salt and water, he certainly would not proceed even to begin. Yet this is what that little pin's-head bud of multiplying cells, the starting embryo, proceeds to do. And in a number of weeks it will have all....... There are not many anatomical organs where exact shape counts for so much as with the eye. Light which will enter the eye will traverse a lens placed in the right position there. *Will* traverse; all this making of the eye which *will* see in the light is carried out in the dark...And the whole structure, with its prescience and all its efficiency, is produced by and out of specks of granular slime arranging themselves as of their own accord in sheets and layers, and acting seemingly on an agreed plan. (pp.105-7)

The eye has a predetermined structure or form. So too the *visual life* that is mediated by eye and brain has a form definable in advance of the baby's birth. Seeing is a constitutional aspect of human vitality paced into being by a growing nervous system interacting with its environment. Mysteriously, the brains and retinal systems of human beings receive and actively translate patterns of light and shade so that they see, in common, objects and characteristics of the physical world. Metaphorically we may speak of the human brain observing innate rules for ordering retinal patterns in terms of objects and thus we may speak of a grammar of vision. This draws attention to the complex skilful activity involved in actually seeing (Over and above our constitutional competence) and to the fact that visual experience has a uniform structure however unique particular experience may be.

When the words, *grammar* and *rules,* are used in reference to unconscious psycho-physiological processes their primary sense must be modified of course. In using 'depth grammar' one is choosing a phrase which is strongly associated with a special linguistic theory of Noam Chomsky. In the course of presenting the primary sense of 'depth grammar' Chomsky clarifies the general concept of grammar also:

> A distinction must be made between what the speaker of a language knows implicitly (what we may call his *competence)* and what he does (his *performance*). A grammar, in the traditional view is an account for the ability of a speaker to understand an arbitrary sentence of his language and to produce an appropriate sentence on a given occasion. If it is a pedagogic grammar, it attempts to provide the student with this ability; if a linguistic grammar, it aims to discover and exhibit the mechanisms that make this achievement possible. The competence of the speaker—hearer can, ideally, be expressed as a system of rules that relate signals to semantic interpretations of these signals. The problem for the grammarian is to discover this system of rules; the problem for linguistic theory is to discover general properties of any system of rules that may serve as the basis for a human language, that is, to elaborate in detail what we may call, in traditional terms, the general *form of Language* that underlies each particular realization, each particular natural language.
>
> Performance provides evidence for the investigation of competence. At the same time, a primary interest in competence entails no disregard for the facts of performance and the problem of explaining these facts. On the contrary, it is difficult to see how performance can be seriously studied except on the basis of an explicit theory of the competence that underlies it, and, in fact, contributions to the understanding of performance have largely been by products of the study of grammars that represent competence. (*Topics in the Theory of Generative Grammar, p.73)*

The traditional aim of a grammar is to specify the class of properly formed sentences and to assign to each what we may call a *structural description* that is, an account of the units of which the sentence is composed, the manner of their combination, the formal relations of the sentence to other sentences and so on. If we hope to go beyond traditional grammar in some significant way, it is essential to give a precise formulation of the notion *structural description of* a *sentence* and a precise account of the manner in which structural descriptions are assigned to sentences by *grammatical rules.* The rules contained in a traditional grammar are of widely diversified kinds and there is no clear indication of what is to be the exact nature of a structural description. Modern linguistics has devoted a great deal of attention to clarifying the latter question, but has not considered with any seriousness the notion *grammatical rule.* Inattention to the process by which structural descriptions are generated and assigned to sentences leaves a serious gap in linguistic theory, however, and leaves open to serious doubt particular decisions about the inventory of elements in actual descriptive studies, since clearly such choices should not be independent of the complexity of the system of rules by which the structural description of each sentence is specified. In any event, it seems that a really insightful formulation of linguistic theory will have to begin by a determination of the kinds of permitted grammatical rules and an exact specification of their form and the manner in which they impose structural descriptions on each of an infinite set of grammatical sentences. *(On the Notion 'Rule of grammar',* *p.* 119)

There is a suitability in describing logic as a depth grammar. It is not concerned with performance. Psychologism distorted logic in trying to anchor it to concrete psychic life. Newman also failed to see that the claim of logic is not that it is a grammar of assent, a grammar of actual inference, but that it is a grammer of rationality. What it deals with is not how, psychically, we do think or should think but rather the quality of rationality and the nature of processes that are rationality-preserving. In this way it does reveal something of the constitutional competence that is exercised in every performance that has a rational character. Boole put it that it reveals something of the constitutional of the human mind one feels that he would have found the phrase, depth grammar, very acceptable and forceful.

Basically, it is the development (since 1930) of a natural deduction format for logic that has endered *grammar* and *depth grammar* extremely suitable images for depicting logic. As we have seen in metalogic this is arguably the format which most properly displays the character of logical truth and logical processes. It takes the medium of logical language (which since the time of Frege is not simply a set of symbols but the essential design and theory of any medium for processing rationality) and formulating natural deduction movements as rules it evolves from them the standard content of logical truth. Thus it purports to give a combined presentation of the proper medium for expressing logical truth (logical space as Wittgenstein would term this medium) and the proper format for its principles. This format is linguistict—rule, logical argument formula LAF), schema—but there is a reality signified, namely human vitality in its aspect or quality of being rational, the ultimate ground and justification of logic. What is given in logical language, in logical principles and in logical systems is a *form* of life—the rational form. And the rules are not merely 'regulative' in type, the prescriptions for a higher quality or standard of rational life but are 'constitutive'—they express and interpret in symbols something of the essence of rationality, of basic rational competence.

While using the conceptual models of grammar and rule it is of the utmost importance to be alive to the essential difference that obtains between grammar and logic, grammatical structure and logical structure, grammatical rule and logical rule. Generative grammar has rendered obsolete many comparisons which totally relativized grammar to actual language and has established itself as a fundamental study of a human competence. This is the competence to create a medium of life that 'sounds right', and 'makes sense', grammar being the study of this medium of language as a constructed, coherent, understandable entity. This medium, however, is simply a context in which the reality and phenomena studied by logic are present, and indeed it is not the only context: in the psychic medium of thought the quality of rationality is also present and rational competence exercised. It follows that a grammatical study of the medium of language is not a study of logical realities that can exist in that medium: it is the *saying* that is polished and grammatical, it is *what is said* (the thought content, the *Stoic lekton)* that is formally valid or invalid. And if logic designs a special language for itself it is precisely as a *means* to process thought content more clearly. To lake a particular example, while in ordinary life language mediates a great deal of argumentation and discussion, grammar does not study the phenomenon of implication and yet this phenomenon has beer so central in the history of logic that some (e.g. Kneale) would be prepared to define logic as the pure science of principles of involvement. Similarly, where grammatical rules guide us to a proper *use* of language and more fundamentally, formalize our innate language competence logical rules are concerned rather with the rationality that is mediated by language (and indeed may not be confined to this medium).

Of course speech and thought are in actual fact more unified than can be represented in the sciences which are inevitably highly selective in their concerns. It is interesting to note that in tradition there have been two recurring views. One links speech and thought merely by association: meaning is associated with words; words are loaded with meaning, and language is a public transport system. In the second view speech and thought are much more unified: thought is internal speech., and speech is verbal thought—an externation and elaboration of internal speech: 'I have drawn from the well of language thoughts I had not' The practice of medieval logicians was to describe logic, in terms of its dual context thought and language as a science of discourse, mental and verbal. Without rejecting this practice two medieval schools of thought grew apart through emphasis on one or other context. For one school, thought is the primary locus of logical entities and phenomena; depicting thought through the metaphor of stretching the bow and aiming the arrow in archery, a distinction was made between the first stretching *(intention)* of our minds which is to our environment (disclosing objects of the world and their attributes and expressing this disclosure through object-language) and its second-level activity or intention (focusing the conditions of being known or thinkable, the properties and features which things have when they are conceived by a mind or spoken). Second intentionality gives rise to the distinction between real and logical properties. In its first intention the mind is dealing with objects Which *are* this or that; in its second intention it is dealing with signs which *mean* this or that—its disclosures are of sign reality, and the properties and structures it discovers belong to signs which are constituted by people in the process of thinking or saying something. These properties and structures are logical and the distinction between them and real properties is basic in both Greek and medieval logical theory. Thus the first medieval view (associated with, e.g. Aquinas and strongly advocated in recent years by Veatch's *Intentional Logic*) defines logic as a science of second intentions, a study of thought not, of course, in its psychic, entitative existence but in its aspect of disclosing and signifying, of being meaningful and intentional.

The second medieval view, associated with, e.g, Occam and Buridan, sees the overt, linguistic character of logic as paramount, defining, logic as a science constructed throughout in a meta language and dealing with syncategorematic terms. It became customary to speak of these terms (our modern logical constants) as determining the form of propositions, where categorematic terms (which functioned as subjects and predicates) constituted their matter or particular reference, Bochensk—comments

Expressed in modern terms, the difference betweer

the two conceptions of logic that have been exemplified is that the first is semantic, the second syntactical for the first uses the idea of reference, the second determines logical form in a purely structural way. According to the second the *logical constants* are the subject-matter of logic, while on the view of Thomas [Aquinas] this object is their *sense*. On either view Scholasticism achieved a very clear idea of logical form and so of logic itself. *(A History of Formal Logic, p.159)*

The controversy was valuable in separating and exploring the two loci of logical phenomena, although it did not explain their unity as a dual context. Some aspects of this unity are clarified in the conception of logic as a depth grammar of rationality. Logical experience is not an experience of thought as such, or of speech as such. it is an analytic experience of rational content and rational structure. Reaching to the basics and the building blocks in meaningful thought and expression, it may be described, procedurally, as a miroscopic and genetic type of experience. Since the time of Leibniz and Frege, indeed, logicians have felt themselves in such basic contact with meaning, that they have confidently discarded the imperfect tools of vernacular languages and have created a logical language for mediating the constitution and complexification of meaning. Bertrand Russell has expressed his vivid sense of the potency of symbols, axioms and rules that are very simple and very few. In modern times this experience has been made operational: logicians have engaged in reducing areas of human enquiry and activity to simple beginnings; their experience and their projects have been foundational with regard to modern computerization. One might sum up by saying that logic has displayed systematic thought and speech as the evolution of an initial input of rationality and it has become conscious of itself as a grammar governing such evolutions.

This has tended to make the logician very much aware that one's system of thought in any context is, to an important extent, a function of elementary beliefs, schemas of reasoning and modes of expression. They may be there by choice or be assimilated culturally; they may be articulated or not, be in the focus of consciousness or never more than tacitly known. But wherever there is system, it can be displayed, analytically, as an evolution from genetic rationality.

III. LOGIC AS AN ONTOLOGY OF THE POSSIBLE

A tautology is such that it is unconditionally true, e.g. *ApNp*. Such statements are built up from variables, they do not bear a reference restriction to any particular world and their formality guarantees their truth in every context. Propositional Logic is a body of tautologies. A reference restriction governs the laws of Standard Predicate logic, however, as it presupposes that it is dealing with a non-empty world, i.e. that at least one individual exists; accordingly some of its theorems can be proved true only conditionally on the presupposition being true. Thus not all truths of standard logic are tautologies. The tendency of logic is, of course, to transcend contexts rather than to prescribe their nature in any way however general. Lesniewski indeed has devised a system contrasting with Standard Predicate Logic in not assuming the existence of any object and in being valid for an empty universe.

The concern of logic is to analyse rationality, not to tell us about a particular existing world: it does not seek to be informative in this latter sense. What ontological content then has a depth grammar of rationality? Ontological content arises from two basic facts:

Firstly, the rational *can* be real, i.e. that which in thought is not characterized by unreason can be an actual fact. Taking 'state of affairs' as any item that can be expressed in a proposition, a state of affairs is possible when, being conceptualized or linguistically described, there is no formal inconsistency, no self-cotradiction, present either explicitly or implicitly.One can analyse this understanding of possibility more basically by reference to the modal notion of, necessity equiparating 'It is possible that this state of affairs be actual' to 'It is not necessary that this state of affairs be not actual'. Real possibility is decided, then, by the presence or absence of unreason. This approach of Aristotle (in *On Interpretation,* xiii, 22b) has been the most prominent one in history down to contemporary times. It is not at all the psychologistic one of Descartes who identifies the possible with that which, psychically, is clearly and distinctly conceivable.

Secondly, the real *must be* rational. This operates as an assumption in ordinary life and in science; there are systems of metaphysics, traditional and contemporary, in which it is axiomatic; it certainly constitutes part of a faith implicit in rational living. In theoretical science, indeed, this assumption is strengthened to the point that the more rationally aesthetic a theory is the more it is favoured as giving the best understanding of facts. Dirac puts it: 'It seems to be one of the fundamental features of nature that fundamental physical laws are described in terms of a mathematical theory of great beauty and power, needing quite a high standard of mathematics for one to understand it ... The research worker, in his efforts to express the fundamental laws of Nature in mathematical form, should strive mainly for mathematical beauty.' ('The Evolution of the Physicist's Picture of Nature'; and 'The Relation between Mathematics and Physics': for full details see Bibliography, p.417 below.)

It follows that

(a) No existing world can be in conflict with the corpus of logical truth or with any fragment of it. If a world is rational it fulfils the exigencies of pure rationality (e.g. *ApNp);* if an expression is a logical truth then no genuine instantiation of it can be false.

(b) Every existing world instantiates logical laws that have absolutely no reference restriction. These are the type of laws that logic seeks to discover: as a grammar of rationality it seeks to be free of presuppositions about existence.

Thus logic has ontological content. In being a depth grammar of rationality it is positively a science of the conditions of possibility and thereby provides insight into the limits of our existing world. It is described here as an ontology of the possible, rather than as a metaphysics, to stress the fact that its knowledge is evolved not from the experience of actual being and from an analysis of the *concept of being* as, traditionally, in metaphysics but from an analysis of the quality, rationality. Guido Küng notes and follows this distinction in usage: 'We prefer to use the terms "ontology" and "metaphysics" in the sense in which metaphysics is the science making existential assertions about the different kinds of entities which ontology merely describes without deciding whether they actually exist.' *(Ontology and the Logistic Analysis of Language,* p.9, n. 30)

Celebrated passages from Wittgenstein's *Tractatus* come to mind supporting the conception of logic as an ontology of the possible:

> 4.461 Propositions show what they say: tautologies and contradictions show that they say nothing.
>
> A tautology has no truth conditions, since it is unconditionally true: and a contradiction is true on no condition.
>
> Tautologies and contradictions lack sense.
>
> 4.4611 Tautologies and contradictions are not, however, non-sensical They are part of the symbolism, just as 'O' is part of the symbolism of arithmetic.

(It is emphasized here that tautologies do not provide a new experience or particular information about the world. There is nothing extrinsic to the symbolism of a tautology conditioning its truth-value. It fulfils logical syntax but it does not have a sense referring to an actual condition of the world.)

> 6.112..The correct explanation of the propositions of logic must assign to them a unique status assign all propositions.

> 6.113..It is the peculiar mark of logical propositions that one can recognize that they are true from the symbol alone, and this fact contains in itself the whole philosophy of logic. And so too it is a very important fact that the truth or falsity of non-logical propositions *cannot* be recognized from the propositions alone.
>
> 6.1222... logical propositions cannot be confirmed by experience any more than they can be refuted by it. Not only must a proposition of logic be irrefutable by any possible experience, but it must also be unconfirmable by any possible experience.

(The propositions of logic simply do not deal with the particular world in which we live and it is not meaningful to describe our experience as evidence for or against them.)

The penetrating thought of the *Tractatus* is narrowed beyond simple acceptance, however, not only by the fact that it must be interpreted in terms of the Picture Theory, but also by Wittgenstein's passionate assumption of an un changing *a* priori order in the world and by his unsubstantiated identification of logical propositions with tautologies (The propositions of logic are tautologies. Therefore the propositions of logic say nothing.'—6.1 and 6.11). In his *Investigations*, Wittgenstein recalls, very beautifully, the earlier constricting assumption:

> Thought is surrounded by a halo. Its essence, logic, presents an order, in fact the *a priori* order of the world: that is, the order of *possibilities,* which must be common to both world and thought but this order, it seems must be *utterly simple.* It is a *prior* to all experience, must run through all experience; no empirical cloudiness or uncertainty *can be* allowed to affect it—it must rather be of the purest crystal. (97)

Noting, in his *A Companion to Wittgenstein's* Tractatus, that Wittgenstein's identification of logical propositions with tautologies is unsubstantiated and indeed inaccurate, Max Black adds:

> . . the need for known decision procedures for checking on putative logical truths is an integral and indispensable feature of Wittgenstein's philosophy of logic. For he would find it intolerable that we might understand a proposition without knowing in advance how to find out whether it was a tautology or a contradiction; he could never admit that the tautological character of a proposition might reveal itself by accident, as it were, after we had stumbled upon a proof of it. But subsequent research in logic has shown that a universal decision procedure is impossible, even in the relatively simple case of the predicate calculus. This result is fatal to Wittgenstein's philosophy of logic. It shows that any adequate account of the nature of logical truth must be more complex and more sophisticated than that contained in the *Tractaus.* (p.319)

Finally, an ontology of the possible can appear trivial only to one who conceives reality and life in a static way and is content with a purely observerculture. To one who conceives the world as evolving and who believes that in the calendar of evolution a new critical phase has arrived calling for more human control and an actively humanizing culture, this ontology of limits is of fundamental importance both in content and in the orientation and discipline it provides for thought.

IV. LOGIC AS THE SCIENCE OF FORMAL TRUTH

This description integrates the two previous ones of logic (as a depth grammar of rationality and an ontology of the possible). It requires a richly philosophical interpretation of the term 'formal' which goes back to Aristotle substantially but avoids an essential narrowness inculcated by the Greek theory of knowledge.

For Aristotle, any intelligible aspect of a thing is a form, and intelligibility is exemplified not only in physical things but also in the process of understanding them. As we sense things higher processes of cognition are brought into play. Firstly there is an act in virtue of which the object sensed appears in an intelligible perspective. This activity may be called insight. It is not the act of knowledge itself, but an activity in virtue of which the object is present intelligibly. Secondly, the mind reacts to this presence: it conceives, produces within itself, the meaning displayed in the sense-data. Actually, the mind may need many concepts to express adequately the meaning present to it in a single insight.

This mental conceiving constitutes the simplest activity of intellectual awareness: it does no include a recognition that the intelligibility conceived is that of a real object. The conscious reification of meaning, the conscious identification of intelligibility and object, is accomplished in the act of judging, the personal assertion or denial. This is a more complex act than conception but it is the simplest act that is capable of being true or false.

Conceiving and judging develop into a more complex movement of thought—inference, Structurally, inference is a movement from evidence to conclusion, a movement of the mind to new knowledge through the impetus of implication.

Thus the higher thought processes are insight, conception, judgment and reasoning. Through these processes we become *informed* about the world. They constitute a reactive vitality through which an intelligibility that is in things is duplicated mentally. An inherent narrowness in this psychological theory was that it did not explain and analyse the distinction between thought that apprehends, reactively, forms of actually existing things and thought that expresses forms but does so endogenously, i.e. with independence of what may or may not exist It was this narrowness which stirred and shaped the modern Cartesian controversy of how to prove that there is really, as we think, a world external to us. More significantly in post-Kantian times there has been a reduction of the exaggerated hellenic dichotomy in the subject object relationship; this has meant an acceptance of an essential relativization attaching to what is denoted by the terms, *knowledge* and *existence,* and an explicit study of the bipolar nature of each.

The narrowness of the mirror theory of knowledge confines Aristotle's philosophy of firm to the range of abstracted forms but does not otherwise diminish its validity. For him (in the reactive context of knowing actual things as they are) one and the same intelligibility (form) is in an external thing, materially, and in an understanding person mentally. It is in the thing as that which it is; it is in the person as the content, the meaning, of his idea. A form or plan which is materialized, in, e.g. this individual Ford motor-car, has been conceived mentally in the mind of a trained mechanic: the real metal object *is* a Ford motor-car; the consciousness of the mechanic *discloses* to him all that is intelligible about such a car; The Ford Manual of Instructions makes the same disclosure available to the reading public.

In reactive conception not only is there formal identity, there is knowledge also, i.e. not only is the mental from one which is also real, it is essentially a disclosure of the real form: it means it, signifies it. The idea of a Ford car is not itself a Ford car, rather it is a disclosure of what a Ford car is. In the judgment indeed one proceeds to state that the real is as one conceives it to be and accordingly the values true or false may be put on one's judgment.

In contrast with reactive thought, a natural deduction system is worked cut without reference to any particular world. It is endogenous rather than reactive in character: it is the most generalized reaction to facticity; it seeks to discover and to follow the evolution of principles of rationality; the type of truth it readies is not what is *so actually* in our world but what *cannot be otherwise in any world.* Its forms are forms of the possible. Mapping them on to reality we may say that they are the logical scaffolding of the real world in respect to the conditions of possibility that are relevant to it and which it, accordingly, fulfils.

Ideally, logic probes the most universal laws of intelligibility and *these* laws apply to every rational world as formal truths of it. Humanly, of course, sections and systems of logic may make some ontological commitments, however general, and so their law: are formal truths not of any world as rational but of a type of world. The limiting description may be wide and generic, such as modern Predicate Logic's commitment to deal only with a non-empty world, a world with at least one individual in it. On the other hand it may be quite narrowing as in the abstractive logic of Aristotle. However, the tendency of logic is to discover such formal truths as evolve from principles of reason. Ontological commitment is kept at the minimum that is technically possible at a particular time, technical possibilities being determined by the design of the language used and the range of operations available. The freer a system is from ontological presupposition the m6re perfectly formal are its truths. It is an accurate summary of the history of logic to say that it has always been tending towards the objective of being a corpus of perfectly formal truths, i.e. of propositions which are such that what they say is so and can be seen to be so purely on the basis of principles that govern intelligibility.

In the *Tractatus* Wittgenstein gives a penetrating analysis of how tautologies are formal truths:

6.113 It is the peculiar mark of logical propositions that one can recognize that they are true from the symbol alone, and this fact contains in itself the whole philosophy of logic. And so too it is a very important fact that the truth or falsity of non-logical propositions *cannot* be recognized from the propositions alone.

> 6.12 The fact that the propositions of logic are tautologies shows the formal—logical—properties of language and the world.

(The tautological character of given combinations of symbols shows that reality what is so is being known in formal aspects which belong to it.)

> 6.124 The propositions of logic describe the scaffolding of the world, or rather they represent it. They have no 'subject-matter' ... It is clear that something about the world must be indicated by the fact that certain combinations of symbols—whose essence involves the possession or a determinate character—are tautologies. This contains the decisive point. We have said that some things are arbitrary in the symbols that we use and that some things are not. In logic it is only the latter that express: but that means that logic is not a field in which *we* express what we wish with the help of signs, but rather one in which the nature of the natural and inevitable signs speaks for itself. If we know the logical syntax of any sign-language, then we have already been given all the propositions of logic.
>
> 6.1251 Hence there can *never be* surprises in logic.

Thus given as contingent facts that we *think* things and *say* things, and given the tautological possibilities of thought and language it is clear that what-is-so (reality) has formal aspects and that the limits of our knowledge of these aspects derives from the limits of the language we use. Max Black sums up Wittgenstein's position:

> The 'connexion' of logic with the world is an identity of logical form, and has nothing to do with the contingent features distinguishing the actual world from the other possible worlds that might have existed in its place. That is why *we* do not express anything by means of logical propositions: the substance of the world shows *itself* through them (6.124 g). And that is why there can be no surprises in logic (6.125 1); for in order to he surprised, we must entertain suppositions that *turn out* to be false. The language of 'surprise' and 'discovery' is appropriate in the natural sciences, where contingent falsifications sometimes clash with reasonable expectations; in logic there is nothing to be expected and nothing to cause disappointment or produce gratification. *(A Companion to Wittgenstein's Tractus, p.30)*

It is an index of the rich philosophy of form in Aristotle that we find in it a philosophic counterpart to Gödel's demonstration that arithmetic, and any formal system which requires it, is necessarily incomplete. For Aristotle only a system confining itself to formal aspects of reality can be complete: a formal system cannot deal with the material quantitative as such and be complete. The reason is that material things are not totally formal; we cannot conceive and duplicate in our minds the basic individuality of anything for this individuality is unique and incommunicable while a concept has a universal meaning and is applicable to many. Material reality is not completely conceptualizable therefore; it is not totally formal. Thus no corpus of formal truth can contain complete knowledge of it. It is the core of Aristotle's Hylomorphic (Matter-Form) Theory that each material extended thing has two irreducible aspects: (1) the aspect of being this individual which one can designate by pointing or by the pronoun 'it' (considered exclusively in this aspect a material thing is named Primary Matter by him); (2) the aspect of being intelligible in ways that are common to other things (considered exclusively in this aspect a material thing is a complex of forms, its basic intelligibility being named its essence).

The data investigated by logic is form—not as materially existent in individuals but in its generalized state as content of thought and language. In this generalized state form is properly described as rationality. The truths logic reaches evolve from principles that govern intelligibility; accordingly they refer to what can be what can not be otherwise rather than what actually is unless (as, e.g. in predicate logic) it confines itself, in however general a manner, to our particular world.

Not only is logic a corpus of formal truths, these truths at the same time elucidate the principles and evolution of such truth. As Boole notes: 'In one respect, the science of Logic differs from all others; the perfection of its; method is chiefly valuable as an evidence of the speculative truth of its principles.' (Preface to *The Mathematical Analysis of Logic)* Thus logical truths permeate every other discipline and science as rules of general intelligibility by which movements are made from evidence to conclusion in particular contexts; they govern implication, conflict, compatibility and subordination of meaning everywhere.

We find in the human vitality of thought not simply the power to be intelligible but the power to conform, in its intelligibility, to what can be, what cannot be otherwise, and what is. This is a power consciously exercised, possessing the quality of commitment and assertion, and so patient of the values, true and false. Humanly, it is the function of logic to exercise this vitality in the context of general intelligibility and in accordance with its principles; it is the science of formal truth.

Chapter-3

The Nature of Logical Space, of the Proposition and of Logical Operators

Chapter-3

I. THE NATURE OF LOGICAL SPACE

In its primary sense the word, space, is grounded in the fact that material things are extended, spread out, and that the total extension of the universe may be *viewed, mentally,* as forming a container for the individual objects. The force of the word consists not in conveying that there is anything over and above individual objects and their quantities but in fashioning a medium in which we can talk and reason about various interrelationships, of, e.g. place and magnitude. One might reasonably interpret the word as expressing the set of possibilities of such interrelationships.

The phrase, logical space, maintains contact with the primary sense of the word, space. It denotes a medium brought into existence by rational thought and by logical language which is specially designed to mediate the systematic presence of thought content. It is only thought content that cm be expressed and brought into this medium and the interrelationships in which it stands there are all logical ones.

Together, Frege and Wittgenstein provide a clear general idea of the genesis and nature of logical space. In introducing his special logical notation Frege says:

> The most reliable way of carrying out a proof, obviously, is to follow pure logic, a way that, disregarding the particular characteristics of objects depends solely on those laws upon which all knowledge rests. Accordingly, we divide all truths that require justification into two kinds, those for which the proof can be carried out purely by means of logic and those for which It must be supported by facts of experience... Now when I came to consider the question to which of these two kinds the judgments of arithmetic belong, I first had to ascertain how far one could proceed in

arithmetic by means of inferences alone, with the sole support of those laws of thought that transcend all particulars. My initial step was to attempt to reduce the concept of ordering in a sequence to that of *logical* consequence, so as to proceed from there to the concept of number. To prevent anything intuitive *[Anschauliches]* from penetrating here unnoticed, I had to bend every effort to keep the chain of inferences free of gaps. In attempting to comply with this requirement in the strictest possible way I found the inadequacy of language to be an obstacle; no matter how unwieldy the expressions I was ready to accept, I was less and less able, as the relationships became more and more complex, to attain the precision that my purpose required. This deficiency led me to the idea of the present ideography. Its first purpose, therefore, is to provide us with the most reliable test of the validity of a chain of inferences and to point out every presupposition that tries to sneak in unnoticed, so that its origin can be investigated. That is why I decided to forgo expressing anything that is without significance for the *inferential sequence* ... I called what alone mattered to me the *conceptual content* [*begrifflichen Inhalt*]. Hence this definition must always be kept in mind if one wishes to gain a proper understanding of what my formula language is. That, too, is what led me to the name 'Begriffsschrift'. Since I confined myself for the time being to expressing relations that are independent of the particular characteristics of objects, I was also able to use the expression 'formula language for pure thought'...

The mere invention of this ideography has, it seems to me, advanced logic. I hope that logicians if they do not allow themselves to be frightened off by an initial impression of strangeness, will not withhold their assent from the innovations that, by a necessity inherent in the subject matter itself, I was driven to make. These 'deviations from what is traditional find their justification in the fact that logic has hitherto always followed ordinary language and

> grammar too closely. *(Begriffsschrjft. a formula language, modelled* upon *that of arithmetic, for pure thought,* Preface*).*

What Frege sought to provide was a language, the grammatical use of which would, of itself, show up logical relationships and certify validity. Using terms derived from leibniz he emphasized that his language was not simply a *calculus ratiocinator* translating into formulas but requiring to be supplemented by intuitive reasoning; *it was* a *lingua characterica* directly and immediately appropriate to displaying thought contents in logical relationships:

> My intention was not to represent an abstract logic in formulas, but to express a content through written signs in a more precise and clear way than it is possible to do through words. In fact, what I wanted to create was not a mere *calculus ratiocinator* but a *lingua characterica* in Leibniz's sense. (Ueber den Zweck der Begriffsschrift, 1882). *(Ueber den" Zweck der Begriffsschrift,* 1882)

In brief, the use of such a language brought thought content into a medium which made it readily subject to logical experience. Speaking picturesquely, it gives thought contents their situations in logical space. It is not likely that Frege would have objected to this metaphor which is a dominating one in Wittigenstein's *Tractatus.* Commenting on the origin of the metaphor, Max Black says:

> The basic ideas are suggested by the systems of representation used in 'coordinate geometry'. Any material particle, occupying a point in physical space, can be located, in a way that has become commonplace since Descartes introduced the technique, by means of a set of three numerical coordinates (e.g. by the distances of the point from three fixed lines, the 'axes of references'). Wittgenstein thinks of each point in physical space as a possibility the possibility—of the existence of a material particle at that position. Similarly, he conceives of an elementary proposition as an atomic possibility—a 'point' or 'position' or

'place' (ein *Ort)* in a *logical* space: the proposition is the possibility of the corresponding atomic fact. According to this conception, logical space is the ordered system of all atomic situations. The 'logical coordinates' of a proposition ought therefore to be a set of specifications sufficient to determine the proposition's sense..... An important implication is the inseparability of a proposition from the 'logical space' in which it is located (3.42). The proposition's logical relations partially determine its sense and are not something superadded when the proposition combines with other propositions in truth-functions. (A *Companion to Wittgenstein's Tractaus, pp. 154-5)*

Just as a solid body denies the use of the space it occupies to any other body, so a proposition may be said to occupy all points of, logical space at which it excludes something incompatible with it. Thus if there were only three elementary propositions (*p,q,r*) in logical space, the proposition *Apq* would occupy the two points *KKNpNqr* and *KKNpNqNr* (there would be a total of eight points, each being a conjunction in which each elementary proposition or its negation occured). Wittgenstein expresses his point as follows:

4.463 The truth-conditions of a proposition determine the range that it leaves open to the facts.

(A proposition, a picture, or a model is, in the negative sense, like a solid body that restricts the freedom of movement of others, and, in the positive sense, like a space bounded by solid substance in which there is room for a body.)

A tautology leaves open to reality the whole—the infinite whole—of logical space: a contradiction fills the whole of logical space leaving no point of it for reality. Thus neither of them can determine reality in any way.

4.464 A tautolgy's truth is certain; a proposition possible, a contradiction's impossible,

For Wittgenstein there is one logical space for what can

be called 'the world', 'thought' and language' The making intelligible which in lanuage effects is a verbalization alike of real possibility and of mental conception. The 'logos' of our language is the 'logos' of the world and the 'logos' of thought. One cannot be and one cannot adopt an intelligible position in thought or language, without being in logical space, subject to its relations. The form of logical space brought into human existence by the design and development of a logical language gives us access also to the structure both of the world and of thought:

> 5.6. *The limits' of my language* mean the limits of my world,
>
> 5.6 .1. Logic pervades the world: the limits of the world are also its limits.

Thus just as one could interpret the word, 'physical space', as expressing the set of possible relations generated by quantitative existence, so one could interpret 'logical space' as the set of relations generated in intelligible existence, intelligibility being exemplified in the world, thought and language.

To sum up the comparison between physical space and logical space: It is quantified things that are situated in physical space; the kind of things in logical space are propositions: thus 'proposition' is *the* logical universal, the summum genus, and propositional logic is the basic section of the science.

Wittgenstein writes:

> 5.47.One could say that the sole logical constant was what *all* propositions, by their very nature, had in common with one another.
>
> But that is the general propositional form.
>
> 5.471. The general propositional form is the essence of a proposition.
>
> 5.4711 To give the essence of a proposition means to give the essence of all description, and thus the essence of the world.
>
> 5.472 The description of the most general propositional

form is the description of the one and only general primitive sign in logic.

In physical space a place is the inner surface of surrounding bodies; this surface is made possible and determined by the quantified nature of all the bodies. Correspondingly, the logical place of a proposition is the set of propositions incompatible with it: they are excluded by it, are outside it, diminish its range, box it in. such a place is *indicated by the* nature of the sign construct expressing the proposition and of course, is ultimately *determined* by the sense of the proposition itself. Finally, spatial relationships are intuited in the course of ordinary sense-experience; logical relationships (the relation ships of logical space) are experienced best in the course of designing logical language, of forming sign-constructs and of making systematic calculations.

Thus our appreciation and experience of logical space, and of the situations and relationships in it, requires (a) a grasp of the signs and sign constructs which characterize linguistic competency in logic; and (b) a grasp of the conceptual content which is formalized and processed in logical sentence construction and logical calculation.

Examining modern logical notation we are confronted immediately with the need of a theory of the proposition, explaining what is formalized by the propositional variable and with the need also of a theory of the operators which are formalized by, e.g. connectives, quantifiers and predicates.

II. THE NATURE OF THE PROPOSITION

Any thought-content which has the form of a potential truth-claim is a proposition. Traditionally, logic has always been concerned with the fact that in our speech and in our thought we can achieve an intelligibility that is appraisable also as a truth-claim. It has not concerned itself with all forms of thought or meaning, e.g. with those that constitute prayers, commands, exclamations. Its notation is such that the grammatical formation of complex meaning is always the processing of a potential truth-claim and the propositional variable conceived as formalizing the type of entities which are such claims. Thus, technically in calculation, the values which can be substituted for propositional variables are required to possess an invariant aspect of being potential truth-claims.

How is that a proposition is in a principle capable of being asserted, capable of being appraised as true or false? The reason is twofold: firstly, since form (intelligibility) characterizes language and thought as well as reality, a proposition cannot fail to express that which is possible or impossible, actual or non-actual; secondly, since linguistic forms and thought forms are also intentional (i.e. are disclosures), of their nature they can become the content of actual truth-claims. Thought-content is complete and propositional through possessing and disclosing form.

A further characteristic of the proposition is that it can be the object of many attitudes: I can be certain that *p* is the case, doubt it, opine it, assert it, deny it, believe it, be convinced of it, be sceptical of it, assume it, suppose it, surmise it. Indeed propositions exist only in so far as they are brought into existence by psychic and linguistic processes and they are arrived at by analysis of the end results of these processes. However, a study of, e.g. belief is very different from a study of thought content. This is evident in the contrast between a grammar of assent such as Newman's classic, and a grammar of rationality, such as a modern standard logic. It is evident also in the impossibility of applying Standard logical rules to belief statements: granted that 'John believes that *'the Prime Minister of England* is *going to visit America* it does not follow that John believes that *Mr Heath* is *going to visit America';* the familiar rule of substitution cannot be applied to propositions which are linked indisolubly to a belief co-ordinate so that actual equivalence is not sufficient for substitution unless the believer is aware of it. These facts justify the use of a judgment-stroke before theses in logic to signify (a) that one is not dealing with the sign-structure but with its thought-content (we have seen already that the sign-structure of itself does not express anything, it must be thought; the symbolism itself is not the proposition); and (b) that one is not subsuming it under any attitude but that of an actual truth-claim. Interpreted in this way the judgement stroke makes explicit facts that must otherwise be taken for granted. This seems to be essentially the point of Frege's symbol |–. He says, in *Begriffsschrift*:

> If we *omit the* small vertical stroke at the left end of the horizontal one, the judgment will be transformed into a *mere combination of ideas [Vorstellungsverbindung]* of which the writer does not state whether he acknowledges it to be true or not... *The horizontal stroke* that is part of the sign |– combines the signs that follow *it into a totality, and the affirmation expressed* by *the vertical stroke at the left end of the horizontal one refers to this totality* let us call the horizontal stroke the *content stroke* and the, vertical stroke the *judgment stroke.* The content stroke will in general serve to relate any sign to the totality of the signs that follow the stroke. *Whatever follows the content stroke must have a content that can become a judgement.* (As in *From Frege to Gödel*, pp.11-12)

It is quite arguable that in setting out logical formulae as theses in a system and numbering them as such we render a symbol such as Frege's judgement—content stroke redundant, but Wittgenstein seems to underrate rich facets of its significance when he writes:

> Frege's 'judgment-stroke' |– is logically quite meaningless: in the works of Frege (and Russell) it simply indicates that these authors hold the propositions marked with this sign to be true. Thus |– is no more a component part of a proposition than is, for instance, the proposition's number. It is quite impossible for a proposition to state that it itself is true. (*Tractatus*, 4.442)

With Frege, proposition is conceived and symbolized as

thought-content that can be appraised as true or false; it may function as content in many personal attitudes but these of logic process it in the simple attitude of assertion or actual truth claim.

III. THE NATURE OF LOGICAL OPERATORS

Thought-content combines the feature of disclosing intelligibility with that of being intelligible in itself. From the matter aspect it presents itself as a unity which is explained in terms of formative processes that have been called, metaphorically, operations. We have no direct experience of such processes; indeed conclusions about the existence and nature of the proposition itself are reached only through reflection on our thought life and through analysis of it. We postulate logical operations to explain the formation of thought content (which it is the business of logical language to process Accordingly our belief in them and our theory of them must be mediated by our experience of the symbols we invent and the sign-constructs which we constitute to express thought.

Logical language presents propositions in and through its wff's and distinguishes specific wff's as *C*-statements, *K* statements, predicative statements, existential statements, modal statements, etc. This suggests that propositions have specific formations also and the word *operation* is used, to be not both (i) the formative construction of specific wff's; and (ii) the specific formation of the thought-content signified: 'operation' in this letter sense is a conceptual construct, a theory grounded in our experience of logical language which is precisely expressive of proportions. A theory the general propositional form (i.e. of the generic form of all propositions) focuses, as we have seen, the invariant feature that all propositions have of being intentional and thereby potential truth-claims. The Term *operator* connotes any element deemed to be used fromatively in making logical sense, general or specific—e.g. (at the level of propositional *signs*) connectives such as C,K, etc. quantifiers, predicate-letters.

It must always be remembered that a wff has meaning only in use (i.e. only when it is thought by writer, speaker, reader or hearer does it actually signify) and that therefore, of itself, it is not actually expressive of thought. It is interesting to note St. Augustine's observation (*De Magistro*) that rational thought cannot be fully exposed in any formal system, that no sign by which a person communicates his thought can make us understand without a personal effort of understanding on our part. In *The Blue Book* Wittgenstein says :

> It seems that there are *certain definite* mental processes bound up with the working of language, processes through which alone language can function. I mean the processes of understanding and meaning. The signs of our language seem dead without these mental processes; and it might seem that the only function of the signs is to induce such processes, and that these are the things we ought really be interested in....we are tempted to think that the action of language consists of two parts, which we may call understanding these signs meaning them, interpreting them, thinking. These latter activities seem to take place in a queer kind of mechanism, the mind; and the mechanism of the mind, the nature of which it seems, we don't quite understand, can bring about effects which no material mechanism could. (p.3)

Indeed between the *Tractatus* and the *Investigations* Wittgenstein moved, in his understanding of language, from a conception of it as (merely) a system of signs (*zeichensprache*) to the con-ception of it as intentional thought, a disclosure of world (*Hermeneutik*) and his objective became one of surmounting the traditional dualism of signs and meaning, language and thought. This objective is widely shared today and marked it entirely natural to construct a theory of logical operations and logical operators *vis-à-vis* thought-content that is grounded in our experience of the linguistic role and behaviour of *C*, *K*, etc. for in thinking and uttering, e.g. *Cpq* the thought-content is formed indissoulbly with the sentence.

Certainly as one ranges over the main sections of logic the wff's present meaning in a variety of formations. There is truth-functional meaning, formed by the connectives; predicative meaning, formed simply by the predicator and complexified in generality by the quantifiers; modal meaning, formed by the modal operators; and many-valuate meaning, formed by operators whose force is defined otherwise than by truth-tables. In wff the function of variables is of course not formal at all; the functor or operator is the formal way by which we both isolate a thought-content and also express it. The more technically precise, in definition, an operator is, the more clearly present in the specific thought content. An operator need not have a special sign, however; in a predicative sentence logical language symbolizes predicate and argument but not predication (in virtue of which there actually is a predicate and an argument)—it simply juxtaposes predicate—letter and argument conveying in this way that they are now formed into a predicate argument unity,

One may categorize and analyse the main operators appearing in logical systems as follows:

(a) Truth functional operators. The kind of meaning brought into existence by truth-functional formation is such that its truth-value is always a specific function of the truth values of the constituent propositions. Of course, strictly speaking the proposition *Cpq* is a unit and the propositions symbolized *p* and *q* do not exist as such. For the purpose of testing and displaying the truth functional relationships one has to analyse it into constituents. Logical operation is a metaphor for formation in the strictest sense of the world: if one likes to use the Aristotelian model of latter from and echo the medieval traditional one can speak of *p* and *q* as potential matter for formations symbolized by *Cpq*, *Apq*, *Kpq*, etc.

(b) The predicator and the quantities. Eliminating the verb of existence modern notation has achieved a clear simplicity in the representation of predication, e.g. *Fa*, and of generality within predication e.g. *(x) Fx, (Ex) Fx*. There is a welcome departure also from grammatical symbolism, and generality is displayed as formation,the function *Fx* being incomplete potential material for generalization. It may be tempting to view atomic thought content or meaning as being universally predicative. One must remember however that linguistic scholars are not satisfied that all peoples do use their natural language in this topic-comment way. Further, the tradition of logic has always avoided reductionism here. It has been predominantly concerned with that which has significance for the inferential sequence (Frege) and in this context what is basic about every proposition is its character as a potential truth-claim. This basic characteristic does not presuppose a further single basic formation of meaning as is evidenced by the fact that propositional logic functions as the fundamental section of logic.

(c) The negator. Negation is of fundamental importance it is a remarkable fact that of all the possible statements we can make about the world one half of them is false, for given any meaningful statement we can always form another statement which together with it exhausts logical space. Negation is not (like denial) a psychological event: as Frege pointed out, in criticism of psychologistic interpretations, it is not the opposite of assertion, but rather is formative of the asserted proposition. Being positive or negative is a feature of meaning and is quite distinct from being true or false which is a feature of *correspondence* between meaning and the facts meant. A positive statement can be denied and can be false; a negative statement can be asserted and can be true. Testing a theory by the method of falsification, by focusing and trying to establish its negation, shows the human importance of negations within logical space.

There is of course no negation in physical space and this gives rise to the need of explaining its significance in logical space. For Plato the force of negating a statement is to both reveal its meaning and to express otherness to it: all forms of meaning refer to facts and opposing forms refer to different facts. He was adhering to Parmenides, principle: 'you will not find thought without being, in whose presence it is uttered'. Technically, for him the 'not' in 'that is not true' is governing the predicate-term rather than forming the proposition as a whole.

The problem of explaining true negative statements is recurring one in history, discussed in ancient times not only by the Greeks but also by Indian logicians who spoke of 'negative facts', and in modern times by a line of philosophers and logicians before wittgenstein: Frege, Meinong, Peirce, Russell, Husserl, Moore. Wittgenstein's analysis was very penetrating: of itself negation does not represent anything in reality: 'My fundamental idea is that the "logical constants" are not representatives; that there can be no representatives of the *logic* of facts.' (*Tractatus* 4.0312) Negation is not something that occurs in the world: it is an operation mapping out the area of logical space. While not providing a new experience of reality it does form and order a content of our thought about reality. Some modern philosophers, such as the Phenomenalist Paul Ricoeur, would put it that negation is not part of the given, it is contributed by spirit in the world: 'To know being is not merely to let it appear, it is to shape it intellectually, to order it, to utter it.' Yet negation has a referential force: Wittgenstein speaks of it as casting a shadow on the world:

> That shadow which the picture as it were casts upon the world: How am I to get an exact grasp of it?
>
> Here is a deep mystery.
>
> It is the mystery of negation: This is not how things are, and yet we can *say* how things are *not*. (Note-books, p.30)

P and *N*p lead us to the same state of affairs; they have sense through presenting different possibilities and the stare of affairs verifying the asserted proposition falsifies its negation and vice versa. The existence of the state of affairs is a positive fact; its non-existence is a negative fact. Exactly the same investigation tests both propositions:

> 2.04 The totality of existing states of affairs is the world.
>
> 2.05 The totality of existing states of affairs also determined which states of affairs do not exist.
>
> 2.06 The existence and non-existence of states of affairs is reality. (we also call the existence of states of affairs a positive fact, and their non-existence a negative fact) (*Tractatus*)

P and *Np* determine the situation of each other in logical space for they totally exclude each other and thereby surround each other. Thus together they map a state of affairs on to logical space, its logical place being determined according to whether it verifies the positive or then negative proposition:

> 4.064 Every proposition must *already* have a sense: it cannot be given a sense by affirmation. Indeed its *sense* is just what is affirmed. And the same applies to negation, etc.
>
> 4.0641 One could say that negation must be related to the logical place determined by the negated proposition.
>
> The negating proposition determines a logical place *different* from that of the negated proposition.
>
> The negating proposition determines a logical place with the help of the logical place of the negated proposition. For it describes it as lying outside the latter's logical place.
>
> The negated proposition can be negated again, and this in itself shows that what is negated is already a proposition and not merely something that is preliminary to a proposition.
>
> 4.1.Propositions represent the existence and non-existence of states of affairs. *(Tractatus)*

In summary, negation is a logical operation, a formation of thought content; it is characterized by revaluing the meaning of the corresponding positive proposition in a formative act which reverses that meaning. It is the resulting proposition as a whole *(Np)* which is negative in form and so performs the function of negating.

(d) Operators in class-calculus and in many-valued logic. Symbols that appear in calculi or logic as functors do not all signify logical operations or logical operators. In e.g. class calculi sign-constructs fall under two main categories: (1) Names of complex classes generated by Boolean operations on simple classes, e.g. '$a + b$', '$a \times b$'. The operation here is not formative of a proposition and so is not a logical one. The unit constructed is, of course, valuable in class calculation. (2) Statements which chart class space by expressing various possible relationships between classes, e.g. '$a= b$', '$a \neq$o'. Here the statements are, in their propositional form, predicative, i.e. this is their form as disclosures, the form through which they mean or say something at all and which grounds their appraisablilty as true or false. The Boolean relationships of class equality or inequality are material or facts expressed through the propositional form of predication: the signs, = and ≠, formalize and represent non-intentional relationships. They are not logical, i.e. processes postulated to explain the formation of a disclosure as such; rather, they construct the stated relationships i.e the relationships which we mean, say, intend.

Similarly, in many-valued logic, statements are always subject to bivalent evaluation because the operators which form them as propositions are logical, two value ones; what many-value Operators construct is non intentional relationships. In many valued logic a *C*-statement asserts a proposition or thought-content which is joined by the *C*-operator. In many-valued logic the symbol *C* is defined in a framework other than the propositional one of appraisability as true or false; as an operator it is a principle of construction for non-intentional relationships which require to be expressed through logical forms such a predication. A logical operation is one whose whole being consists in forming a disclosure, i.e. an intentional sign which means, discloses, says something. Its origin or ground is in rationality: it is a form of life, specifically of rational competence to think and say something. What is referred to in the disclosure, the *matter* of the disclosure (to use an Aristotelian and medieval image) may be abstract, e.g. mathematical facts. Such facts too have their own construction and symbolic representation; the non-intentional operations which form the sign-constructs may be Boolean, or many-valued, etc.

(e) Modal operators. The operations postulated to explain modal propositions *(Lp, Mp, Up, Zp)* are logical but in a complex sense of the word *logical.* In *Lp* (it is necessary that *p*) the proposition as truth claim is certified in a special way, i.e. as being necessarily so: *Lp* signifies a proposition under the specific certificate of logical necessitation. Other certifications are of impossibility *(LNp* or *Up),* simple compatibility with necessitation *(NLNp* or *Mp)* and of falling under neither necessitation nor impossibility (*KNLNpNLp*). Clearly, modal operators presuppose formed propositional meaning they are not postulated as logical operators in the direct, primary sense of the term; what they specify is the *form* of assertion. Since the phenomenon of implication of necessitation in the context of meaning, is a central concern of logic modal operators are *material* which it is the direct concern of logic to study. Thus a modal proposition presupposes *formations* of both the proposition and its assertion which in their different senses, are called logical operations.

Chapter-4

Logic and Subjectivity

Chapter 4

I. INTRODUCTION

With Frege modern logic succeeded in moving explicitly and completely away from the influence of a Psychologistic perspective which, for over two hundred years, had stunted its growth and distorted its work. It has not succeeded however in achieving a self-concept which defines the relationship between logic and subjectivity, the link between the science and the life of the human person. Indeed on the whole a fear of being psychologistic seems to have operated against a development of this aspect of the philosophy of logic. For the general philosophies of such logicians as Aristotle and Leibniz might be expected to stimulate interest in this matter, as might also contemporary person-centred philosophies, the movements of Phenomenology and Structuralism, and the development of Wittgenstein's thought between the *Tractatus* and the *Investigations.*

II. ARISTOTLE AND LEIBNIZ

For Aristotle, reality is not totally formal. If we use the word, interiority, for that in the individual thing which is furthest away in our knowledge of it, then the most interior aspect of every material thing is its subjectivity. One can 'imitate' the forms of an individual, i.e. reproduce them in the psychic medium of thought through a perfect understanding of them, but one cannot conceive deep subjectivity which is in composition with from but is, in itself, formless—unique, rationally inimitable, incommunicable. This subjectivity is the supposit of predications, designated by the pronoun, *it,* and dignified in the case of human beings with the use of personal pronouns I, *you, he, she.*

Leibniz accepted this pluralistic conception of the world as one of myriads of subjectivities. Predication, the subject-form structure in which we most frequently express our awareness of the world, was important evidence for it. Indeed Leibniz conceived the world to be so truly represented in predication (where the subject *has* all its predicates, comprehending all the predications that can be possibly made of it) that, in his monadology, he endeavours to see the vast changing universe as interiorized in subjectivities—in pre-established generative grammars of activity that were private but harmonious. He used the word, *monad,* to designate subjectivity; everything is condensed and collected in monads: to apply metaphorically the language of his differential calculus, each monad is an integral embracing an unending series of characteristics and events as differentials. Phenomenal development (like predication) is rational through and through, concentrated in antecedently given rules of the monads, nothing happens without a reason and so the science of logic is the analytic mirror of universal rationality.

The general philosophies of Aristotle and Leibniz invite us, then, to consider logic, depth grammar of rationality, as *a form* of life, essentially relativized to a human subject.

III. WITTGENSTEIN

In the *Tractaus* Wittgenstein uses 'world' for reality in so far as we contact it in the medium of language and thought. It is a fact that we can, in the Aristotelian sense of the word, imitate it: reproduce it in these media; we can say it, think it, and what we say and think can be eval vated as true or false. Thus reality is amenable to rational imitation: it can be objectified in rational processes and this potentiality to disclose itself in rational media is always there, is pre-linguistic, pre-epistemic. Considered precisely as having this potentiality realities, individually and collectively, are described as *objects*; so considered a reality has not actually any particular character; it cannot be described and is symbolized by a variable:

4.1272 Wherever the word 'object' (thing', etc.) is correctly used, it is expressed in conceptual notation by a variable name.

For example, in the proposition, 'There are 2 objects which....', it is expressed by '(*Ex,y*)...'.

To *know a reality as an object is to conceive it precisely in its potentiality to* disclose itself in rational media. In a process of analysis then, actual and possible worlds presuppose objects or, in other words, actual and possible worlds and everything in them have a radical objectivity—their formal aspects and actual properties as worlds do not exhaust their being: that which through mediation or imitation is this world, is also that which *can be* mediated or imitated and *can* disclose itself in *any* rational medium.

Further it is because actual and possible worlds are objective that they have indispensable characteristics causing irrational propositions about them to be false, and proposition certified by rationality to be true. Thus objectivity, the fact that reality is such that it can disclose itself in any rational medium, guarantees that a grammar of rationality will be an ontology of the possible.

Wittgenstein's theory of objects is difficult, but it is a penetrating grounding of a quality that attaches to logical laws: they express that which is *so*', whether as a possibility, or in all possible worlds, or in any world in which there is at least one individual. The source, guarantee and ground of quality is that, radically, reality is always and everywhere that which can appear, can be disclosed, in any rational medium a grammar of rationality can, therefore, speak for it.

It is interesting to note that Aristotle in speaking of reality in its primary state of potentiality to rational form, described it in terms of being subjective. Wittgenstein's context was thought and language where reality is naturally presented at the objective pole of a relationship with a thinker or speaker.

After the *Tractatus* Wittgenstein de-escalated his absorption in the objectivity of reality, in its constitutional amenability to be imitated in any rational medium, its *potential* rationality (not to be identified with *formal* rationality which characterizes reality as mediated, i.e. our *world).* We find instead an escalation of interest in the other pole of life (the subjective one) with language again as the point of departure language is not viewed as a medium in which reality is imitated (pictured and thereby said); the emphasis is now on language as a form of personal and social vitality exercised in interaction with reality. Its roots and forms are followed backwards towards the human subject.

This new direction brought balance and completeness into Wittgenstein's philosophy of language. His insight into the objectivity of reality remained as valuable as ever, but the picture theory was abandoned and a much broader conception of language emerged.

We do not use language exclusively to communicate truth, to say what is so and what can be so. Such however was the static *Tractatus* conception of language giving rise to the goal of ideal descriptions by ideal languages, which

> sounds as if these languages were better, more perfect than our everyday language, and as if it took the logician to shew people at last what a proper sentence looked like. All this, however, can only appear in the right light when one has attained greater clarity about the concepts of understanding, meaning and thinking. For it will then also become clear what can lead us (and did lead me) to think that if any one utters a sentence and means or *understands* it he is operating a calculus according to definite rules. (*Philosophical Investigations,* I, § 81.),

Further, meaning cannot be explained simply through a correlation of words with things: a word can be used as a name but it can also be used in various other ways:

> ... in fact we do the most various things with our sentences. Think of exclamations alone, with their completely different functions.

> Water!
> Away!
> Ow!
> Help!
> Fine!
> No!
>
> Are you still inclined to call these words 'names of objects'? (Ibid, § 27)

For Wittgenstein, we have the habit of looking at language without looking at the language game; we must study language empirically as an ordinary human phenomenon, getting back to 'rough ground', i.e. looking to actual examples and learning from them:

> But how many kinds of sentences are there? Say assertion, question and command? There are countless kind countless different kinds of use of what we call 'symbols', 'words,' 'sentences.' And this multiplicity is not something fixed, given once for all; but new types of langauge, new language games as we may say, come in to existence, and others become obsolete and get forgotten.
>
> Here the term 'language-*game*' is meant to bring into prominence the fact that the *speaking* of language is part of an activity, or of a form of life.
>
> Review the multiplicity of language-games in the following examples, and in others:
>
> Giving orders, and obeying them
> Describing the appearance of an object, or giving its measurements
> Constructing an object from a description (a drawing)—
> Reporting an event—
> Speculating about an event—
> Forming and testing a hypothesis—
> Presenting the results of an experiment in tables and diagrams—
> Making up a story; and reading it—

Play-acting—
Singing catches—
Guessing riddles—
Making a joke; telling it—
Solving a problem in practical arithmentic—
Translation from one langauage into another—
Asking, thanking, cursing, greeting, praying—

It is interesting to compare then multiplicity of the tools in language and of the ways they are used, the multiplicity of kinds of word and sentence, with what logicians have said about the structure of language. (Including the author of the *Tractus Logico-Philosophicus*). (Ibid.,§ 23)

Wittgenstein conceives language as a medium of self-expression in which we live and move and relate to others. There is no such thing as a correct form for language: such an ideal arose from the mistaken conception of language as essentially a depicter of fact:

> ...it is clear that every sentence in our language is 'in order as it is'. That is to say we are not *striving after* an ideal, as if our ordinary vague sentences had not yet got a quite unexceptional sense, and a perfect language awaited construction by us. (Ibid.,§98)

The form of language derives from the user ; as such it is not something private and esoteric, for the user has human life and lives in a social milieu with shared skills and agreements in vocabulary, grammar, tones of expression, gestures, etc. But it is the user who decides how to use words for the purpose of communicating to his hearer and it is this use which is the life, meaning and form of the particular sentence uttered:

> Every sign *by itself seems* dead. Wh*at* gives it life? In use it is *alive*. Is life breathed into it there? Or is the *use* its life? (Ibid., § 432)

It follows that the word, language, refers to an indefinite range of language games. They have no common defining property but between them is a family resemblance:

> Here we come up against a great question that lies behind all these considerations. For someone might object against me: you take the easy way out. You talk about all sorts of language games, but have nowhere said what the essence of a language-game, and hence of language, is: what is common to all these activities, and what makes them into language, or parts of language. So you let yourself off the very part of the investigation that once gave you yourself most headache, the part about the *general form of propositions* and of language. (Ibid., § 65)
>
> Don't say: 'There *must* be something common, or they would not be called games'—but *look and see* whether there is anything common to all. For if you look at them you will not see something that is common to *all,* but similarities, relationships, and a whole series of them at that. To repeat: don't think, but look! (Ibid., § 66)
>
> And the result of this examination is: we see a complicated network of similarities overlapping and criss-crossing: sometimes overall similarities sometimes similarities of detail. (Ibid.)
>
> I can think of no better expression to characterize these similarities than 'family resemblances'; for the various resemblances between members of a family: build, features, colour of eyes, gait, temperament, etc. etc. ovelap and criss-cross in the same way. And I shall say: 'games' form a famiy. (Ibid., § 67).

Speaking a particular language is part of a form of life it expresses a range of living activities—ordering, questioning, describing, etc. As forms of life, language-activities are logical primitives: they cannot be justified, for they are bedrock:

> It is easy to imagine a language consisting only of orders and reports in battle. Or a language consisting only of questions and expressions for answering yes and no. And innumerable others. To imagine a language means to

> imagine a form of life. (Ibid., § 19)
>
> If I have exhausted the justifications I have reached bedrock, and my spade is turned. Then I am inclined to say: 'This is simply what I do' (Ibid, § 217)
>
> What has to be accepted, the given is—so one could say—forms of life. (Ibid., II, p.226)

IV. STRUCTURALISM

It has been said that everyone is born, intellectually, into the world either a Platonist or an Aristotelian. It could be said with equal justice that anyone who dedicates himself to explanation must identify with either the Wittgenstein of the *Tractatus* or with the Wittgenstein of the *Investigations*, or must become an integral Wittgenstein—the solitary person, perhaps, of real life.

The movement, Structuralism, seems to possess in its own way, at the present day, the main tensions that were felt and pressing in the philosophical development of Wittgenstein. Responsible for *avant garde* movements in the human sciences, with hardly any contemporary scientist or philosopher who does not accept the value of structuralist investigation everywhere, structuralists have been known more for their opposition than for their openness to theories which have recourse to the human subject. The fact is, however, that the question of the origins of structure is a central problem as yet unresolved in the movement.

The concept, *structure*, here is of course a very special one which moves away both from the simple etymology of *structure* (*struere*, to build) and from the static connotation of *form*. Piaget points out:

> ... once we focus on the positive content of the idea of structure, we come upon at least two aspects that are common to all varieties of structuralism: an ideal (perhaps a hope) of intrinsic intelligibility supported by the postulate that structures are self-sufficient and that, to grasp them,

> we do not have to make reference to all sorts of extraneous elements; second, certain insights—to the extent that one has succeeded in actually making out certain structures, their theoretical employment has shown that structures in general have despite their diversity, certain common and perhaps necessary properties ....in short, the notion of structure is comprised of three key ideas; the idea of wholeness, the idea of transformation, and the idea of transformation, and the idea of self-regulation. (*structuralism*, pp.4-5)

Structuralism repudiates the atomistic tendency of many current disciplines to explain structures as 'composites formed of elements that are independent of the complexes into which they enter' (Ibid.) A structure is a whole and it is through the relations among elements that we conceive it properly; the elements of a structure are subordinated to laws which define the whole and explain its overall properties. Through these laws the structure is constituted not only as a whole but also as a whole in process of transformation. Structures are systems of transformational their laws both structure them and simultaneously govern their transformations:

> ....all known structures from—mathematical groups to kinship systems—are, without exception, systems of transformation. But transformation need not be a temporal process: 1+1 'make' 2; 3 'follows hard on' 2; clearly, the 'making' and 'following' here meant are not temporal processes. On the other hand, transformation can be a temporal process; getting married 'takes time'. Were it not for the idea of transformation, structures would lose all explanatory import, since they would collapse into static forms. (Ibid., pp.11–12)

And transformations of a structure conserve it since the elements to which thy give rise always belong to the structure and are always governed by its laws:

> These properties of conservation along with stability

> of boundaries despite the construction of indefinitely many new elements presuppose that structures are self-regulating. (Ibid., p.14)

In the vision of Structuralism, philosophy, logic, mathematics, the physical sciences, the life sciences, the psychological and social sciences, the humanities (literature, history and linguistics) would form a continuum of knowledge, each discipline employing the structuralist method of investigation and ultimately seeing its sector of reality as a self-regulating transformational system or 'structure'. The success of the structuralist method (e.g. in anthropology and linguistics), the importance of Structuralists (such as Ferdinand de Saussure, Claude Lèvi-Strauss, Roman Jakobson, Jean Piaget, Francois Jacob, Roland Barthes, Edmund Leach, Louis Althusser, Jacques Lacan), the explanatory potency of structure (as a deep rather than a surface reality—that which itself cannot be seen but nevertheless can only be derived from what is seen): these facts compel respect for the Structuralist vision. Indeed standard logic, in the format of a natural deduction system, is a structure in the full Stucturalist sense of the word, and in its own domain is already a consistent and complete system of knowledge.

However at this point, a fundamental problem on which Structuralist opinion is unclear, unsure and divided, arises. Is structure an ultimate p: imordial reality? Does it, itself, call for *formation*? What, ultimately, is its genesis or is it an ungenerated whole? It is easy to think of the elements of a structure as changing while the transformation laws applying to them remain immutable. But the very existence of transformation rules poses the same fundamental problem; and the word *innate* poses formidable problems of formation for biology and physiology to answer. Piaget comments:

> Now the implicit hope of anti-historical or anti-genetic structuralist theories is that structure in the end be given a non-temporal mathematical or logical foundation (Chomsky has, in fact, reduced his grammars to a formal 'monoid'

> structure). But if what is wanted is a *general* theory of structure, such as must meet the requirements of an interdisciplinary epistemology, then one can hardly avoid asking, when presented with such non-temporal systems as a mathematical group or a set of subsets, how these systems were obtained—unless, of course, one is willing to stay put in the heavens of transcendentalism. One could proceed by postulate, as in axiomatic systems, but from the epistemological point of view this is an elegant way of cheating which takes advantage of the prior labor of those who constructed the intuitive system without which there would be nothing to axiomatize (Ibid., pp.12–13)

Thus while some contemporary structuralists oppose theories based in any way on the reality of 'subjects' and 'subjectivity', the movement itself, being a method and not a finished doctrine, does not exclude such theories. Piaget, for instance, asserts:

> Structure is simply a system of transformations, but its roots are operational; it depends, therefore, on a prior formation of the instruments of transformation—transformation rules or laws ... The subject exists because, to put it very briefly, the being of structures consists in their coming to be, that is, their being under construction. (Ibid., pp.140–41)

It is interesting to note two other problems which structuralist investigation cannot fail to encounter. Firstly, since mathematics and logic are used to explain physical laws, what is the relationship between structures in mathematics and logic and structures that are ascribed to the real? Are they the same? Are real structures *there* independently of us? Wittgenstein spoke of the world having logical form but *world* has a specific meaning in his philosophy and *form* is a static concept. The parallel question for the structuralist is whether formal transformations of logic and mathematics account within the observed facts for change and persistence.

The second question concerns the interrelationship between

linguistic and logical structures. And here Chomsky's rationalism has replaced the view of logical positivists and of linguistic scholars like Bloomfield who reduced mathematics and logic to linguistics, and mental life to speech. In Chomsky's view since the speaker-hearer's normal use of language is creative he must 'be in control of what is now often called a generative grammar of his language'. The roots of such a grammar are in reason and in an innate reason. Thus rational vitality is the source of language, and logic (the grammar of rationality) is the source of linguistic grammar.

V. HUSSERL

The broad task which the movement of Phenomenology set before itself was the descriptive investigation of phenomena, both objective and subjective. Those who were phenomenologists in the strictest sense paid particular attention to what it means for objects to appear subjectively in experience, and (on the basis of an operation called phenomenonlogical reduction) studied how the appearances of an object are constituted in and by consciousness. Thus Paul Ricoeur defines the movement as follows:

> Fundamentally, phenomenology is born as soon as we treat the manner of appearing of things as a separate problem by 'bracketing' the question of existence, either temporarily or permanently. *(Esprit XXI,* 821)

It is obviously a movement with a strong belief and interest in subjectivity. With Husserl indeed subjectivity is 'the wonder of wonders', the central mystery:

> Whether we like it or not, whether (for whatever prejudices) it may sound monstrous or not, this (the 'I am') is the fundamental fact *(Urtatsache)* to which I have to stand up, which, as a philosopher, I must never blink for a moment. For philosophical children this may be the dark corner haunted by the specters of solipsism or even of psychologism and relativism. The true philosopher instead

> of running away from them, will prefer to illuminate the dark corner. *(Formale und transcendentale Logik,* p. 209}

Throughout his life (if we disregard his *Philosophie der Arithmetik of 1891)* Husserl was resolutely set against psychologizing, i.e. translating objects is to psychological experiences, and as early as *1895,* through contact with Frege, abandoning a plan to derive arithmetic from psychology, he had begun his celebrated critique of logical psychologism—the view, as he put it, that 'the theoretical foundation for the construction of logic ... is supplied by psychology, and specifically by the psychology of knowledge.' He was equally opposed to 'objectivism'—failure to take proper account of the subjective aspect of knowledge; and the problem to which he gave his attention, as being the most fundamental one, was reconciling the objectivity of truth with the subjectivity of the act of knowledge. Pivcevic sums up his philosophical development as follows:

> If we glance back at Husserl's philosophical development from, his *Philosophy of Arithmetic* onward, we shall see that, at root, all his analyses were concerned with one basic problem: the problem of the relation between the objective content of knowledge and the acts of meaning and knowing. Or, to repeat one of his own questions: How are we to understand the fact that the "in-itself" of the objectivity can be thought of by us and moreover "apprehended" in cognition, and thus in the end yet become "subjective"? It was this problem that led the young mathematician Husserl to interest himself in the soetic presuppositions of mathematics and to inquire into the origin' of the concept of number. He was made aware by Brentano of the importance of intentional relations, and in exploring these relations he found himself in the domain of that 'object-constituting subjectivity' (*die leistende Subjekitivität*, as he came to call it) which was to remain the focal point of his phenomenological analyses. (*Husserl and Phenomenology*, p.91)

An intentionally active meaning giving, object constituting subjectivity—*die leistende subjectivität*—is central in Husserl. 'Subjectivity' here refers not to particular subjectivities but to subjectivity as such (which he finally interprets in the, context of a transcendental Ego). He believes it is of fundamental importance to study its constitutive activity, and, for logic, to study in particular the categorial activity which produces logical concepts and logical schemata.

However although Husserl outlined his concept of a Pure Logic (i.e. of a logic that accepted human subjectivity as its source but was free of psychologism) the details of his work were epistemological in character, being concerned with an elucidation of knowledge rather than with a systematic development of logic. Acknowledging that Kant, Herbart, Lotze, Leibniz and Bolzano had also worked on blueprints for a pure logic. Husserl sketched his own two-level structure. Spiegelberg writes:

> The first level is that of the propositions or 'truths' studied by the logic of statements *('apophantics')* as composed of meanings and their various combinations. The second level consists of the 'things' to which these statements re-fer, i.e., of the states of affairs *(Sachverhalte)* which they assert, the relations, complexes and other configurations which they can enter and which are to be investigated by what Husserl calls a *formal ontology.*
>
> Actually, this two level pattern incorporates two one level conceptions of pure logic, formulated most impressively by Bolzano and by Meinong respectively. Bolzano had organized his pure logic on the propositional level around representational ideas, propositions and truths *(Vorstellung* an *sich, satz* an *sich, Wahrheit an sich).* Meinong knew only of the 'state of affairs,' which he had named *'Objectiv,'* and of other categories of formal ontology. Husserl's conception incorporated both these levels, that of the propositions, which are valid or in valid, and that of the states of affairs, which do or do not 'subsist', as Bertrand

> Russell rendered Meinong's term. ('To be the case' might be a less hypostatizing equivalent of the rather harmless German word '*bestehen*'.) (*The phenomenological Movement: A Historical Introduction*, vol. 1,p.96)

Later (1929) in his *Formale und Transcendentale Logik* Husserl added a third level: this would be a study of the designata of logical symbols within the context of idealized speech.

Husserl's contribution did not go beyond his argument for the need and possibility of a pure logic. But it is an important point of view. It argues that the science of logic has traditionally been conceived on the basis of a confrontational model of knowledge generally, where science simply faces and observes reality so that its findings are the already-out-there-now-real. Subjectivity is forgotten so that the objectivism is blind.

On final analysis and taking this view in its essentials, there is not in it anything invalidate modern formal logic and metalogic but its assimilation would force logic to work out a richer philosophical perspective.

VI. SUBJECTIVITY IN CONTEMPORARY PHILOSOPHY

This is a central concept for phenomenologists and existentialists and indeed is frequently burdened with enormous philosophic tasks as when, for instance, Merleau-Ponty speaks of behaviour as 'embodied subjectivity' or speaks of the existence of an 'art hidden in the depths of the human soul and which, like all art, is only known through its results'. In traditional systems which acknowledge their origins in Greek and medieval philosophies, self is also a fundamental concept grounded in conscious activity; for a conscious act presents itself as a subjective act which is object oriented: concomitant with, e.g. the objective awareness or the objective anger there is a disclosure of self *as subject*. (There never occurs a subjective act which is also subject oriented; the result is that the concomitant awareness we have of self cannot be elaborated into direct, insightful, thematic knowledge such as we have of objective realities.)

Undoubtedly today's philosophical milieu is suitable and stimulating for exploring the grounding of logic in the human subject.

Of particular interest to logic are some writings of Heidegger (for the parallelism that is evidenced between contemporary philosophy and Wittgenstein) and of Jaspers (for his conception of the highest logic as Reason becoming-conscious-of-itself).

Heidegger, a student of Husserl and widely regarded as the central figure in contemporary existentialist thought, is representative of the strong movement depicting self not as an isolated (Cartisian) *worldless* I but as inseparable from the world, living authentically only when I make situations vitally *mine* instead of being buried and hidden by surrender to the enslaving tendency of routine life. The programme of Heidegger's *Sein usd Zeit* is not unlike that of Wittgenstein's *Investigations*—the bringing back of philosophy to a view point from which one can see the human subject as always participant. For Heidegger himself this means retrieving the Pre-Soctratic viewpoint when truth was *alethia*, the unhiddenness of being, before it became with Aristotle a mere property of propositions—correspondence with facts. Language is not simply an instrument for communication: Heidegger rejected such linguistic occasionalisms, the conception of language as extraneous to the vitality of thought; for him (Holzwege, pp. 60-61) language is our access to being:

> It does not merely present in words and sentences things obvious and things concealed as meant in some particular way; on the contrary, it is language which beings things as such into the open in the first place. Where no language prevails as in the existence of stones, plants and animals, then there is no access to things either... Any given language is the occurrence of the word in which its

own world dawns historically on a community... the event in which things as such become intelligible for man in the first place.(F. Kerr's translation, in 'Language as Hermenutic in the later Wittgenstein'. see Bibliography)

Jaspers writes succinctly of the indissocialibility of subject and object:

> What is then the meaning of this mystery which is implied at each moment by the subject-object-dichotomy? It can only mean that Being as a whole is neither subject nor object but must be the *Enveloping,* which reveals itself in this dichotomy.
>
> Clearly then, Being as such cannot be an object. Everything that becomes an object for me breaks away from the Enveloping in confronting me, while I myself emerge from it as a subject. An object is a definite kind of being for the subject, whereas the Enveloping remains obscure for my consciousness. It is brought to light only through objects, and takes on greater and greater clarity to the extent that the objects become more sharply present to consciousness. The Enveloping itself does not become an object, but it appears in the cleavage of the subject and the object. It is a *background* which is incessantly illuminated through the appearance of objects, while remaining forever the Enveloping. *(Einfuhrung in die Philosophie,* p.30)

With regard to Jaspers' conception of a higher logic, Sebastian Samay analyses its nature and origin:

> Under the joint impulse of Reason and Existence, thought is able to explore its own transcendental possibilities, possibilities that lie beyond the limits of ordinary logic. Once these limits are transcended, logic is replaced by a-logic.
>
> We must now briefly examine this a-logic, briefly because its principal elements of paradox and contradiction are already known to us from Existence-elucidation.

However, we must be prepared to meet some insurmountable difficulties in trying to show the rapport between ordinary logic and rational a-logic. All of these difficulties originate in the fact that the relationship between these two modes of thought is actually transcendental and enveloping. A-logic constantly envelops logic, without really absorbing it, so that their relationship cannot be described logically.

...it would seem that it is logic itself that demands this final leap of thought into Being where, instead of enveloping its object, itself is enveloped by it. It appears that this last exertion of thinking is made on logical grounds, so that the resulting a-logic is really a rational one. A-logic is not the abdication of Reason, rather the expansion of it. Reason in all its forms is indispensable even for a logic. They may explain, at least partially, one of Jaspers' often quoted cryptic phrases, 'I have non-knowledge itself only through knowledge, and perfect non-knolwedge through a maximum of understanding...

This process of Reason becoming conscious of itself should not be understood as a simple psychological self-reflection. It requires an act of transcendental reflection. Transcendental reflection forces knowledge to return upon itself, away from its objects. This is not as natural and easy as it may sound, because what Reason finds in returning upon itself is not an object but a source *(Ursprung)*. Transcendental reflection requires a veritable about-face,inversion *(Umkehrung)*,or conversion *(Bekehrung)* of our object-bound natural attitude.This conversion demands a great deal of exertion on the part of Reason. The new logic is a matter of struggle. 'Reason is not easy but difficult to realize,' says Jaspers.

It can be realized only if individuals make it part of their personal formative process. They must become 'wholly involved and interested in it, if this logic is to succeed.' In other words, it cannot be learned or taught from a detached and safe distance. Philosophical logic, as we already know, is an act of Existence. *(Reason Revisited: the Philosophy of Karl Jaspers.* Published by Gill and Macmillan, pp.210, 214, 220)

VII. CONCLUSION

Formal logic is a corpus of truths discovered and systematized by methods that are objective in quality. If the objectivism is blind, however, logic as human wisdom will be deficient. It is proper that at the level of philosophical reflection the formal systems be seen not only as an ontology of possibility (ground in the objective) but as a grammar of rationality (grounded in the subjective). This will not lead, quantitatively, to more theorems within formal logic but it will lead, qualitatively, to a perspective that is integral

Of course many logicians have difficulties in conceiving logic as having a ground in subjectivity. The fact that this conception does not lead to an enlargement of formal logic is automatically a minus against it. (Since the time of the Greeks it has been explained that subjectivity is not amenable to 'imitation' in rational media so that its functioning as source to logic could not be expressed in a formal system.) Again, conceptions (such as Jaspers) of a logic, higher than traditional and modern logics, in which Reason becomes conscious of itself and which is characterized by paradox and contradiction, may easily appear to lack any real solidity. Further, logicians experience their science as a formal system grounded on itself: to go outside the system and ground it in subjectivity seems to be an exercise in psychologism. Indeed Beth and Cavailles conclude that, for the logician, phenomenonlogy is psychologism developed in a new language.

Notwithstanding the dangers it does not seem impossible to reach a perspective in logic which would do justice to subjectivity. Such a perspective would assimilate in substance both the *Tractatus* (which itself summarizes so well the historical tendency of formal logic) and the *Investigations* (which possesses so much of the spirit of contemporary movements to the subjective pole of life).

The *Tractatus* is right in emphasizing that reality is objective in the sense of being amenable to imitation in any rational medium. And logic is the most fundamental science to display this, for it is at the same time both a grammar of rationality and an ontology of the possible. Science supports this view simplicity by its efforts to express the laws of nature in mathematical laws of the greatest rational simplicity and beauty possible; but also by its faith that the universe and every event in it is, in principle, patient of rational explanation. This faith is shared broadly, indeed, by ordinary people throughout their daily lives.

when it is the objectivity of reality that is the centre of interest, our concern with language tends to be limited to the descriptive, propositional use of it—to our rational capacity to say what is so or can be so. This is a limited viewpoint from which the clarity and cogency of logic is very impressive. However, just as reality is amenable to rational *description* (description by a human observer) so human life in all its facets is amenable to rational *expression* (i.e. formed communication by the human subject). Looking at language from the direction of the human person, one sees it as a multifaceted expression of life with reality. And from here logic is seen as potentially, for the logician, a glimpse into the art of our own subjectivity.

Chapter-5
Validity

Chapter 5

Our second run through the Strategy is nearly complete. You can speak Predicate or, more accurately, you can write it; you can translate English into it. All you need now is a way to te st Predicate arguments for validity. That is the main business of this article. Also, since we have already discussed translation into Predicate, we might as well complete the application of the Strategy in this chapter. That is, we will combine the tasks of validating Predicate and natural language arguments.

5.0 WHAT ABOUT TRUTH TABLES?

A first thought might be: why not just use the truth tables familiar from Sentential to test validity. Alas, while it would be very nice if we could use them, a little thought will show that Predicate has outgrown them. And I mean this quite literally.

Start with this very simple argument:

All men are mortal
Socrates is a man
___
Socrates is mortal.

(So well-known is this example that its absence from the book would shock logicians and I wasn't willing to do this.)

Translating this into Predicate would give us this:

$(\forall x)\ (Fx \supset Gx)$

Fa
___
Ga.

How would you use truth tables here? The first thing to do is to work out how many different basic sentences there are in this argument. The conclusion counts as one, and so does the second premise. That is, from the perspective of Sentential, these can be treated as, say, P_1 and P_2 But what about the first premise? There do not seem to be *any* basic sentences in it; there is a quantifier and a non-basic *predicate* which is itself made up of two basic predicates. But no basic *sentences* at all. Of course, the *whole* of this first premise could be treated as, say, P_3. but. in doing this, we would destroy any possibility of showing the argument valid. Its validity quite clearly comes from the structure of elements *within* the quantified sentence; the argument

$$\begin{array}{l} P_3 \\ P_1 \\ \hline P_2 \end{array}$$

would not be validated by truth tables.

Still, you may think, all is not lost. From our discussion of universal quantification, you know that this premise is like a long conjunction; it is of the form

$(Fa \supset Ga) \& (Fb \supset Gb) \& (Fc \supset Gc)...$

Each of these conjuncts contains basic sentences: you can count six different ones in the display. Unfortunately, that is just the trouble. If there are an infinite number of items in the universe of discourse, there are going to be an *infinite* number of basic sentences hidden (so to speak) in the universally quantified premise. And it would be rash to insist, in our logic, that there are only a finite number of things in the universe. Remember, since we want the logic to apply to mathematical reasoning, numbers must be counted as items, and there is certainly an infinite number of them.

In consequence, when you come to compute the number of rows of the truth table for this argument, you will get:

2^{∞}, i.e., $(2 \times 2 \times 2...$ infinitely)

and this is a very large number indeed. Any truth table with that many rows would be unwritable. So, even for the very simple Predicate argument above, the truth table method is no use.

NOTE. It is even worse. You can only think of a universally quantified sentence as equivalent to an infinite conjunction if you also think that everything in the universe could have a designator. However, there are good reasons to think that this is not so. 'The number of what mathematicians call 'real' numbers is said to be uncountably infinite. and this would preclude their all having designations. (Because the number of possible designators in the universe is 'smaller' than the number of reals, i.e. there is plausibly only .a countable infinity of designators.)

5.1 DEDUCTIONS

We have drawn a blank with truth tables, so you will not be surprised to hear that the next option is to look at the use of deductions. Sentential arguments could be shown to be valid by either method; we have now to see whether deductions can help us with Predicate.

Something that came out of the failure of the truth-table method does give us a reason to be hopeful. To see what I am getting at, reconsider the discussion of the argument about Socrates, and, in particular, the conjunctive expansion of the first premise. The first conjunct in the infinite expansion is

$$Fa \supset Ga.$$

This is simply a conditional constructed from two basic sentences. If we had this conditional as a premise, then we could use the other premise to reach the conclusion in three quick steps, viz.

1	(1) $Fa \supset Ga$	Premise
2	(2) Fa	Premise
1,2	(3) Ga	1,2 $\supset$E

(You may well be a bit rusty on the rules and score-keeping used in deductions. It might be a good idea to have a quick review.)

So, if we had a rule which allowed us to go from

$(\forall x)(Fx \supset Gx)$

to

$Fa \supset Ga$

it would be an easy matter to derive the conclusion. Moreover, there doesn't seem to be any reason why we shouldn't have the rule. Given that it is true that every man is mortal, it is surely true that each designated man is mortal including Socrates.

With such overwhelming reason in its favour, we are certainly entitled to have a rule of inference that sanctions the move from a universally quantified sentence to one without quantifiers. Such a rule would be a Universal Quantifier Elimination Rule (E, for short) and could be used to construct the following deduction.

1	(1) $(\forall x)(FX \supset Gx)$	Premise
2	(2) Fa	Premise
1	(3) $Fa \supset Ga$	1. $\forall$E
1.2	(4) Ga	1.2 $\supset$ E

The only thing that stands in our way is that we haven't yet got the means to formulate the rule in an appropriately *general* way. You remember how careful one has to be about the presentation of the rules. It must not turn out that $\forall$E is appropriate to the above argument, but not to other more complex arguments. The statement of $\forall$E and other Predicate rules is the business of the next sections. The point of the present section is to show how rules like $\forall$E can be combined with the ten from Sentential to give us a way to construct deductions for Predicate language arguments. (Can you guess how many quantifier rules there are? Four. There are two quantifiers and we will need an Elimination and an Introduction rule for each of them.)

One last point: we will assume that the rules of Sentential do carry over to Predicate. For example, the argument

$$\begin{array}{l} Fa \supset Ga \\ Fa \\ \hline Ga \\ \hline \end{array}$$

counts as an instance of ⊃E. We could be more precise about this; we could re-introduce the rules, one by one, having re-defined the notions of basic and non-basic sentence for Predicate. However, having pointed out this assumption. I think we can let matters rest.

5.2 A NOTATION FOR PREDICATE RULES

What we need to display Universal Elimination in the most general way is to represent Predicate arguments in schematic form. Remember that in giving the Sentential rules we used the letters 'A', 'B' and 'C'. These were not themselves sentences, they are rather like the blanks on a questionnaire which have to be filled in with sentences. However, unlike Sentential, Predicate sentences have components which are not sentences. (In saying this I am ignoring logical components such as '⊃'. They are, of course, parts of sentential sentences, even though they are not themselves sentences. In the schematic presentation of Sentential rules, they were not replaced by schematic letters they—portrayed themselves, and will continue to do so in Predicate rules.)

The required schematic presentation of designators, predicates, and variables is achieved as follows.

(i) 't' will be used as a blank for designators. This letter is chosen because designators are often called *terms* by logicians.

(ii) 'Φ' (Greek phi) will be used as a blank for predicate expressions, however complicated. That is, 'Φ' holds a place for any expression that has at least one free variable in it. Here are some possible substitutions for 'Φ'.

Fx. Fx & Hx, Hy ⊃ Rxy, (∀y)(Fy ⊃ Rxy)

Notice that the last of these has a quantifier, but the whole of the expression still counts as a complete predicate expression because of the free 'x' in it. (There can, of course, be multiple occurrences of 'x' as in the second example above.)

(iii) 'v' will be used as the blank for variables. (Subscripts are allowed if needed.) In particular, we can understand

Φv

as a place-holder for a predicate with a *one* free variable. If you see

$\Phi v_1 v_2$

this means that the predicate has *two* free variables in it.

These conventions will allow us to write out the rules of inference so that they are completely general. For example, the claim that all men are mortal, in Predicate

$(\forall x)(Fx \supset Gx)$

could be a filling for

$(\forall v)\ \Phi v.$

But this same schematic form would serve for

$(\forall y)(\exists x)((Fy \ \&\ Hx) \supset Rxy).$

The variable 'y' takes the place of 'v', and

$(\exists x)((Fy \ \&\ Hx) \supset Rxy)$

takes the place of 'Φv'.

Notice that the quantifier symbols are treated as place-holders for themselves. They behave in schemata exactly like '$\supset$' and the other Sentential connectives.

5.3 UNIVERSAL QUANTIFIER RULES

A. Universal Quantifier Elimination (∀E)

We can now state the Universal Quantifier Elimination rule that allows the move from every person's mortality to that of Socrates.

$$\frac{(\forall v)\ \Phi v}{\Phi t}$$

SCORE-KEEPING The conclusion depends on whatever premises '(∀v)Φv' depends on, so you have to indicate this on the left-hand side of the line number of 'Φt'. Also, you have to cite the line number of '(∀v) Φv' on the right-hand side of the deduction.

NOTE We will assume that 't' replaces all and only occurrences of v'. This convention in the formulation of the rule will apply to the other rules unless it is expressly overridden. The reason for it should be fairly obvious; without it, the following would be an instance of ∀E.

$$\frac{(\forall y)\ (Fy \supset Hy)}{Fa \supset Hy}$$

and we would have a free variable in the conclusion. In essence, this would be a case where a predicate was inferred from a sentence. We cannot make sense of such an inference as valid, since validity requires the preservation of truth, and a predicate isn't assessable as true or false. The convention that t' and 'v' replace each other in each and every occurrence will be called the *replacement convention.*

The deduction we constructed for the mortality example, unsurprisingly, turns out to be in line with this rule. However, it would be as well to consider a more complicated example.

All logicians are pedantic.
Everyone who is pedantic is hard to live with.
Fred is not hard to live with.
Therefore, Fred is not a logician.

Translation

$$(\forall x)\ (Fx \supset Gx)$$

$$(\forall y)\ (Gy \supset Hy)$$

$$\frac{\neg Ha}{\neg Fa}$$

Deduction

1	(1) $(\forall x)(Fx \supset Gx)$	Premise
2	(2) $(\forall y)(Gy \supset Hy)$	Premise
3	(3) $\urcorner Ha$	Premise
1	(4) $Fa \supset Ga$	1, $\forall$E
2	(5) $Ga \supset Ha$	2, $\forall$E
6	(6) Fa	Assumption
1,6	(7) Ga	4,6 $\supset$E
1,2,6	(8) Ha	5,7 $\supset$E
1,2,3,6	(9) $Ha \ \& \ \urcorner Ha$	3,8 &I
1,2,3	(10) $\urcorner Fa$	6,9 $\urcorner$I

Here we used two applications of the new rule and then introduced 'Fa' as an assumption. This was done because it was obvious that we could use this assumption to derive 'Ha' and this stands in direct contradiction to the third premise. The final line uses this contradiction to derive the wanted conclusion, the negation of the assumption. As you can see from the left of the last line, the conclusion depends only on the original premises since the assumption is discharged by the use of $\urcorner$ I.

B. UNIVERSAL QUANTIFIER INTRODUCTION ($\forall$I)

Not all of our reasoning proceeds from the general to the specific; often we use general premises as the basis for general conclusions. Below is an example.

All jobs worth doing are worth doing well.
Anything worth doing well is time consuming.

All jobs worth doing are time consuming.

Translating this into Predicate, we get

$(\forall x)(Fx \supset Gx)$
$(\forall x)(Gx \supset$

$(\forall x)(Fx \supset Hx)$.

If we proceed using the means at our disposal, we get the beginning of a deduction which looks like this.

1	(1) (∀x) (Fx ⊃ Gx)	Premise
2	(2)(∀x)(Gx ⊃ Hx)	Premise
1	(3)Fa ⊃ Ga	I, ∀E
2	(4)Ga D Ha	2, ∀E
5	(5)Fa	Assumption
1,5	(6)Ga	3,5 ⊃ E
1.2,5	(7)Ha	4.6 ⊃ E
1.2	(8)Fa ⊃ Ha	5,7 ⊃ l
	(9)??	

Here we are stuck. We have established a connection between 'Fa' and Ha', just as the conclusion seems to require. But we can hardly jump from this specific connection to the universally general conclusion of the original argument. 'Then again, perhaps we can.

It is well-known that people are always jumping to general conclusions, and it is no less well-criticized. After all the care we have taken, we cannot allow ourselves a rule which would allow as valid such inferences as this one.

The butcher on the corner is dishonest.
Therefore, all butchers are dishonest.

Yet, the earlier ,argument seems quite different from this blatantly invalid one. If we could capture that difference, we could formulate a rule that would prevent the butcher' inference while allowing the earlier one. This requires some further thought.

It is often easier to reason with particular things in mind, even when the reasoning is general in spirit. An instructor of veterinary medicine may well find it easier to get his message across by saying

Fido has sweat glands in the pads of his paws.
Fido has 13 thoracic, 7 cervical and 7 lumbar vertebrae.

In these remarks, 'Fido' is a proper name. Yet, it has a role unlike that of any ordinary proper name: it would be only funny if one of the students in the class asked whose dog Fido was. (I suppose the lecturer would be justified in saying that Fido was everybody's dog.) Names used in this way are called *arbitrary names* because they purport to designate arbitrarily chosen representatives of some collection of things. The idea is that if you want to make a point about, for example dogs, you can do so by imagining a representative of the species. This representative, however, must be chosen carefully; it must have only characteristics true of any dog chosen at random.

Of course, when proper names are used in this way, we don't actually choose a representative; we just speak as though we have one in mind. That is why it is a gross misunderstanding to wonder to whom Fido belongs. First, there is no specific dog answering to the name, and, second, the point of this use of a name is precisely to exclude non-general features.

Arbitrary names are very closely related to universal quantification. The lecturer could as well have said: 'all dogs...' He didn't, presumably because he wanted to make his point in a graphic way; arbitrary names are commonly used for this purpose. (Think of how some instructions for filling up forms use names like 'John Doe'.) However, our present interest is solely in the relationship between arbitrary names and universal quantification. If we could formulate a rule of inference that allowed a universal conclusion only from a premise that had an arbitrary name, this would give us what we need while avoiding 'butcher' inferences.

The first step is to introduce a new category of designator: arbitrary designators. In honour of Fido, we will use 'f' (with subscripts, if needed). This means that terms, items that fill the 't' position, can either be designators like 'a', 'b', 'c' or arbitrary designators like 'f'. In the rule of Universal Elimination, the slot for the conclusion, viz.

Φt

could be filled by something like

$Fa \supset Ga$

or by

$Ff \supset Gf$.

We can now state the Universal Quantifier Introduction Rule (I).

Φt

$(\forall v)\ \Phi v$

WHERE: (i) 't' is an arbitrary designator.

(ii) 'Φt' does *not* depend on any line in which 't' occurs.

SCORE-KEEPING In using this rule, '$(\forall v)\Phi v$' depends on whatever 'Φt' depends on, so you *put* the relevant line number(s) to the left of '$(\forall v)\Phi v$'. To the right, you cite the line number of 'Φt'.

The statement of this rule seems complicated, but a closer look should show that it is really quite straightforward. Condition (i) demands that the designator we are generalizing about is arbitrary. This condition helps to keep out 'butcher' inferences.

Condition (ii) makes sure that we do not smuggle in 'butcher' inferences while using arbitrary designators. If 'Φt' does depend on a line in which 't' occurs, then it may well be the case that the arbitrary name is not so arbitrary after all. Here is a blatant example.

Rover is a dog with three legs.
Therefore, all dogs have three legs.

Translation

$Ff_1\ \&\ Gf_1$
— — — —
$(\forall x)(Fx \supset Gx)$
— — — —

'Deduction' (the error is marked in line 5)

1	(I) Ff_1 & Gf_1	Premise
I	(2) Ff_1	1, &E
I	(3) Gf_1	1. &E
1	(4) $Ff \supset Gf$	2.3 $\supset$1
**1*'	(5) $(\forall x)(Fx \supset Gx)$	4, $\forall$I

Of course. I'm sure that you would not have used an arbitrary name in the premise of this argument, since you would have recognized that Rover is hardly an arbitrarily chosen dog. However, not everyone is as clear-thinking as that, so we have to state the rules without loopholes. Condition (ii) rules out this attempted deduction because (4) depends on (1) 'which has f_1 in it.

The argument we considered earlier, the one about jobs worth doing well, can be shown to be valid by this deduction.

1	(1) $(\forall x)(Fx \supset Gx)$	Premise
2	(2) $(\forall x)(Gx \supset Mx)$	Premise
1	(3) $Ff \supset Gf$	1, $\forall$E
2	(4) $Gf \supset Ht$	2, $\forall$E
5	(5) Ff	Assumption
1.5	(6)Gf	3,5 $\supset$E
1.2.5	(7)Hf	4,6 $\supset$E
1.2	(8)$Ff \supset Hf$	5,7 $\supset$I
1.2	(9) $(\forall x)(Fx \supset Hx)$	8, $\forall$I

Here we introduced an assumption with 'f in it at line (5). This caused no harm, since it was discharged before we got to the line to which $\forall$I was applied. That is, line (8) is the 'Φt' line with the arbitrary designator, and it depends on lines (1) and (2). Neither of these. however, has 'f in it, so all the conditions for $\forall$I are met. This is unsurprising. The original premises of the argument were universally general. so we would expect to be able to derive a universal conclusion from them.

Also, notice that I used $\forall$E in lines (3) and (4) to derive sentences with arbitrary designators. This is because I anticipated the need for such designators at the end of the deduction. Had I used 'a' instead of f'. I would not have been able to finish the deduction. However, if you ever get yourself in that position, you need only go back and change the ordinary designators to arbitrary ones. Just make sure, though, that you do not thereby violate condition (ii). The possibility of such replacement is more significant than it might seem. It is precisely because the deduction up to step (8) could have had any designator in it that it is all right to make the universal claim in step (9). That is, because there were no special assumptions made about the item designated in line (8), there is no reason to doubt the universally general claim in (9).

Just like ∀E, ∀I requires thc replacement convention. That is, 'v' in 'Φv' must replace each and every occurrence of 't' in Φt'. However, the need for the convention has a different basis in the case of ∀I. For ∀E, we required it because we wanted to block the deduction of non-sentences from sentences, since this would not have accorded with our conception of validity as truth preserving. This would not be a problem for ∀I, though, because one always begins with a sentence (with arbitrary names), and adds quantification. So, the question is why do we need the convention to block moves like that from 'Rff' to '(∀y) Rfy'. The following unquestionably *invalid* argument and its supposed deduction provide the answer.

Everyone resembles themselves.
Therefore, everyone resembles everyone.

Translation

(∀x)Rxx
____
(∀x)(∀y)Rxy

'Deduction' (violation of convention is marked)

1	(1)	(∀x)Rxx	Premise
1	(2)	Rff	1, ∀E
1	(3)	(∀y)Rfy	2, ∀I
I	(4)	(∀x)(∀y)Rxy	3, ∀I

Only the replacement convention blocks the construction of a deduction for this invalid argument.

5.4 EXISTENTIAL QUANTIFIER RULES

A. Existential Quantifier Introduction (∃I)

After the lengthy discussion of ∀I, it will be a relief to get back to a simpler case. The following inference seems obviously valid, and does not need to be hedged about with all sorts of special conditions.

Tony is late.
Therefore, there is at least one person late.

The move from the specific to the existentially general is bound to be valid. Or is it?

There is one fly in the ointment. What would you say about this argument?

Santa Claus does not exist.
Therefore, there is at least one thing that does not exist.

On the face of it, the conclusion is self-contradictory. Yet I suspect that the premise would be judged true, and the argument seems to follow the same pattern as the one about Tony. To be honest, this example raises a problem that I have so far kept from you: what to do about 'designators' that fail to designate. We can't simply disallow them in Predicate, since the sentence about Santa Claus is a perfectly intelligible natural language claim which we ought to be able to translate into Predicate. For the present, however, I will continue to ignore the mess they make, neither dealing with it, nor sweeping it under the rug. Everything I say now about the existential rules of inference will be applied only to designators which *do* in fact pick out an appropriate item.

The rule of inference for Existential Quantifier Introduction (∃I) follows.

Φv

$(\exists v)\Phi v$

WHERE: it is *not* required that 'v' in 'Φv' replace *every* occurrence of 't'.

SCORE -KEEPING When using this rule, '(∃v)ϕv' depends on whatever 'Φt' depends on, so you put the relevant line number(s) to the left of '(∃v)Φv'. To its right you cite the line number of 'Φt'.

Notice that we have here relaxed the convention about 'v' in 'Φv' replacing all and only occurrences of 't' in Φt'. It is worth explaining this.

We can relax the replacement convention for ∃I because, unlike ∀I, the existential rule doesn't generate conclusions 'strong' enough to lead us astray. Here is the premise that we used in discussing the issue with respect to ∀I.

Everyone resembles themselves
Translation (∀x)Rxx.

We can use ∀E on this premise to get

Rff.

Now, without the replacement convention, ∃I allows the move to any of the following:

(∃x)Rxx
(∃x)Rfx
(∃x)Rxf.

Taking the second one as an example, we could use ∃1 as a final Introduction step to get

(∃y)(∃x)Ryx.

It was this sort of multiple quantification that got us into trouble when ∀I was used without the replacement convention. Here there is no trouble at all. The multiple existential says simply that someone resembles someone, and this certainly is true given that everyone resembles themselves.

Could you have used ∀I instead of ∃I in the final step? Of course, and I chose 'f' in the application of ∀E to allow this possibility. what you would end up with is

(∀y)(∃x)Ryx.

This says that everybody resembles somebody or other, and this seems a perfectly reasonable consequence of the claim that everybody resembles themselves. What you could never get is the existential on the *outside,* i.e. having wide scope. Try it and you will see that the ∀I replacement convention stops you.

B. Existential Quantifier Elimination (∃E)

Smith and Jones are sitting at a table in a pub when they are told

someone at this table is a raffle winner
Translation (∃x)(Fx & Gx).

Quite clearly, it would be a mistake to conclude from this that Smith is a raffle winner. Equally, it would be a mistake to conclude that Jones is. The original claim is general, and makes no reference to a specific individual. So, if 'a' designates Smith, we would not be justified in inferring

Fa & Ga.

If *Smith* 'eliminated' the existential quantifier in this way, the inference would be a case more of wishful than of logical thinking.

However, suppose that Smith and Jones know that all raffle winners will be toasted. They can surely conclude from this, and the previous claim, that someone at this table will be toasted. That is, the following is a valid inference.

(a) Someone at this table is a raffle winner.
All raffle winners will be toasted.
Therefore, someone at this table will be toasted.

Translation

$(\exists x)(Fx \,\&\, Gx)$
$(\forall x)(Gx \supset Hx)$

$(\exists x)(Fx \,\&\, Hx)$

Our task will be to work out a rule for eliminating existential quantifiers so that we can construct a deduction for this argument. But it must be a rule that doesn't involve the sort of wishful thinking that Smith engaged in when he heard that someone at the table was the raffle winner. That is. the rule must not allow inferences from existential claims to claims about known individuals.

Even though the elimination of existential quantifiers cannot be accomplished in the way that Smith thought, there is a useful clue in his reasoning. Suppose that Smith and Jones are both given to wishful thinking. That is, Smith thinks

Fa & Ga

and allowing 'b' to designate Jones, Jones thinks

Fb & Gb.

Each of them might then reason as follows.

Smith			*Jones*		
1.	(1)Fa & Ga	Premise	1	(1) Fb & Gb	Premise
2.	(2)(∀x) (Gx ⊃ Hx)	Premise	2	(2) (∀x) (Gx ⊃ Hx)	Premise
1	(3)Fa	1 & E	1	(3) Fb	1 & E
2	(4)Ga ⊃ Ha	2 E	2	(4) GB ⊃ Hb	2 ∀E
1	(5)Ga	1 & E	1	(5) Gb	1 & E
1.2	(6)Ha	4,5 ⊃ E	1.2	(6) Hb	4.5 ⊃ E
1.2	(7)Fa & Ha	3,6 ⊃ 1	1,2	(7) Fb & Hb	3,6 ⊃ 1
1,2	(8)(∃x) (Fx & Hx)	7 ∃I	1,2	(8) (∃x) (Fx & Hx)7 ∃ I	

These two deductions are precisely the same *except* in one respect: where the one on the left has claims about Smith, the one on the right has claims about Jones.

As I said earlier, we cannot could one the move from someone at the table won to Smith won, nor can we condone the inference from someone won to Jones won. All we know is that at least one person won: we don't know who won. However, if we did know who it was, then a deduction like those above could be constructed, and it would validate an argument very close to argument (a). It would be just like (a) except for having a non-general premise in place of '(∃x)(Fx & Gx)'.

In this example, it was either Smith or Jones who won. This made it easier to see what is going on, but it isn't essential. Suppose that the number of possible winners was indefinitely large. Still, as long as someone won, a deduction of the above form can be constructed by using a designator of the relevant individual. After all, an existentially quantified claim such as

(∃x)(Fx & Gx)

can be understood as an open-ended disjunction

(Fa & Ga) V (Fb) & Gb) V (Fc & Gc). . .

If the existential is true, then somewhere in the disjunction there must be at least one true sentence of the form

F_ & G_.

Since there is some such sentence, you will be able to use the deduction pattern which is exemplified above in Smith's and Jones's reasoning. All you have to do is to find out what name fills in the '—'

In view of this, does it really matter for the argument in question whether you know who *actually* won? It would seem not. As long as you know someone won *and* you can construct a deduction that goes from a designator of that individual, *whoever, it is* to the conclusion. you can count yourself as having reached that conclusion simply from the fact that someone won. That is, given

someone at the table is a raffle winner

and given that you can construct a deduction FROM

_ is at the table and is a raffle winner

AND

all raffle winners will be toasted

TO

someone at the table will be toasted

you can take yourself to have shown how to construct a deduction for the original argument (a), viz.

Someone at the table is a raffle winner.
All raffle winners will be toasted.
———————————————
Someone at the table will be toasted.

This is justified because the first premise tells us that there is a person who won, and the deduction shows us how to get from the claim that a *particular* person won to the desired conclusion.

But what are we to make of '—'? We cannot construct deductions with blanks in them. It is meant to be filled in by a designator of the raffle winner. We know that someone won the raffle. We just don't know the name of the winner, and that is why we needed the blank. Does this sound familiar? Why not use an arbitrary designator in place of '—'? As long as we are careful, we can formulate a rule for Existential Elimination using arbitrary designators and following the reasoning described with'—'. Here is the formulation of the rule for Existential Quantifer Elimination (∃E).

IF you can show that

(I) Φt
— — — —
C

THEN you have shown this:

(2) (∃v)Φv
— — — —
C

WHERE: (i) 'Φt' is obtained by replacing all and only occurrences of 'v' in 'Φv' by an arbitrary designator 't'. That is. the replacement convention is in force.

(ii) C is any sentence of Predicate which does not contain 't'

(iii) C is deduced from 'Φt' without depending on any line containing 't' except, of course, the line

where 'Φt' itself is introduced.

SCORE-KEEPING: C in (I) may well have depended on lines besides that of 'Φt'. You must write these dependencies to the left of C in (2). In doing this you do *not* include dependency on the line where 'Φt' was assumed, but you do not include the line with '(∃v) Φv'. On the right you cite the line with '(∃v)Φv', the line where 'Φt' is assumed, and the line in (1) where C is deduced.

This is the most complicated of our rules. Since it is easier to see in operation, here is the correct deduction of argument (a) using it.

1	(1)	(∃x)(Fx & Gx)	Premise
2	(2)	(∀x)(Gx ⊃ Hx)	Premise
3	(3)	Ff & Gf	Assumption
2	(4)	Gf ⊃ Hf	2 ∀E
3	(5)	Gf	3 &E
2,3	(6)	Hf	4,5 ⊃E
3	(7)	Ff	3 &E
2,3	(8)	Ff&Hf	6,7 &I
2,3	(9)	(∃x)(Fx & Hx)	8 ∃1
1,2	(10)	(∃x)(Fx & Hx)	1,3,9 ∃E

This deduction contains both stage (1) and stage (2) as described in the rule, but they are squashed together. Stage (1) goes from line (3) to line (9). These constitute a deduction of C which, in this case, is '(∃x)(Fx & Hx)' from 'Φt' which is 'Ff & *Gf*. As the rule says, once you have such a deduction, you are entitled to draw the conclusion C from the original *existential* premise, wiping out any dependency on the assumption made at line (3). Line (10) embodies this move. It re-asserts C, but it no longer depends on the assumption; instead it depends on the existential premise and any other premises used in the deduction of C.

In using arbitrary designators as part of Existential Elimination we have to be very careful. Arbitrary designators were introduced to allow for Universal Introduction, and we must ensure that there is no illicit move from existential to universal quantification. This is where conditions (i)-(iii) come in. I won't stop to justify each of them separately but, to give you some idea of their importance, consider this argument:

Something is green.
Therefore, everything is green.

Translation

$$\frac{(\exists x)Fx}{(\forall x)Fx}$$

If it weren't for condition (ii), it would be easy to construct a deduction for this unquestionably invalid argument. Here is how.

1	(1)	$(\exists x)$ Fx	Premise
2	(1)	Ff	Assumption
1	(3)	Ff	1,2,2 $\exists$E
1	(4)	$(\forall x)$Fx	3, $\forall$I

The third step is marked to show that it falls short of being a proper application of $\exists$E. The trouble is condition (ii). In this 'deduction', 'Ff' is treated as C, and this violates the requirement that 't' (in this case 'f') must not occur in C.

5.5 OPERATING WITH THE RULES

The quantifier rules are much more difficult to formulate precisely than the Sentential rules. However, they are not difficult to work with. You will find deductions are often easier in Predicate than in Sentential, and, while you must understand the conditions that effect each quantifier rule, you are not likely inadvertently to violate these conditions. The most appropriate use of a rule in a specific case will probably satisfy the conditions.

In this section, there are three worked out examples, which should help you extend your skill in constructing deductions. Before presenting these examples, however, I have to ask an important question, a question which may have already occurred to you: *what about identity?* In all this talk about quantifier rules, I have so far left out of account any rules for inferences involving this relation. It is easy to see that some such rules are needed. The rules we now have would not help us with even this simple example of a valid argument.

Mark Twain wrote *Huckleberry Finn.*
Mark Twain is Samuel Clemens.
Therefore, Samuel Clemens wrote *Huckleberry Finn.*

Translation

Rab
$a=c$
―――
Rcb

The premises of this argument are non-quantified sentences of Predicate, and they are each different basic sentences when viewed from the perspective of Sentential. So, the fourteen rules we now have would not suffice to validate this argument. In spite of this, I will not stop here to formulate the rules for identity. For reasons you will appreciate, they are more naturally part of the subject matter of the next chapter. Now for some examples.

Example I

Some deductions are not easy.
Anything not easy is a challenge.
Therefore, some deductions are a challenge.

Translation

$(\exists x)(Fx \ \& \ \neg Gx)$
$(\forall y)(\neg Gy \ \& \ Hy)$

$(\exists y)(Fy \ \& \ Hy)$

Deduction

1	(1)	$(\exists x)(Fx \ \& \ \neg Gx)$	Premise
2	(2)	$(\forall y) (\neg Gy \supset Hy)$	Premise
3	(3)	$Ff \ \& \ \neg Gf$	Assumption
2	(4)	$\neg Gf \supset Hf$	2 $\forall$E
3	(5)	$\neg Gf$	3 &E
2,3	(6)	Hf	4,5 $\supset$ E
3	(7)	Ff	3 &E
2,3	(8)	$Ff \ \& \ Hf$	6,7 &I
2,3	(9)	$(\exists y)(Fy \ \& \ Hy)$	8 $\exists$1
1,2	(10)	$(\exists y)(Fy \ \& \ Hy)$	1,3.9 $\exists$E

At line (3) we made the assumption necessary for the first stage of Existential Elimination. Using the other rules, we finally got line (9) which depends on the assumption and the universal premise. Since line (9) does not contain ‘f’. It can count as C in the Existential Elimination rule. All that is needed is to make that explicit as was done in line (10). Here we are entitled to re-assert the sentence in line (9) as depending on lines (1) and (2).

Example 2

John likes something made of chocolate.
Everything made of chocolate is fattening.
Anything fattening is not good for you.
Therefore, John likes something that is not good for him.

Translation

$(\exists x)(Fx \ \& \ R_1ax)$
$(\forall x)(Fx \supset Gx)$
$(\forall x)(y)(Gx \supset \neg R_2xy)$

$(\exists x)(R_1 ax \ \& \ \neg R_2xa’)$

WHERE 'Fx' is 'x is made of chocolate
'R_1xy' is 'x likes y'
'Gx' is 'x is fattening'
'R_2xy' is 'x is good for y'.

NOTE In the third premise, we have an interesting case. What is the function of 'you'? As a pronoun it could be used to designate the addressee of the remark, but it is unlikely that this is its function here. After all, it isn't clear who the addressee is. A more reasonable interpretation is that it is used as a mark of generality, rather as one uses 'one'. As such it is understood as implicity universal and that explains the second universal quantifier in the translation. Note, additionally, that the domains of quantification have been restricted to 'things' for x and 'persons' for y.

Deduction

1	(1)	$(\exists x)\ (Fx\ \&\ Rax)$	Premise
2	(2)	$(\forall x)\ (Fx \supset Gx)$	Premise
3	(3)	$(\forall x)\ (\forall y)\ (Gx \supset \neg R_2Xy)$	Premise
4	(4)	$Ff\ \&\ R_1af$	Assumption
2	(5)	$Ff \supset Gf$	2 $\forall$E
3	(6)	$(\forall y)\ (Gf \supset \neg R_2\ fy)$	3 $\forall$E
3	(7)	$(Gf \supset \neg R_2\ fa$	6 $\forall$E
4	(8)	Ff	4 & E
2,4	(9)	Gf	5.8 $\supset$ E
2,3,4	(10)	$\neg R_2fa$	7,9 $\supset$ E
4	(11)	R_1af	4 & $\exists$
2,3,4,	(12)	$R_1af\ \&\ \neg R_2fa$	10,11&1
2,3,4,	(13)	$(\exists x)\ (R_1ax\ \&\ \neg R_2xa$	12 $\exists$1
1,2,3,	(14)	$(\exists x)\ (R_1ax\ \&\ \neg R_2xa$	1,4,13 $\exists$E

Here line (4) is the assumption needed for Existential Elimination The steps from (4) to (13) are those necessary to show that the conclusion follows from the premises and the assumption. Having established this, and given that the conclusion does not itself contain 'f', we are entitled to re-assert the conclusion in line (14). However, as per the rule for

Existential Elimination, this line depends on (1) and the other premises and no longer on (4). Thus, it is only in line (14) that the conclusion of the argument is shown to follow from the originally given three premises.

Example 3

Somebody kissed everybody at the party.
Therefore, everybody at the party was kissed by somebody or other.

Translation

$$\frac{(\exists x)\ (\forall y)\ Rxy}{(\forall y)\ (\exists x)\ Rxy}$$

(Notice that, in translating this argument, simplifying assumptions were made about the domain of quantification. There is no need to include predicates such as 'x is a person' and 'x was at the party' when simpler translation with restricted domains of quantification suffices for showing validity.)

Deduction

1	(1)	$(\exists x)(\forall y)Rxy$	Premise
2	(2)	$(\forall y)Rf_1y$	Assumption
2	(3)	$Rf_1\ f$	2 E
2	(4)	$(\exists x)Rxf_2$	3 ∃1
1	(5)	$(\exists x)Rxf_2$	1,2,4 ∃E
1	(6)	$(\forall y)(\exists x)Rxy$	5 I

In this deduction, we make the assumption at line (2) as the first stage in Existential Elimination. This assumption is then stripped of its universal quantifier (line (3)) and the existential quantifier is re-introduced at line (4). This is a most important line. It contains no occurrence of 'f_1', so it can legally count as C in the ∃E rule. But it also has the existential quantifier in the inside position and this is what the conclusion requires. Line (5) is the final stage in Existential Elimination. It confirms our right to assert the sentence in line (5) as the consequence of the original existential premise, and that is why we are allowed to say that line (5) depends on (1) and no longer on (2). The final line applies Universal Introduction to line (5). This is perfectly legal; line (5) depends only on line (I) and there is no occurrence of f_2' in line (I). In effect, the last line merely re-introduces the universal quantifier that was dropped in line (3). but the quantifier is now on the outside as required.

What would happen if we tried to deduce the converse of the above? That is, what would happen if we tried to Construct a deduction for the following argument?

Everyone at the party was kissed by someone or other.
Therefore, someone kissed everyone at the party.

This is a blatantly invalid argument; the premise guarantees that a lot of kissing took place, but it does *not* point to one particular person responsible for all of it. For this reason, you would expect the rules to block any deduction in this case, and that expectation is not disappointed. Here is the beginning of an attempted deduction.

1	(1) $(\forall y)(\exists x)Rxy$	Premise
1	(2) $(\exists x)Rxf$	I E
3	(3) Rf_2f_1	Assumption

At this point the deduction cannot proceed further. What is wanted is $(\forall y)Rf_2y$', but you cannot use $\forall$I to get it. Because line (3) depends on itself (it is an assumption) and contains 'f_1', you are not allowed to use $\forall$I.

5.6 Logical Truth and Vanishing Premises

Some sentences of Sentential were tautologies, their truth tables had T in every row. For example, the following is a very simple tautology:

$P \supset P.$

Using $\models$, we were able to indicate this by writing

$\models P \supset P.$

The double-bar turnstile says that the truth of the sentence(s) on the left *impose* truth on the sentence on the right. It is this property that allows us to use it when the set of sentences on the left are the premises of a valid argument and the sentence on the right is the conclusion. When there are no sentences on the left, as in the above example, we are forced to understand it as saying that *no sentences at all* are required to impose truth on the right-hand sentence. That is, the sentence is true in and of itself, its truth is self-imposed or *necessary*. In Sentential. the only sentences that are like this are tautologies and that is why the above use of the double-bar turnstile is a convenient way to indicate that a sentence is a tautology.

Also, you will remember this sort of assertion:

$\vdash P \supset P$.

The single-bar turnstile asserts that the sentence(s) on the left allow the construction of a deduction of the sentence on the right. More pedantically, it asserts that there is a deduction in which the right-hand sentence is the last line, and in which this last line depends on the line(s) containing the sentences on the left. In the above case, there are no sentences on the left. Hence, what is claimed is that there is a deduction in which the above sentence is the last line, and in which this last line depends on no previous line. Here is such a deduction.

(1) P	Assumption
(2) $P \supset P$	1,1 $\supset$I

Though we haven't actually proved it, it is provable that every assertion made about sentences in Sentential with the double-bar turnstile can be matched by an assertion with the single-bar turnstile (and vice versa). In every case in which a set of sentences imposes *truth* on another sentence, we can construct a *deduction* of this latter sentence using those in the former set, and vice versa.

Unsurprisingly, then, when the set of sentences on the

left is *empty*, as in the above cases, we would still expect the truth turnstile to be assertible whenever the deduction one is (and vice versa) and this is precisely how it turns out in Sentential. But what about Predicate?

The only way we have of showing an argument valid is by constructing a deduction. Thus, if you did the **EXERCISE** above you are now sure that

$$(\forall x)Fx \vdash (\exists x)Fx.$$

Does this entitle you to assert the following?

$$(\forall x)\ Fx \vDash (\exists x)Fx$$

That is, does the existence of a deduction in Predicate entitle you to assert that the premises of the deduction impose truth on its conclusion? Of course. What would have been the point of my long explanations of the quantifier rules if this wasn't so? Strictly speaking all of this is informal, we haven't the advanced logical machinery needed to prove it, but you can take my word for it.

Suppose now we were to construct a Predicate deduction which had no premises at all? This is easily done.

1	(1) $(\forall x)Fx$	Assumption
1	(2)Fa	1$\forall$E
1	(3)$(\exists x)Fx$	2 $\exists$I
	(4)$(\forall x)Fx \supset (\exists x)Fx$	1,3 $\supset$ I

This deduction entitles us to assert

$$\vdash (\forall x)Fx \supset (\exists x)Fx$$

and, following our discussion above, we are also entitled to assert

$$\vDash (\forall x)Fx \supset (\exists x)Fx.$$

But what are we to make of this assertion? Strictly, it says that this conditional imposes truth on itself, it cannot but be true. However, unlike such sentences in Sentential, it is not a tautology. This is because the method of truth tables is not applicable to the quantified sentences of Predicate, and a tautology is, by definition, a sentence whose truth table has T in every row.

What we need is a notion of a sentence which cannot but be true even though it is not a simple tautology. Such sentences will be called *logical truths.*

Logical truths can be very useful. For instance, in chapter 11, we discussed the relationship between the universal and existential quantifiers and came to the (informal) conclusion that '$(\forall x)$' means the same as '$\neg(\exists x)\neg$'. If we can construct a deduction to show that

$$\vdash (\forall x)Fx \equiv \neg(\exists x)\neg Fx$$

then by our earlier reasoning this equivalence will be counted as a logical truth. We will have proven something that we took on trust. Here is how to do it.

First, think of the task as broken down into two smaller ones, viz. showing that

(i) $\vdash (\forall x)Fx \supset \neg(\exists x)\neg Fx$
AND
(ii) $\vdash \neg(\exists x)\neg Fx \supset (\forall x)Fx$

It is easier to see what you are doing in each of these and they can be put back together at the end by $\equiv$ I. The deductions presented consecutively, and with the stages indicated, are as follows.

1	(1)	$(\forall x)Fx$	Assumption
2.	(2)	$(\exists x)\neg Fx$	Assumption
3	(3)	$\neg Ff$	Assumption
1	(4)	Ff	1 E
1,3	(5)	$Ff \;\&\; \neg Ff$	3,4 & I
3	(6)	$\neg(\forall x)Fx$	1,5 $\neg$I
2	(7)	$\neg(\forall x)Fx$	2,3,6 $\exists$E
1,2	(8)	$(\forall x)Fx \;\&\; \neg(\forall x)Fx$	1,7, & I
1	(9)	$\neg(\exists x)\neg Fx$	2,8 $\neg$I

(i)	(10)	$(\forall x)\ Fx \supset \urcorner (\exists x) \urcorner Fx$	$1,9 \supset I$
11	(11)	$\urcorner (\exists x) \urcorner Fx$	Assumption
12	(12)	$\urcorner Ff$	Assumption
12	(13)	$(\exists x) \urcorner Fx$	$12\ \exists I$
11,12	(14)	$(\exists x) \urcorner Fx\ \&\ \urcorner (\exists x) \urcorner Fx$	11,13 & I
11	(15)	$\urcorner\urcorner Ff$	$12,14 \urcorner I$
11	(16)	Ff	$15 \urcorner E$
11	(17)	$(\forall x)\ Fx$	16 I
(ii)	(18)	$\urcorner (\exists x) \urcorner Fx \supset (\forall x)\ Fx$	$11,17 \supset I$
	(19)	$[(\forall x)\ Fx \supset \urcorner (\exists x) \urcorner Fx]\ \&$	
	(19)	$[\urcorner (\exists x) \urcorner Fx \supset (x)\ Fx]$	10,18 & I
	(20)	$(\forall x)\ Fx \equiv \urcorner (\exists x) \urcorner Fx$	$19 \equiv I$

This is the longest deduction we have had, and it repays study. As is so often the case, the secret of success lies in the assumptions made. In the first stage, we assume the antecedent of the conditional (i), the conclusion without its initial negation, and '$\urcorner$Ft' which is needed for Existential Elimination. The strategy is to get a contradiction (line (5)) and blame the assumption in line (1). At this point, Existential Elimination can be applied to discharge the '$\urcorner$Ff assumption. By re-using the assumption in line (1), we can get a second contradiction (line (8)) and this is now blamed on the assumption in line (2). The result is '$\urcorner$ (3x) $\urcorner$ Fx' depending on line (I), so we can discharge all assumptions to get the conditional in line (10). This completes stage (i).

The second stage requires the assumption of the antecedent of (ii) and the assumption of '$\urcorner$ Ff. By Introducing an existential quantifier, we get '($\exists$x) $\urcorner$ Fx' and this contradicts the first assumption. Negation Introduction is effected on $\urcorner$ Ff' giving us ' $\urcorner\urcorner$ Ff' i.e. 'Ff'. Since this last sentence depends only on line (11) which does not contain f, we can Introduce a universal quantifier to get '(x)Fx'. The deduction is then completed by discharging the assumption at line (11) to get (ii), and then putting (i) and (ii) together to get line (20) by Equivalence Introduction.

5.7 PREDICATE, RULES AND ALGORITHMS

Truth tables are an effective and mechanical way to decide the validity of Sentential arguments; they provide an algorithm for validity. Constructing a deduction in Sentential seems altogether different. To see how to proceed in a deduction can require considerable thought. Also, if the argument you are working on is invalid, you will never be able to construct a deduction. Yet, you would not know how to distinguish this case from one in which the argument is valid, but the construction of its deduction is beyond your ability. The deduction method seems non-effective and non-mechanical.

However, as I pointed out, this appearance is deceptive. Though it is beyond the scope of this hook to prove it. the deduction method for Sentential is mechanical and effective. For any given argument, valid or not, you can mechanically go through every possible application of the rules to the premises. generating thereby every possible deduction. There will be a no doubt large but *finite* number of these, so all you have to do is systematically search through them. If one is a deduction of the conclusion, the argument is valid; if there is no such deduction, then the argument is invalid.

Crucial to this procedure working are:

(i) the systematic application of the rules to any given set of premises generates only a finite number of possible deductions;

(ii) the rules suffice to construct a deduction for any valid argument of Sentential, they are *complete*.

Of course, we do not go about constructing deductions in this way. It would take a great deal of time and would be tedious beyond belief. Instead, we exercise our ingenuity in examining the premises and the rules. With sufficient skill, we can see how to construct the deduction for a valid argument without going through too many detours. Nonetheless, it is worth your knowing that, in respect of Sentential, the rules can be shown to constitute an algorithm for validity, even if it is only in principle and not in practice. It is worth your knowing this partly because matters are different with respect to Predicate.

It can be shown that the application of the rules to Predicate language arguments cannot be arranged so as to constitute an algorithm for validity. The skilful use of these rules is a necessity and not merely a convenience. Further, the reason for the difference between Sentential and Predicate has nothing to do with completeness. It has been demonstrated that a deduction can be provided, using the fourteen rules, for every valid argument of Predicate. The problem is not the completeness of the rules, but the fact that there is no guarantee of a *finite* number of possible deductions for any given set of premises. Since we cannot depend on finiteness here, we cannot describe an algorithm which asks us to check over every possible deduction to see if there is one that meets our requirements. Remember, an algorithm must be a procedure with a finite number of steps.

Nor is this all. Logicians have been able to show, not only that the deduction method is not an algorithm, but that *there cannot be any algorithm for validity in Predicate.* This is a very interesting result. It means that in developing a sufficiently rich language - Predicate - to give the Strategy some hope of dealing with natural language arguments. the possibility of an algorithm for validity has disappeared. I suppose some of you might think this an unfortunate result for the Strategy. but I urge you to reconsider. It is only because of the Strategy that we are in a position to appreciate this fact about natural language arguments. Our patient working through the Strategy has helped us to discover that natural language arguments of a certain degree of complexity cannot be tested for validity by any algorithmic procedure.

NOTE Everything in this section depends on results in logic (such as completeness) which cannot be demonstrated in this book. For those interested in pursuing these matters, consult the Reading List at the end of the book.

The Main Points of Chapter 5

(1) We first showed why truth tables could not be used to decide the validity of Predicate arguments. The obvious next move is to consider the method of deduction.

(2) A notation for expressing the Quantifier Rules was then introduced. This included schematic presentations of variables and predicates.

(3) The four Quantifier Rules were presented and justified as truth preserving.

(4) Since Predicate does not allow us to use truth tables, there are no Predicate tautologies except in the trivial sense of sentences of Sentential which we count as incorporated into Predicate. However, there are sentences of Predicate which cannot but be true, since they are deducible from *no* premises or assumptions. These are called *logical truths.* In calling sentences which are deducible from no premise or assumptions logical *truths*, we depended on the fact that the Quantifier Rules are wholly truth preserving. In more advanced logical texts, this fact, called *soundness*, can be demonstrated in detail.

(5) Though we haven't the tools needed to prove it, Predicate is *complete*, every logical truth is deducible. In this sense, Predicate is just like Sentential. However, Predicate differs from Sentential in an important respect: there can be no algorithm for validity in Predicate, whereas both truth tables and deduction are algorithms for validity in Sentential. This lack of any possible decision procedure for Predicate can be demonstrated, but, as with soundness and completeness, you should consult the Reading List if you want to track down the advanced texts which contain such demonstrations.

Chapter-6

Logic and the Ideal Rational Life

Chapter-6

I. INTRODUCTION

It is proper that logic should distil from its mass of truth a contribution to perspective in human life. Certainly it is a vantage point from which one can understand the benefits and limitations that occur when life expresses itself in any rational form. For an important part of its work is study of the structure of formal systems; further it formalizes very exactly its own methods and truths; and its role in the creation and operation of our computer world has been very important. For all these reasons it is proper that a contemporary philosophy of logic should have the function of providing perspective on formalism and wisdom in the human disposition to formalize.

This chapter will analyse, firstly the human value and necessity of formalization and the efficiency of logic as a science here then it will and the limitations of formalization. These analyses will be a basis for presenting a logical ideal for rational living, the ideal being named meta formalism. This ideal has strong affinities to a new contemporary scientific method which will be described.

II. FORMALIZATION IS INHERENT TO RATIONAL LIVING

To be rational is to be operating some formal system; logical procedures in logical language are an extension of natural procedures in natural language. For instance, one aspect of thinking rationally is that we think in accord with what we already know: previous knowledge is a continuous rational constraint—we bring it to bear in a quasi-axiomatic way. We accept systematic consistency as a condition of rationality in daily life, i.e. that principles, explicit or implicit, which are present at the start should be held rigorously throughout the context. The rational expectancies of our daily life have, indeed, the logical character of theorems and instantiations from our *weltanshauung*. Little conscious effort may be involved in the daily exercise of systematic thought, for the knowledge used is habitual and the procedures of judging and testing in the light of that knowledge are habits too.

The very language we use involves a viewpoint, materializes a systematic outlook, is by nature a vehicle of models. Wittgenstein would put it that behind any contemporary language lies the history of a nation's forms of life in the language of Teilhard de Chardin these constitute a noosphere. It is inherent in human living that live in particular cultures and that, accordingly we think systematically. And indeed characteristics of nature, sovereign, thinking are present when we are systematic: commitment to principle and to procedure, generality and tenslessness of statement, precision and consistency in content.

Logic itself bears witness to our strong rational impulse both to elaborate truth, transmitting it to consequences, and to diagnose flasehood, locating its roots in a false principle. If not a definition of the science, it is certainly an important aspect that it is a theory of derivability and that this theory is necessarly operational (to varying degrees) in the other sciences and in daily life.

III. THE LIMITATIONS OF FORMALIZATION

Formalization has, however, important limitations—essentially, historically and psychologically.

A radical incompleteness in human formalizations has been indicated both techniclly and philosophically. In Aristotle's view material reality is not completely conceptualizable, is not totally formal; this led him to the hylomorphic theory of matter.

For Aquinas, similarly, no reality is known fully in concepts, is completely formalizable; thus our rational point of view shows up the things of our experience as being composite; if one speaks of that in them which is conceptualizable as essence, then one has to say that *to be* is not identical with *being of this essence*—there is a real distinction between the rationality of a thing and its actual being.

An essential point in Frege's theory of predication was the observation that a concept has not the complete reality ('saturation') of the object conceived. Gödel's famous incompleteness theorem established that arithmetic, and any formal system which requires it, is necessarily incomplete. For Wittgenstein an indefinite number of language games is possible, for languages are forms of life and life is too rich for complete formalization. Introducing an abstract computing device, now called a Turing machine, Turing showed that the application of such machines to theories other than arithmetic is effected by an arithmetization process and that there are an uncountable infinitude of non-computable arithmetic functions. These varied and important conclusion point to a common fact, namely that formalization is always an asymptotic movement, if one takes as its goal a complete grasping of reality; they indicate that over-control by an particular formal system or device is not natural to the human mind and underrates the range of its power.

In conceiving the possibility of science (logic) which would transcend contexts and abstract from the impact of lived experience, Boole implicity underwrote the importance of not identifying logicality with total rationality. And Leibniz distinguished accurate knowledge and adequate knowledge drawing attention to enormously important elements in our life and in the world which cannot be put in scientific terms. However, the Western world has pursued rationality predominantly in the form of logicality. With its ideal of quantitative exactness and complete objectivity or exteriority in knowledge it has achieved technological control over nature, but its rationality has not been sufficient for understanding the complex unity of human life and the world: it has not integrated into a single culture the clarity and simplicity of exact science with humanistic sensibilities, and it has not retained human properties and values in an era of technology. Rather, mental enquiry and technology has moved forward too much on rigid formal tracks, driven by a logic of intensification and incrementation which prescinded largely from human consequence. According to contemporary thinkers such as Polanyi and Merleau-Ponty we are coming to the end of this epoch of exaggerated objectivism; Marjorie Grene writes:

> We are in the midst of a new philosophical revolution, a revolution in which, indeed, the new physics too has had due influence, but a revolution founded squarely on the disciplines concerned with life: on biology, psychology, sociology, history, even theology and art criticism... we have had to free ourselves from the bonds of Newtonian abstraction, to dare, not only to manipulate abstractions, to calculate and predict and falsify, but to *understand*. The revolution before us is a revolution of life against dead nature, and of understanding as against the calculi of logical machines .... The conceptual reform in which we are now engaged must restore our speech about the world to intelligible discourse and the world it aims at describing to significant and coherent form. Nature must be understood once more as the multifarious scene, not only of an invisible billiards game played by chance against necessity, but of a vast variety of forms, energies and events, living and non-living, sentient and insentient, of processes alive, active and striving, as well as of conditions, dead, passive and inert (*The Knower and the Known*, pp. 13-14)

The analytic aspect of formalist thinking has been particularly cultivated by the West. This carries with it the habit of dissecting, and of separating everything from everything else, ourselves from the world and from one another. It is natural that this has contributed to the creation of psychic distances, alienating us from the world and from others, and to the felt need for restoring interconnectedness and achieving integrated social living. Certainly, analytic habits can act like an over-efficient grindstone on the cutting surface of the mind. It seems that the great Asiatic cultures have avoided this characteristic of Western thought, have expressed themselves in fluid analogies rather than in well-defined concepts and have sought *union* with nature in an intuitive, subjective, mystical approach.

Psychologically, there is such a thing as mental cramp, the mind being locked in a particular orientation by, e.g. a set of principles that was never fully understood and chosen, by what is implicit in the language system we use, by a less than adequate objective which keeps us moving with considerable intent in one direction (e.g. towards maximum efficiency in locomotion or towards complete computerization). Such 'sets' may be cultural and individuals may be unconscious of the fact that they are not in the nature of things. They may also be generated by personal assumptions or habits never duly examined. Their common result is that under the spell of a deductive compulsion we constantly reapply narrow attitudes of the past, justify repeatedly the characteristic theorems of our lives, relive the same decisions, go through the same behaviour until a good deal of our life is quite spiritless. A most difficult thing for each person is maintaining human proportions, being in all things human not simply rational and exact on one's own terms, but adequate.

The contrasting logical structures of rationalization and self-deception show, each in its own way, how great an effort is required to confront the fact that we are acting inconsistently with some axiom or rule in our lives. In rationalization, the reasons for an action or decision which we present and acknowledge have the quality of consistency with our principles but they fail to express what really motivates us. Our individual form of life presses us to defend it, in this way, against the inroads of our own freedom. The structure of self-deception displays a different mechanism of defence employed in the same cause. Herbert Fingarette points out that the term, invites us to think of the phenomenon as a form of lying to oneself, to conceive it on the model of 'other deception' and to describe it in terms of belief and perception language:

> For example, at is quite natural to speak of the self deceiver as one who doesn't *perceive* his own fakery, who can't *see through* the smokescreen he himself puts up. We also *say* that in a way he sincerely *believes the* story *he* tells while 'deep inside him' he *knows* it *is* not true. He makes it appear to himself that something is so. We say the self deceiver is unaware of his own deception; and, in straight psychoanalytic language, we Speak of his *unconscious* wishes and fantasies. Though in general this is a bag of quite various words, their remarkable interchangeability in the context of self-deception justifies, in this context, our grouping them initially as a single family of terms. (*Self-Deception*, pp.34–5)

Fingarette takes as a basic fact that to become explicitly conscious of some-thing is to be exercising a certain skill, namely the skill of expressing a particular life situation of ours in langauge (-like) form.

> We then state that the self-deceiver is one whose life situation is such that, on the basis of this tacit assessment of his situation, he finds there is an overriding reason for adopting a policy of not spelling-out some engagement of his in the world. As with any reasonably well developed skill, so in this case, too, the action suits the tacit assessment: he does not, therefore, spelout the matter in question; and by virtue of this policy, he is further obliged not to spell out the assessment or the policy. The consequence is that he may be observed as one who is in fact engaged in the world in a certain way such as carrying out a destructive campaign against some person ... yet he is unable (by virtue of his tacit commitment) to spell this fact out to himself or to anyone else. Thus when the issue is raised, he does not, cannot, express the matter explicitly at all. He is in this respect in no better position than anyone else. He tells us nothing but what he tells himself. *(Self-*

Deception, p.62)

The person has, generally speaking, three options in a situation in which he is strongly inclined to a way of acting which is radically inconsistent with his avowed explicit outlook and aims. One option is to totally forego the way of acting in question; a second is to avow it as *his.* In this second option one becomes a radically divided and vulnerable being; one faces a spiritual crisis in the Kierkegaardian sense of a crisis of the shaping, or the betraying, of the self The third option is to leave the stalemate between inclination and personality and to move into self-deception the—individual engaging himself in the way to which he is inclined, but the person refusing to acknowledge the engagement as his.

Interpreted in this way as motivated strategy, i.e. as something the ego does rather than as something which happens to the ego, one sees the powerful role of system within human life and the tensions it creates in authentic living. This is especially true if one views the skill (witheld in the situation of self-deception) of spelling-out, of being consciously clear and explicit, as being intimately associated with the highest level of organization and unification of the individual human life.

Finally, there is such a thing as putting an excessive value on clarity, on the clarity that formalization provides. It is difficult to sustain the excessive clarity of someone else's formalizations: the system (within its own terms of reference) is so wholly present, so cogent that the hearer is robbed of potentiality. No one is clearer in mind than a person with an obsession. And the clarity of our own thinking too may blind us to its narrowness of scope.

IV. METAFORMALISM AS AN IDEAL FOR RATIONAL LIVING

The basic fact is That formalizations neither fully contain the material object's reality nor do they express the human subject's vitality completely. A formalization is incomplete both as description and as expression. This indicates that subjectivity, open to all viewpoints, has a wider receptivity than can be accommodated by a sum total of formal systems, and that the human person is meant to maintain this basic openness and receptivity.

As subject I seem to have an indefinite openness to life. I remain a mystery to myself, in my subjectivity, in that I can never completely formalize myself, to myself. I can objectify and understand the range of capacities I display; with others I can subjugate my environment to myself and constitute social life on our planet as I wish. But while I must live in *some* environment and constitute some particular kind of social life, my subjectivity is not really comprehended in terms of my particulars limited circumstances and specific achievements—I could be living a very different kind of life and be a very different kind of being, mentally and bodily. There is no bipolar (subject-object) life of which I can say that I could not be subject in it, that it could not be personally my life.

Thus the subjection of life to system is not the rational ideal for life. We demonstrate a greater rationality by looking on form not as fulfilling but as enriching, not as the goal and termination of effort but as a base for further ascent, not as bringing to rest our desire and search for truth but as incr-easing, endlessly, our potentiality for it. Such a perspective may be called *metaformalism* since it is justified by reflection on the value and limitations of formalization in human life.

It is a striking fact that today studies of diverse sciences are drawing attention to how much of ourselves is in our world: to the process of objectivization and to the fact that the world in which we live and move and have our being is an objective world, encountered by us in a bipolar (subject-object, from-to) experience. The act of being that is formalized in human knowledge is being-revealing-itself to human-consciousness; the human view point (sensitive and rational) is an intrinsic part of the formalization. Today interest in the mind's synthetic function in objectivization has displaced and dated the traditional controversy of Idealism and Realism. The complexities of objectvization are conceived to invalidate, as oversimplifications, both poles of this controversy.

The fact is that, as human beings, all we can say is what is or is not objectively so, and to understand the nature and range of objective truth we must understand objectivization. Just as in physical science, relativity theory points out that there is no such thing as a brute fact, the simplest entity in science being an observed fact, so too logical experience at the level of theoretical thought is that an essential relativity or proportion attaches to the world in which we live and move and have our being. Every objective fact is being-revealing-itself-to-consciousness the simplest fact expresses *a priori* conditions and terms of the rational viewpoint. Experience of formalization has drawn attention, within the science of logic, to rationality as input and, indeed, formal recognition of this input constitutes a radical difference between the axiomatic procedure and that of natural deduction.

Thus logical experience does not support the positivist belief that scientific knowledge possesses a total exteriority any more than it supports belief in an irrational, arbitrary subjectivity it suggests to the logician that, as an ideal and master movement in rational living, we should maintain a freedom and mobility of viewpoint (which would be compatible with a further theistic expectancy of, and 'waiting for', a revelation of absolute unobjectified, unformalized being).

For some philosphers the discovery of so much that is of ourselves in the world, the extended awareness of the raw material from which life is built, has given rise to a sense of emptiness and futility a pessimism. For Cioran western civilization is in a state of paralysis; every idea and movement works itself out formalistically and then crumbles. Reason is 'the rust of our vitality—'it is by undermining the idea of reason, of order, of harmony that we gain consciousness of ourselves'. 'An individual, like a people, like a continent, dies out when he shrinks from both rash plans and rash acts, when instead of taking risks and hurling himself towards being, he cowers within it, takes refuge there.'

Logical experience does not support this pessimism. The objective world is our world: it can be as optimal as we make it; always it is *possibly* the best of worlds. Again, the limits of objectivization, sensitive and rational, which are coming more and more into focus, point to ineffable possibilities in unobjectified, undisclosed, being. Further, and very practically, logical experience draws attention to our faculty of transcending the objective, and it suggests that the vitality of transcendence may be of central importance for contemporary well being. Nowadays the multiplicity of systems (beliefs, values, ways of life) has a pessimising effect—for many people it has become difficult to so believe that it would be logical and a worthy thing to die for their belief. Logical experience, following the natural grain of human life, suggests that the central skill of that life consists in combining a definite choice and dedication in objective living with cultivation of our capacity for transcendence.

Transcendence is threefold. We have the capacity to move out of the gravitational field of our objective circumstances and on to contact, feeling and enjoyment of our own subjectivity. Transcendence of this type may be explicitly practised; it is also implicit in the development of ego strength, the maturation of personality. There is also the transcendence of objectified being that moves towards unobjectified, undisclosed being. It is a function of philosophy to be transcendent in this way. Finally, for the theist, there is the transcendence that moves towards God and divine life, in the hope that our obediential capacity for the ineffable life of God will be actualized.

Thus logical experience is hospitable to the ideal of a life that has bi-polar strength that integrates dedication and transcendence, temporal achievement and everlasting freedom. Life points to the future. The capacity to assimilate the past as potentiality for the future, to orientate ourselves with great flexibility, with heuristic curiosity about a reality that is only partially disclosed—these are important human qualities at every moment of evolutionary time.

The word, *evolution,* underlines a basic function of any logical system or social structure—to contain an elaborated point of view and to mediate development to a wider point of view with richer content. It is the spirit of a dynamic conservatism to recognize that the past justifies itself by leading to a better future. Such a spirit needs the service of a section of logic which is pluralistic, i.e. which is a science of integrating different formal orientation, which designs 'system-operators' (analgous to propositional operators) studying the connectivity of systems, and which achieves a technique of systematic and contemporary questioning of structures that mediates genuine development. We tend to use a restricted logic for thinking in closed systems: we prove what we like and we like what we prove, expecting that a principle of logical osmosis will bring others to the same logical consistency. The ground of a pluralistic logic, however, is not the closed system but mela-formalism; the space of such a logic is peopled by myriads of (elaborated) viewpoints: it is the grammar of the connectivity and integration of viewpoints, the technical embodiment of magnanimity and love.

V. METAFORMALISM AND THE NEW LOGIC OF FRAMEWORK TRANSPOSITIONS WITHIN SCIENCE

Current scrutiny of the notion and validity of objectivity has served to present scientific knowledge no longer as a single system expressed in a single language but as a collection of contexts each with its own formal point of departure, conceptual framework, language and elaborated content. The question and need arises: is there a process of integrating whole conceptual frameworks—a formal logical process? Is there a rational grammar for combining context-languages? Important beginnings have been made in working out a new logic of framework transpositions.

With regard to literature on this subject: the writings of Polanyi and Popper are well-known general treatments of the notion of objectivity in science; recent studies by Butterfield, Conant, Kuhn, Agassi, Feyerabend, Hanson, Sellars, Wartofsky and Heelan have criticized relevant assumptions of classical science; the writings of Patrick Heelam are a primary source and the following treatment is based on his extremely lucid presentations.

The situation requiring a new logic arose in the first decades of this century with the replacement of classical physics by quantum physics:

> This involved a conversion from the classical model of a subjectless scientific objectivity to the subject-dependent objectivity of quantum mechanics. Quantum mechanics arose as the outcome of Werner Heisenberg's reflection on the role of observables in science. By an 'observable' he meant a quantity that, though not imaginable in a classical space time model, was part of the interpretations of a mathematical model and was measurable in principle. His intution rejected the objectivist presuppositions of classical physics and in a profoundly significant epistemological shift, he conciously placed the measuring subject or observer at the heart of quantum mechanics. The classical physics of his time presupposed either no observer or one separated from matter and outside of history. The quantum mechanical observer, on the other hand, is one of human scale who uses instruments of the same scale to observe, quantum-mechanical events and processes. Quantum-mechanical observers, then, are as manifold as the kinds of instruments a scientist can use. The most significant discovery of quantum mechanics, however, is the fact that it is not possible to construct an instrument or a panel of instruments that will give simultaneously the values of all the observable properties of a quantum mechanical system.
>
> Quantum mechanics thus is concerned with contextual observations or descriptions; that is, every observation of

a quantum-mechanical system is dependent on the context of the observation, which is, namely, the measuring instrument used to make an observation... What looks from the classical perspective to be a restrictive principle expressing, namely, our inability to measure simultaneously the precise position and momentum of a system, turns out, with the quantum-mechanical perspective, to be in the first instance a revelation of the context- or observer dependent character of scientific observations. It also shows that the total scientific horizon is not revealed to any one observer, but that in addition to possible (precise) position states and possible (precise) momentum states there are those imprecise states of position and momentum together revealed in response to mixed contexts of observation. In other words, the synthesis of context results in an enrichment of the horizon vis-a-vis the complementary contexts—taken as thesis and antithesis in their pure dialectical opposition.

(For example, in a mixed position and momentum context precise position or precise momentum cannot in principle be observed, but imprecise position (x) and imprecise momentum (p) can be observed and the systematic variabilities (or 'uncertainties') Δx and Δp of x and p respectively will obey Heisenberg's uncertainty Principle ... which relates the measure of inaccuracy *(Δx)* of a position measurement (x) with the associated measure of inaccuracy (Δp of a momentum measurement (p) according to the inequality of $\Delta x. \Delta p \geq h/2\pi$—Where h is Planck's constant.) *(Nature and its Transformations,* pp.498-9)

Thus there is no basic set of 'observational facts given immediately and indubitably in experience without the involvement of the subject', and there is no privileged set of basic concepts 'considered as irreformable because received passively from the object':

... the contrast between the observational, on the one hand' as epistimically certain and descriptive of reality, and the

> theoretical, on the other hand, as tentative, provisional and not descriptive of reality, cannot any longer be sustained. Certainty is found in the use of both types of predicates, and both are used descriptively of the world... The theoretical explanation of motion becomes an ingredient of our observations of motion. Observational language in fact, becomes laden with theory. That there is in principle no aspect of observational language that is free from the intrusions of theory is the well known theme of a certain group of authors led by Toulmin, Hanson and Feyerabend. In brief, we might summarize their conclusion and ours, that *observational* and *theoretical* are not characteristics of predicates but of predications or uses of predicates: a *theoretical* use being inferential, mediate and circumspect vis-à-vis realistic intent an *observational* use being non-infrential, immediate and realistic in intent. (The *Logic of Framework Transpositions*, p.317).

The progressive theoretical exploration of each domain of fact is stored in a descriptive language which is an historical entity with an historical development. Naturally, over centuries, a vast family of conceptual frameworks and appropriate languages have come into existence. Some deal with the same domain of facts (and historically, perhaps, one replaced another), others do not; some are compatible, some complementary, some incompatible. The question is what is the logic of relationships between frameworks and the possibility, through logic, of integrating them? This question can be formulated in terms of language, for each framework is a linguistic context, generating necessary and sufficient conditions subjective and objective for the use of a descriptive language. So formulated the question is: what are logical models for understanding inter-framework relationships and developmental transpositions between frameworks in history? Further, is it possible with the contributing help of a 'context-logic' to integrate all context languages, securing a cumulative field of vision from a single linguistic viewpoint?

One of the examples Heelan gives of the kind of logical understanding a context logic would provide relates to quantum mechanics:

> Quantum mechanics with its complementary languages illustrates a peculiarity of a wide class of context dependent languages—that they are mutually exclusive yet not absolutely so. They resist combination on the one hand, and on the other, they can be combined within a broader more inclusive language, which, however, is not in a Boolean relation to the original languages, but stands to them in the non-Boolean relation of a non-distributive lattice.
>
> The paradigm case is precise position language L_a and precise momentum language L_b in quantum mechanics. Each corresponds to its own measurement contexts precise position language is the linguistic projection of precise position-measurement-contexts, precise momentum language is the linguistic projection of precise momentum-measurement-contexts. Bohr and Heisenburg and most complementarity physicists claim that these languages are subsets of the Kinematical language of classical physics. That this is mistaken was pointed out by Feyerabend and the present author...the position and momentum languages are subsets of a braoder quantum mechanical kinematical language L_{ab} in which the space-time description of any quantum system can be formulated, whether or not the system is found in a precise position or precise momentum-measurement-context. The author showed that L_{aa}, L_b, L_{ab}, and their complements suitable defined constitute an ortho complemented non distributive lattice of languages. L_a and L_b can then be said to be *complementary in* L_{ab}. This is not the same as what Bohr meant, since L_{ab} neither contains nor is contained by the Kinematical language of classical physics. It simply replaces it.

The relationships between the three languages L_a, L_b and L_{ab} can be illustrated by means of an analogy taken from biology. Two isolated allopatric stable populations *A* and B of the same species exist in different environments, say, on either side of a broad impassable river. Each population has its own set and distribution of genotypes, G_a and G_b respectively. A Boolean union of the two populations would be one where the distribution of the genotypes would be just the set theoretic sum of the genotypes of the two populations. A Boolean union of two such populations if it makes scientific sense at all, makes sense only if the geographical barrier between the two populations remains intact. But if the geographical barrier is removed, say, by building a bridge across the river, each population is able to invade the territory of the other. New selection pressures arise, genes are exchanged, and possibly new hybrids are found. The exchange of genes, hybridization and natural selection work in the course of time to produce a new steady-state distribution of genotypes G_{ab} in the expanded stabilized population *AB*, which now occupies the whole territory. G_{ab} will be quite different from a BooI can union of the two original distributions G_a and G_b. The genotypes of populations A and B, even though presumably they all persist among the genotypes of the united stablized population *AB*, are in a non-Bolean relation to the latter. The non-Boolean relationships between G_a, G_b and G_{ab} constitute what is called a non-distributive lattice. *(Scienitfic Objectivity and Framework Transpositions)*

The concluding comment is:

The value of the analysis I have just gives over other proposals for the use of a non-classical logic in quantum mechanics and elsewhere is manifold. Firstly, the claim that the context languages constitute an orthocomplemented non-distributive lattice is a precise, well-defined claim which is subject to falsifying tests, secondly, it enables classical logic to be retained, it there are good reasons for retaining it, on the level of each of the related object languages, L_a, L_b and the language of the synthetic context L_{ab}. Non-classical logic need enter only when complementary contexts are combined and in this case, it functions solely on the metalinguistic level of a meta context language which is itself a part of the philosophy of the languages concerned and does not affect the use of the languages themselves. Thirdly, the account I have just proposed can be the starting point for many investigations in the philosophy and history of science and in melsascience of science and philosophy (Ibid)

VI. GENERAL CONCLUSION

Two important insights from the history of logic are that the simplest linguistic act is the sentence (the meaning of words being determined by their roles in sentences) and that the simplest logical act is some exercise of the grammar of propositional logic (formalizing a *whole* proposition, connecting whole propositions monadically, dyadically, etc.). This subordination of parts to a whole may continue to leaven the science of logic. For not only has it seen that propositional, and not terminal, logic is basic within standard logic, it is natural also that it try to situate propositional logic itself within a more general context. Technically, it is quite possible that the basic section of future standard logic will be 'system logic' or 'context logic' (the simplest logical act being regarded as an exercise of its grammar), for it is entirely arguable that a whole framework or system is presupposed and is implicitly present in the for malization and connectivity of propositions. There may then be new Stoic and new Fregean explorers reaching a deeper level in the standard analysis of rationality.

This would bring a qualitative change to modern logic—a science which has been widening itself more than it has been deepening in roots. It would be the kind of technical development which would underwrite the view that logic cannot be fully understood without being seen in its relationship with rational competence and human subjectivity. A 'system logic' would perhaps point to this relationship more strongly than propositional logic.

Chapter-7

Logical forms in the Empirical Sciences

Chapter 7

I. INTRODUCTION

The empirical sciences are sufficiently identified as the present-day range of physical, biological and psychological sciences—they purport to deal directly with ourselves and the would we sense and their conclusions are tested in an appeal made (in experiment or observation) to our world. Extra-experiential or *a priori* sciences, on the other hand, either develop without reference to any particular world (mathematics and logic) or refer to realities that transcend human experience and operate from principles that are acceptable only on the ground of being revealed (supernatural theology).

This chapter will seek to summarize the description which empirical science gives of its own structural growth, and to stress the logical forms which appear in this description and which are the source of the logical strength of the empirical sciences. Problems that arise when the logical formation of scientific argumentation or investigation is not perfect or is not completely explicit will be discussed in the following chapter.

II. AN HISTORICAL SURVEY OF THE DEVELOPMENT, STRUCTURALLY, OF PHYSICAL SCIENCE AND OF SCIENTIFIC METHOD GENERALLY

The Greek contribution to this development. In empirical science today one can distinguish very clearly (1) its field investigations where, by observation and experiment, it tries to reach particular laws; and (2) its theoretical work where it seeks to co-ordinate these laws into a concise explanatory system. A scientist today may be either a field scientist or a theoretical scientist—rarely is the same person both to any really great degree. The Greeks were not empirical scientists in the modern sense of the world. Their interest and insights lay not in methods of investigations but in the theoretical organization of knowledge—in science as an explanatory system of propositions. Consequently their philosophy and science were not sharply distinguished, it was not that they lacked observation or failed to appreciate its value but simply that the conception of science as an experimental, mathematical enterprise was a later development.

A great achievement of the Greek period was to objectify the human hope of explaining the world, developing a theory of explanation and providing in Euclid a model of systematic explanation. Primitive types of explanation personifed forces in the world and tended to project features of our mental life into things. The Greeks, however, conceived explanation as essentially a logical thing, rooted in evidence and meaning. For them to explain the world would be to reflect it in a system of propositions where less general propositions would be deducible from the more general ones; to explain any particular proposition would be to situate it under the general principle from which it could be deduced.

Thus empirical science is indebted to the Greeks for the development of its deductive and explanatory character; in particular to Socrates for a theory of definitions, to Plato for a general theory of the hypothetical approach—the deducing and verifying of consequences—and to Aristotle for a general theory of induction. Aristotle saw that the world of nature could always be otherwise than it is and, therefore, that a purely deductive science of it is not possible. He emphasized that while scientific *explanation* is deductive (and can always be formulated syllogistically) ·scientific *investigation* must be an inductive process, a generalization of particular experience. His treatment of the possible types of induction is very important but his description of the rationale of the inductive process in the concrete modern framework of experiment and mathematical calculation. In this description, the object of the inductive process is to abstract and define forms and a fact (or effect) is explained when it can be shown to be the subject of some defined form, e.g. the phenomenon of falling is explained in terms of it being the nature of a heavy body to fall when unsupported in the atmosphere. Forms vary in degree of abstractness and those displayed in the explanations of Physics, Mathematics and Philosophy represent three different levels of abstractness or generalization.

In his treatment of what modern logicians call inntiative induction (a process in which our sense experience of a particular fact is such as to facilitate direct insight into a general principle), Aristotle points out that science is not self-demonstrating but must originate in intuition. The body of scientific knowledge is generated by two complementary processes—intution and inference. Intutions, immediate apprehensions of fact, occur at both the sensory and intellectual levels of knowing. It is the business of sensory intution to supply science with its data; the role of science is to explain the data by presenting it as deducible from general propositions which, themselves, are ultimately situated under primary principles that do not need to be proved because they are intellectual intutions. Thus when scientific knowledge is organized into an explanatory system of propositions, sensory intutions appear as theoretical conclusions, intellectual intutions as primary explanatory principles; and throughout the system there is recurring process of demonstration, i.e. explanation through deduction from propositions that are more general and, therefore, intrinsically more intelligible.

In Aristotle's foundational study of physical science, basic commitments are made:

(1) *to a reality principle*: every proposition of science refers to the real world;

(2) to *an evidence principle*: there are indefinable terms (so obvious in meaning as to require no explanation) and indemonstrable truths (so obvious in truth as to require no proof);

(3) to *a truth principle*: to be scientific a proposition must be

true;

(4) to *a deductivity principle:* every logical consequence of a scientific proposition is also scientific.

This set of postulates commits science to foundations that coalesce experience and logic, but the coalescence itself is not worked out and clarified—unless one holds that scientific principles are within reach of common intution and do not require systematic mathematical research. In Aristotle's own day these postulates were attacked by the School of Megara, and paradoxes that have become famous were urged against them (e.g. the Liar paradox against the truth postulate); historians such as Prantl and Zeller have regarded these paradoxes as trivial fallacies but their significance was appreciated in antiquity. In the event Aristotle's theory (presented in his *Prior* and *Posterior Analytics*) was accepted and remained dominant for centuries even while physical science itself changed, becoming experimental and mathematical in character.

Within the Aristotelian framework physical science was not able to come to a clear-cut concept of itself—to see in what precise ways it is an idealizing, logical discipline and an experiencing, discovering one also. The fact is that modern science may be considered from two widely differing aspects: (a) as an enterprise of discovery; and (b) as an explanatory body of propositions, axiomatization being the standard method for consolidating and transmitting knowledge. When modern science is *explaining* (or demonstrating) what it has already discovered, it is an idealizing, logical discipline; for discovering truth, however, it recognizes and practices both an empirical approach, and a purely rational, imaginative one. The former approach examines experiments and expresses the regularity of results in terms of physical laws; it checks new theories at every stage and modifies them when new results demand it-and this is an important way in which physical theories come to be formulated. The latter approach constructs theories, imaginatively; speaking of Einstein's major discovery, Lanczos says:

> He could no longer doubt that nature is much more than a conglomeration of accidental mathematical equations which serve for the description of this or that natural phenomenon. There are great and sweeping principles acting in nature which, when found, show us the unifying links between the confusing variety of single events. Newton's theory of gravitation was age old, a closed chapter of physics, there was no reason to ponder on it, nothing new came to light in this field for the last hundred years. And yet, purely as the result of a philosophical enquiry, a deep analysis of reference systems, an entirely new light was shed on the old phenomenon, gravitation was something totally different from anything assumed before, a natural and inevitable property of the geometrical structure realized in nature. Would it be imaginable to make such a discovery by mere observation and trying to fit the observations by a mathematical formula? Not in a million years. Constructive and imaginative mathematical reasoning of greatest profundity was demanded for such a discovery. (*Rationalism and the Physical World*)

Thus, quite understandably, Aristotle's foundational studies did not produce an adequate framework for modern science. In him, the Greeks moved from the foundational research of mathematics (completed by Eudoxus and Theaetetus) to a similar research of physical science. But Greek science was simply observational, neither experimental nor mathematical. And the coalscence of the empirical and the purely rational (so essential and intricate in modern science) was assumed but left uncharted.

The medieval contribution in the development of empirical science. The conception of empirical science as essentially an experimental and mathematical enterprise goes back further than the sixteenth and seventeenth centuries to medieval times. In achieving this conception medieval science advanced beyond the Greek and Arabian stage. The conception itself became more technical and operational in the modern period of science.

In Aristotle, Physics and Mathematics were kept rigidly apart. The concrete world was the province of Physics, and physical questions and answers were non-mathematical in character. From the thirteenth century there was a growing insight into the usefulness of mathematics in explaining the physical world and a gradual penetration of mathematical procedures into physical investigations. By the fourteenth century systematic attempts were being made to express and deal with qualities and motion in quantitative terms. Thus while remaining very limited indeed in mathematical technique, the mathematical physics of the fourteenth and fifteenth centuries developed, conceptually, with out a break into that of the sixteenth and seventeenth centuries.

Medieval scientists in Oxford, Paris, Germany and Italy came to understand also that science must become an experimental enterprise constructing and testing hypotheses. The technical standard of experimentation was not high by modern standards, but Robert Grosseteste, Albert the Great, Roger Bacon, Petrus Peregrinus, Witelo and Themon Judaei were all experimental scientists and introduced the experimental method into European science.

As early as the thirteenth century, in Oxford, Robert Grosseteste (1170-1253) formulated a theory of experimental science: Arriving at scientific knowledge is an inductive process. Induction may be based on a systematic analysis of the phenomena or it may take the form of a sudden leap of intution or scientific imagination. Both forms of induction lead to a theory, to seeing the data or facts in an intelligible perspective. A further problem arises now: how distinguish between true and false theories? A discrimination can be made only by posing questions to reality itself in the form of special experiments or (where the natural condition cannot be manipulated as in astronomy) of special observations. By making deduction from various possible theories, it is possible to determine which theories are falsfied by experiment or observation but it is not possible to be certain that any particular theory is true. Science must rest content with approaching closer and closer towards certainty. His method of elimination or falsification (and confirmation) was based on two assumptions about the nature of reality: (1) the principle of the uniformity of nature—agents are always uniform in the effects they produce; and (2) the principle of economy: it is an objective characteristic of nature that it operates in the shortest way possible; further, as a pragmatic principle in explanation, one explanation should be preferred to anther if it is simpler in content and involves fewer assumptions.

This latter question—what basic assumption or postulates are made in science?—was also discussed by John Duns Scotus (c. 1265-1308) who dealt at length with the principle of the unformity of nature. He believed that it is implicit in every inductive investigation.

It is interesting to note that the experimental method came to characterize various medieval medical schools where there was a remarkable interest in the logical structure of the procedures used. Galileo derived much of the logic and terminology of his theory of science from Paduan doctors.

The revolutionary development of science in the sixteenth and seventeenth centuries. In weighing up science in any particular period one needs to ask two questions: (1) what principles about the nature of science and of the proper scientific approach to reality, inspired and directed the scientists of that period? (2) what actual scientific work did they accomplish? Galileo Galilei (1564-1642) is often singled out as the father of modern science. The principles that inspire modern science go back further than Galileo, but he used them openly, consistently successfully and with this general effect that, with him, European science became once and for all highly mathematical, experimental and technological in self conception and method.

Galileo's conception of scientific method had two main

characteristics. Firstly, he eliminated the discussion of essential natures which had characterized Aristotelian Physics and concentrated on describing what he observed. Such words as 'gravity' were for him simply names for certain observed regularities. Secondly, he tried to express the observed regularities in mathematical terms, focusing quantitative relationships in phenomena, studying these, developing mathematical implications and building up a mathematical theory. This abstract mathematical procedure (replacing the effort at immediate and direct generalization about the phenomenon) led to a special kind of experiment—one that would verify of falsify quantitative deductions.

Galileo believed that mathematical theories displayed the enduring substantial reality underlying phenomena. Nature is mathematical; that which is not mathematical is subjective. Indeed the faith that inspired nearly all science until the end of the seventeenth century was that through being mathematical it could discover the basic intelligibility of nature.

With Newton (1642-1727) science was again a strictly empirical and mathematical enterprise, characterized by induction and verification. But he did not believe that it could claim to discover the intrinsic structure of the universe or describe natural forces in their concrete reality. Science must concern itself with aspects of reality that can be treated mathematically, with properties of things (at rest or in motion) that vary quantitatively. There may be other methods of approaching reality, with equal logical claims to true knowledge; but this is a successful method, humanity, and there are no others in prospect.

Simplifying phenomena by formulating them under their mathematical aspects, converts complex reality into a machine like entity something with definite properties that can be isolated measured and duplicated, so that in the end the behaviour of the machine can be predicted. This simplification of phenomena gives a wide scope to mathematical reasoning, the objective validity of which is tested at each stage, by observation or experiment.

Once they are verified the mathematical generalizations become experimental laws. As such they are known to be objective, but they do not reveal to us anything more than mathematical aspects, quantitative relationships. Newton discarded the view, prevalent for two centuries. That the universe is mathematical in its basic structure, and that mathematics is a key opening up the universe in its concrete reality. He felt that there were no grounds to justify this outlook. The mathematical approach to reality was a method, the best one available, with no better one even in prospect. It was saying too much however to describe it as a key. Indeed we do not know that any mathematical deduction gives objective information unless and until we can relate that deduction to the real world by observation or experiment. And the information does not go beyond mathematical aspects, quantitative relationships.

We can speculate of course about the concrete structure of reality about the real causes or concrete realities behind words like 'gravity'. But speculative hypotheses have no place within science where hypotheses are admissible only in so far as they are amenable to experimental testing.

Newton's conception of scientific method may be summarized as follows: He 'conceived scientific method to be analysable into three essential stages: (1) the determination by experiment of those properties of phenomena that vary quantitatively; (2) mathematical reasoning by means of which these variations may be precisely stated in a form capable of further elaboration; (3) exact experiments by means of which the mathematical reasoning may be verified and extended to further cases in accordance with four rules'. (Susan Stebbing, *A Modern Introduction to Logic*, p.313) Newton prefixed the four rules to Book III of the *Principia:*

Rule 1: 'we are to admit no more causes of natural things than such as are both true and sufficient to explain their appearances.' This rule counsels parsimony or economy in causal explanation.

Rule II: 'Therefore to the same natural effects we must, as far as possible, assign the same causes.' This rests on a belief in the uniformity of nature.

Rule III: 'The qualities of bodies, which admit neither intension nor remission of degrees, and which are found to belong to all bodies within the reach of our experiments, are to be esteemed the universal qualities of all bodies whatsoever.' Newton accepts Galileo's distinction between primary or objective qualities and secondary or subjective qualities. In addition to figure, extension and mobility, he lists as primary qualities, hardness, impenetrability and the inertial powers. Given the simplicity of nature (*Rules I* and *II*) and the presence of these properties in all bodies of our acquaintance, we have sufficient theoretical grounds for ascribing them to all bodies in nature.

Rule IV: 'In experimental philosophy we are to look upon proposition collected by general induction from phenomena as accurately or very nearly true, notwithstanding any contrary hypothesis that may be imagined, till such time as other phenomena occur, by which they may either be made more accurate, or liable to exceptions.' In other words, speculative hypotheses, i.e. those for which no experimental evidence is offered, should carry no weight against inductions.

Governing ideas in contemporary physical science. The last 160 years stand out in history as a scientific age, that is to say, as an age in which scientific knowledge is being continually and progressively translated into technology, revolutionizing industrial life and transforming everyday living too. Science never stood in such relationship to life before. Science, of course, includes both technology and pure (theoretical) science. Applied Logic is not concerned with the former. Since 1900, however, the vast development of physical science has produced governing theoretical principles that must be taken into consideration in analysing and evaluating the evidence -conclusion structuring of science. The are:

(1) Modern science is basically mathematical in content and form: its primary idiom is mathematical so are its most fundamental explanations and concepts; and mathematical formalization is the measure of the full scientific maturity of a discipline (such as biology). Theoretical physics requires the coalescence of the higher systems of mathematics with physical intution and imagination. The physical scientist himself is guided by an innate conviction of mathematical order in nature.

(2) A radical uncertainty must attach to any mathematical model of nature we may construct at the atomic level. It is impossible to calculate both the position and the velocity of minute particles; thus we cannot assign to them, in our equations, their exact place and velocity, with the result that our model is essentially deficient in basic measurements. This is Heisenberg's principle of uncertainty: the classical picture of a particle moving along a precise trajectory is untenable because it is *in principle* impossible to determine precisely position without generating uncertainty in the value of velocity and vice versa. As a result of this principle 'there is a shift in science from casual to statistical laws. Science is content to predict the future without stipulating any [observable or verifiable causal] mechanism between the present and the future, without claiming that its computation follows the steps of causal law. Its method is statistical and it recognizes that every prediction carries with it its own uncertainity. But it believes that this undertaintiy is measurable and, consequently, that there is a room for a scientific prediction which defines its area of uncertainty, as contrasted with unscientific predictions which do not.' (*The Common Sense of Science by* J. Bronowski, Penguin Books)

(3) An unavoidable relativity attaches to the fundamental stage of science observation. The building bricks of science are observed facts. In Newtonian Physics no distinction was made, between the fact itself and the fact as observed. For Einstein the facts that go into the building of science are

observed facts and these are relative to the observer—to his position, relative motion etc. As far as any observation is concerned you never have simply a fact or an observer but the joining of the two is an observation. Further, between the event and the observer there must pass a signal—a ray of light, a wave or an impulse—which simply cannot be taken out of the observation. Event, signal, observer: this is the concrete building unit in science. Thus scientific facts—mass, time, space facts—are compound things relative to an observer in a particular system of reference.

The above three principles govern thinking on the degree of certainty and the kind of objectivity attributed by contemporary scientists to thier theoretical conclusions.

A summary description of the structure of physical science as it has evolved historically. Scientific investigation has as its end result an explanatory body of propositions which needs to be evaluated in its explanatory force, in the degree of system it introduces into knowledge, and in the evidence-conclusion relation ships which structure it. It is a mathematical experimental enterprise developing itself out of a material experience of the world and through the dynamism of rational hypothetical constructions which are verified, falsified and modified through observation and experiment. It does not claim that the material approach to reality is the only valid approach, and it does not attach an absolute certainty to its laws but functions as a continously self-testing, self-correcting enterprise.

III. STRUCTURE AND METHOD IN THE BIOLOGICAL AND HUMAN SCIENCES

Scientific concepts of life have changed so much that very little of the nineteenth-century picture remains today. A powerful force in this revolutionary change had been the beginning of an integration of physics, chemistry and biology and the extension to the human sciences of methods of physics and mathematical analysis. The sciences of life have not developed in their revolutionary way by changing scientific method. Just as striking as new discoveries is the continuance of the traditional basic groundwork of mathematical description and analysis the invention of models and hypothetical mechanisms, logical deduction and testing. Nothing comparable to the methodological changes of the sixteenth and seventeenth centuries has taken place in the twentieth century development of science.

As in Physics and Chemistry, conspicuous activities in biology are the making and recording of observations and also experimentation. Observations and experiments are again preceded and followed by the invention of hypotheses which are tested by recourse to further observations.

> At very rare intervals these hypotheses have a tremendous effect: they open up entirely new lines of research—creating new branches of science as well as affecting older existing branches. Familiar examples are the hypotheses introduced into biology by William Harvey, Charles Darwin, Gregor Mendel and Louis Pasteur. The part played by hypotheses in the work of these celebrated men is obscured by the way in which, in histories of science, they are represented not so much as inventors of hypotheses but as discoverers. Thus Harvey is commonly referred to as the discoverer of the circulation of the blood. But what he did was something much more important. He invented a *hypothesis* concerning the action of the heart which had many revolutionary *consequences* for physiology, that there was a circulation of the blood being but *one*. In this way the distinction between the making of observations and the invention of hypotheses tends to be blurred..... some new hypotheses also lead to the invention of new apparatus for observation, and the new observations so made possible suggest further hypotheses, and so on. (J.H. Woodger *in Biology and Language: An Introduction to the Methodology of the Biological Sciences including Medicine: pp.3-4)*

The same basic pattern of operation occurs also in the human sciences, instrumentation being broadened to include statistical techniques, and 'fact' to include that which is reached through the mediation of statistical science (social data being often of this latter nature, and here deduction takes place in a context in which implications are verified or theories falsified against a criterion of 'statistical facts' or probabilities rather than of facts in the classical sense of the word).

As in physics, a higher theoretical development is occasioned in biology by the frequent readjustments between hypothesis and observation and by the need to co-ordinate many hypotheses within a comprehensive theory. At this level the essence of logical process and the objective of logical arrangement is demonstration, explanation and prediction. In physics, which has the most fully developed system of concepts and affords possibilities of axiomatization, rationality is present here to a great extent in the form of logicality. In biology and in the human sciences theoretical rationality is more heavily weighted with the guidance of intution and its cutting edge has been informal conceptual analysis. Axiomatization has not been applied outside physics. With a growing assimilation of the physicist's experience and exactitude one may expect a greater use of mathematics in the life sciences and the development of an appropriate symbolic language capable of mediating precise analysis and providing scope for calculation. Contemporary biology is not only using some of the branches of mathematics that have been developed to meet the special demands of physics, it is also addressing itself to the task of discovering the special kind of mathematics that is required by itself.

It is also noteworthy that, conceptually, both biology and through it the human sciences are feeling the impact of a reductionist tendency based on the reality of a single scientific method and on the ideal of completely unified knowledge.

IV. THE LOGICAL FORMS AND LOGICAL PROCESSES WITHIN EMPIRICAL SCIENCE

Empirical science combines two distinct objectives and its content is accordingly twofold with a two fold logical formation: (a) Firstly it is, as its name implies, knowledge an organized and growing body of general laws which provide an ever increasing understanding of nature; (b) secondly, it is an exploratory enterprise, possessing an enormous capacity or methodology for the acquistion of new knowledge, and dedicated to continous research by methods certified by it as scientific.

(a) As an organized body of knowledge it is explanatory in force, with the logical elements and formation of an axiomatic system. Here is concerned with consolidating and unifying what has been already discovered: it secures clarity by the primitive quality what has been already discovered: it secures clarity by the primitive quality of its basic technical language, and it demonstrates particular laws by situating them under more general laws or theories. 'Demonstrates' has the force of explaining rather than of proving truth: the process (perfect or imperfect) of proving a particular law is carried out earlier in the work of confirming it and in the effort to falsity it; is explained now by being subsumed under more general laws from which it can be inferred, i.e. it is absorbed into a vast inferential network through which science both explains and predicts, prediction being understanding and explanation before the event. One must emphasize the meaning relations that arise (along with truth relations) when a propostition is subsumed under a more general one; these relations constitute the explanation.

Logical experience of axiomatization underlines the importance, first of all, of having a set of explicit axioms which is a complete and adequate basis for deriving the desired range of theorems. In empirical science a set of theoretical principles or comprehensive theory is sought through which it can describe, explain and predict derivative laws and empirical unformities (i.e. Uniformities that have not been shown to be instances of more general laws). Each empirical science must therefore ask itself whether its theoretical principles are adequate as they stand, whether it needs (and is using) any supplementary principle without formulating and acknowledging it as such. Logicians such as Duns Scotus, in medieval times, and John Stuart Mill, in modern times, have felt that a principle of uniformity in nature must function axiomatically in science. In contemporary times P. A. M. Dirac points out that there is an aesthetic criterion for the selection of possible axiomatic bases in Physics:

> It seems to be of the fundamental features of nature that fundamental physical laws are described in terms of a mathematical theory of great beauty and power, needing quite a high standard of mathematics for one to understand it.
>
> What makes the theory of relativity so acceptable to physicists...is its great *mathematical beauty*. This is a quality which cannot be defined, any more than beauty in art can be defined but which people who study mathematics usually have no difficulty in appreaciating. The theory of relativity introduced mathematical beauty to an unprecedented extent into the description of nature...Quantum mechanics [the second revolution in physical thought of the present century] requires the introduction into physical theory of a vast new domain of pure mathematics—the whole domain connected with non commutative multiplication [where things multiplied in one order do not give the same result as when multiplied in the other order] This coming on top of the introduction of new geometries by the theory of relativity, indicates a trend which we may expect to continue. We may expect that in the future further big domains of pure mathematics will have to be brought in to deal with the advances in fundamental physics...The trend of mathematics and physics towards unification provides the physicist with a powerful new method of research into the foundations of his

> subject....The method is to begin by choosing that branch of mathematics which one thinks will form the basis of the new theory. One should be influenced very much in this choice by considerations of mathematical beauty. ('The Evolution of the Physicist's Picture of Nature' and 'The Relation between Mathematics and Physics': for full details of these articles see Bibliography.)

Because of their low degree of formalization a principle of uniformity in nature or Dirac's principle may be classified vaguely as perspective and its logical weight pass unnoticed.

Of course in generating a whole network of deductive connections leading to all the particular known laws, not only do the theoretical principles *explain* these laws but they themselves are *confirmed* or re-enforced by them and accordingly are said to *describe* them also. Even as an axiomatic system science regards itself as descriptive of nature.

Logical experience of axiomatization also underlines the importance of scrutinizing the processes of derivation. This is comparatively simple within logic itself where the context is set indefinitely by a language of variables and the processes are purely formal therefore. But in empirical science what one is deriving are descriptions of the world with greater and lesser degrees of generality. Thus what Boole observed in general about contextual reasoning applies here—however logical, it embodies forces that derive from our experience and knowledge of the context: such a reasoning process can never be purely logical, purely theoretic. The rationality of empirical science cannot be completely reduced to the simple logicality of a propositional system; the variables or blanks in a purely formal system are paralleled by population of concepts in natural science, and the relationship between these concepts are not simply and solely logical ones of implication, conflict etc. Thus an impartial forum of rationality for science must have both formal and informal aspects. Toulmin puts it:

> Any attempt to judge conceptual novelties in science,

> or to make comparisons across the intellecutal boundaries between rival theories soon derives us beyond the range of a purely formal analysis... The progressive historical transformation of our ideas—involving the displacement of one proto arithmetic, physical theory or political doctrine by another—remains to be analysed and judged in other, less formal terms. (*Human Understanding,* vol. I, pp.64-5)

A consequence of the strong contextual character in the deductions and reductions within scientific explanation is that reductivism is a genuine hazard and an inevitable topic of controversy: is too much being explained in terms of too little when biology is reduced to physics, personality to behaviour, mind to matter? Scientific controversies of this kind are all the more difficult to resolve because, in general, scientific method has extended to other disciplines from physics, so that method is from one discipline, the problems from anther.

(b) As an institution for further discovery, empirical science possesses two methods of making progress: (1) the method of experiment and observation, examining particularly experiments, analysing them through mathematical reasoning and expressing the regularity of results in the form of physical laws; (2) the speculative or dialectical method of creative imagination in which a theory is constructed largely independently of experience. Historically both of these methods have been powerful for the formulation of physical theory, the former (empirical) one being continously productive in that it modifies theories as new results demand this.

Both methods lead to the formulation of a theory, and at this point, two logical principle become relevant:

(a) The principle that in a valid deduction truth is preserved and transmitted; in virtue of this principle the implications of a true theory must be true also. Granted that q is an implication of p and also that p is true then q is true also; this is an LAF, a natural deduction form or schema referred to traditionally as *modus oonendo ponens.*

(b) the principle that in a valid deduction an implication cannot be false without falsity being present among the premises; in virtue of this principle a theory of falsfied when one of its implications is discovered to be false. Granted that q is an implication of p and also that q is false, then p is flase: this sequent is proved within propositional logic.

The above are two correct logical principle; the first is, invoked in generating the predictions of a theory, the second is used to falsify a theory. The form used in verification is not a logical form; if the theory is true, these consequences of it are realized; but these consequences of it are realized; therefore the theory is true (If p,q, but q; therefore p.) The use of this form gives rise to the problem of verification which will be discussed in the next chapter.

Thus the precise logical strength of the hypothetico-deductive method may be defined as follows: when an hypothesis is true the validity of the deductive process constitutes a logical certification that the implications are true, and when an implication is known to be false the validity of the deductive process constitutes a logical certification that the hypothesis is false. These are the only logical principles which are relevant to the method and can constitute it as a formally valid process. Thus logically it is best that the method be conceived and practised primarily in accordance with these principles.

No one has seen this as clearly, perhaps, as Karl Popper. In the eyes of many scientists he is one of the great philosophers of science in history, a philosopher of knowledge whom an experimental scientist can read with complete adherence to his views; his writings are accepted as describing the scientific process with accuracy, veracity and clarity and he presents a very penetrating view of its logic.

In this view it is the task of scientists to produce theories and then to use the two relevant logical principles: (1) by deduction to make the theory yield predictions of what future observations or experiments will show; (2) to make and examine predictions as part of a systematic attempt to falsify the theory. For Popper the essential logic that is available to empirical method is one of disproff rather than of proof although empirical general statements cannot be proved they are falsifiable; they are essentially a type of proposition that can be tested. Thus Popper would define a scientific proposition through its relationship with the two relevant logical principles; it is thc type of proposition which being subject to the deductive process cannot but yield predictions to which also it must transmit is its truth, and which is accordingly governed by the second logical principle that a false prediction certifies it also as being false. Thus the primary method of scientific progress is criticism, and science is essentially and continously a self testing enterprise. Popper sums up his view in *Objective Knowledge: an Evolutionary Approach:*

> As a realist took upon logic as the *organon of criticism* (rather than of proof) in our search for true and highly informative theories or at least for new theories that contain more information, and correspond better to the facts, than our older theories. And I look upon criticism, in its turn, as our main instrument in promoting the growth of our knowledge about the world of facts. (p.318)

He analyses this logic of criticism:

> My theory is briefly this I look upon logic as the theory of deduction or of derivability, or whatever one chooses to call it. Derivability or deduction involves essentially, *the transmission of truth and the retransmission of falsity:* in a valid inference truth is transmitted from the premises to the conclusion. This can be used especially in so-called 'proofs'. But falsity is also retransmitted from the conclusion to (at least) one of the premisses, and this is used in dis proofs or refutations, and especially in *critical discussions* ... Now I should distinguish between two main uses of logic, namely (I) its use in the demonstrative sciences—that is to say, the mathematical sciences—and (2) its use in the empirical sciences. In the demonstrative sciences

> logic is used in the main for proofs—for the transmission of truth—while in the empirical sciences it is almost exclusively used critically—for the retransmission of falsity...
>
> Now what I wish to assert is this. If we want to use logic in a critical context, then we should use a very strong logic, the strongest logic, so to speak, which is at our disposal; for we want our criticism to be severe... Thus we should (in the empirical sciences) use the full or classical or two-valued logic. If we do not use it but retreat into the use of some weaker logic—say, the intuitionist logic, or some three-valued logic (as Reichenbach suggested in connection with quantum theory)—then, I assert, we are not critical enough.....
>
> I would assert that not the least important of the achievements of Alfred Tarski is that by introducing two ideas into logic, he has actually made logic very much a realistic affair. The first is Tarski's idea (partly anticipated by Bolzano) that logical consequence is truth transmission. The second I would say, is the rehabilitation of the correspondence theory of truth, the rehabilitation of the idea that truth is simply correspondence with the facts. (pp. 304-5,308)

An important source of logical strength to empirical science lies, undoubtedly, in its being a continuously self-testing disproving enterprise and in the scrupulous and extensive nature of observation and experiment in it. There is a continuous appeal from fact to theory or principle and from theory or principle to fact. In virtue of this continuous give and take everything that is doubtful comes under frequent scrutiny and no hypothesis is regarded as so well supported by evidence that other evidence may not increase or decrease its reliability. The continuous vigilance of an empirical science with regard to fact, and its continuous testing and preparedness to modify theory are important guarantees of its worth. Stebbing comments:

[Pasteur's biographer said] that he had 'a mind, which while pressing forward to establish new facts, was ever seeking arguments against itself, and turned back to strengthen points which seemed yet weak.' It was these self critical qualities of mind that made Pasteur a great experimental scientist. (*A Modern Introduction to Logic, p. 326)*

Chapter-8

The Scope of Applied Logic

Chapter 8

I. INTRODUCTION

While qualities of mind such as clarity, relevance and cogency in reasoning are described as logical, they are also and properly described as qualities of a mind that is judicial, or scientific or mathematical or clinical. They develop quite naturally from any context in which one invests careful thought and therefore do not presuppose a knowledge and application of the science of logic. Logical qualities constitute one aspect of intellectual character and a cursory examination of even ordinary living shows that it challenges us to achieve intellectual asceticism, discernment and decisiveness of a high order. One has to overcome many difficulties, from within and without oneself, in coming to be utterly fair-minded, not least among which is the fact that the average person does not seem to desire a larger measure of good sense than he already possesses. Yet in life the inferential acquisition of knowledge requires the cultivation of both sound intuitive and inferential processes, it being an important insight that we reach truth either by intuition or by inference and predominantly by a combination of both process. A valid inferential process does not necessarily bring us to further truth unless the evidence we believe in is true also. Here it requires what Santayana called intellectual chastity to be free of prejudices—convictions which are not based either on consultation with experts or on due examination and yet function as a prior (*prae*) base from which to reach a conclusion (*judicium*). Inherent in life is the challenge, in adulthood, to confront the assumptions that are fundamental in one's outlook and to accept personal responsibility for any attitudes and beliefs one will apply as evidence. Assumptions which have been generated in the course of one's personal history or by the process of cultural osmosis possess great psychic power and thus in becoming reasonably unprejudiced, one inevitably becomes muscular and competent in thought generally.

Competence, of course, includes being properly informed in each and every context in which we presume to reason. To arrive at true conclusions, one must have sound and accurate information to begin with. Further this information cannot be properly subjected to an inferential process, unless it is well formulated. So life challenges us to acquire reasonable linguistic sensitivity and rectitude in our own reasoning, and critical discernment in regard to that of others, particularly where techniques for mass persuasion or mass indoctrination are employed.

There is a further aspect of the human condition which is limiting in itself but demands that we compensate for it by fostering carefulness in processing the thought content of our arguments. It is the fact that reasoning is a human, personal activity in which one may be both feeling deeply and inferring, confidently, and everyone is subject daily to propaganda in which agencies emotionalize or de emotionalize their statements according as they wish to arouse emotion or to mute it. Thus human life challenges us to acquire the habit of disengaging thought content from the context of feelings and to learn to gravitate to conclusions on evidence alone. The detachment achieved is some what analogous to that resulting from the design and use of logical language which frees itself from particular contexts to concentrate, as Frege put it, on what has 'significance for the inferential sequence'.

Clearly many forms of life provide the opportunity and the need of developing those qualities of thought that are often called logical. And these qualities need to observe the human proportions of life, for too much clarity may be imported into inter personal relationships and it is often unrealistic and burden some to insist on proof—according to a dictum of Aristotle's, indeed, it is a mark of an educated man not to demand in any subject matter more certainty than that subject admits of, humanly. Accordingly, applied logic does not attempt to prescribe formal procedures for living, existential thought: it does not present itself as an art of thinking better and it does not attach special importance to logic for qualities of mind that may be expected to develop through working in this discipline.

The precise content of applied logic follows naturally on the fact that formal logic is a depth grammar of rationality. It consists of (a) a study of the extent to which this grammar can be *identified* in social use (especially in the sciences), and (b) a demonstration of how logical techniques and perhaps logical language too, may be used to clarify and formalize thought content in various contexts of life and science and philosophy

There is room for the study of existential human thinking and reasoning sifting its structures and methods for the rules which are present and identifying the rules which translate logical laws and those which do not. It is not controverted that there should be such a formal analysis of basic rationality as it exists. And although, historically, most attention has been given to the empirical sciences and mathematics, the analysis in applied logic touches every area of theoretical thought, i.e. of thought which has as its objective not doing or making things but understanding state of affairs.

History shows that two kinds of people are needed for an analysis to be adequate and concrete: (1) people who are expert and experienced in the particular contexts or subject matters being studied, and (2) people who are expert in formal logic. The former are needed to describe the rational structure of their desciplines; the latter contribute by matching these descriptions with forms and structures that formal logic presents in its grammar of rationality. At the points where procedures or structures are not perfectly grammatical, there is, logically speaking, a formal eficiency and therefore what has been traditionally called a 'logical problem' for many hundreds of years the problem of induction has been, in one from or another, a central problem. Where there is a formal deficiency the logician is expected to provide an evaluation both of it and of the steps taken to compensate for it (if it is humanly unavoidable). The essential point however, is that applied logic represents teamwork, the formal logician being simply the member who provides knowledge of logical forms.

II. LIMITS IN THE PURPOSE AND FUNCTIONING OF APPLIED LOGIC

Applied logic is concerned with theoretical thought only, i.e. with thought that is intent on understanding reality and on formulating truth-claims rather than with practical thought which is intent on knowing how this or that can be done. Its claim to be concerned here is that theoretical thought is a movement that is (a) inferential, and (b) intent on formulating a coherent system of propositions. Obviously logic has a useful function here, its laws being translatable as directions for the movement of thought, safeguarding truth.

For a conclusion to be true and shown to be true, the evidence must consist of true propositions and the process by which the conclusion is drawn must be logically valid. It is well to bear this double preoccupation in mind as we study existential methods of theoretical thinking; the theoretic process present is not the sole concern in actual life. In empirical science especially the aim is comprehensive—to extend human experience and control of the world as well as to achieve a theoretical mastery of it. Applied logic cannot contribute directly to an experiencing, a technical control or an intellectual mastery of the natural world; it *can* contribute a generalized understanding and evaluation of theoretical processes used.

It is not the function of applied logic to prescribe forms but rather, working within a description given by experts in the discipline whose basic rationality is being examined, to identify those forms which appear in logic as truths or rules or as pertaining to the process of formalization, and to say also what forms do not match with any part of the grammar which logic provides. The main roles of the specialist and the logician are quite distinguishable. It is important above all for the logician not to presume to *describe* the context to which logic is being applied.

For many hundreds of years logicians did presume, with regard to empirical science, both to describe it and to prescribe form and method for it. This was a great weakness in Bacon and Mill who were criticized by scientists for thinking that they could *devise* methods for science and that they could evaluate existing scientific methods without being practising scientists. It would be difficult to surpass Bacon, of course, for a description in broad terms of the empirical and practical nature of science. He understood broadly the direction that science was taking and should take; he divined the technical progress that could come and would come; and he wrote a direct, clear and imaginative analysis of the meaning and utility of science. Also in his works some convictions of contemporary scientists are voiced: science must have the broadest possible basis of fact; the first step in science is to collect facts and to describe them carefully, even with mathematical precision where that is possible. But when he presumed to evaluate actual scientific procedure, in a generalized way, and to advocate a 'new method' (which would be 'such as to leave little to the acuteness and strength of wit, and, indeed, rather to level wit and intellect. For as in the drawing of a straight line or accurate circle by the hand, much depends on its steadiness and practice, but if a ruler or compass be employed there is little occasion for either, so it is with our method.') his writing ceased to be really imaginative and became vague and speculative in quality.

John Stuart Mill was also severely criticized by contemporary scientists for presuming to write a logic of science in complete independence of practicing scientists. His methods, particularly, belong to the level of common sense thinking; they are pre-scientific and could not qualify as a description of, or prescription for, scientific methodology.

Of course perspective on logical structure comes most reliably from the formal logician. It is possible for the specialist not to be aware of the full significance of a formal deficiency in his method of investigation or format of explanation. With regard to the empirical sciences, especially, it is possible to put an exaggerated value on their logical unification and to use the method of reduction in a way that does not do justice to their rich conceptual diversity. Indeed nowadays controversies concerning reductionism and methodological over simplifications are prominent.

In summary, perhaps the most distinctive feature of contemporary applied logic is that it is inter disciplinary a new limited role being accepted by the formal logician.

III. THE SPECIFIC CONTENTS OF APPLIED LOGIC

Since applied logic is concerned solely with theoretical thinking in all its existential forms, its main studies fall naturally into the following categories:

(a) A study of what is positively logical in existential thought. This involves describing the main forms of the latter (especially scientific investigation and explanation, philosophical and mathematical thought) identifying the logical structure that is present and analysing its strength in the light of logical and extralogical experience.

(b) A study of the problems which arise which an evidence conclusion structure which is in use, existentially, does not correspond to the formal grammar of rationality developed within formal logic. These are called logical problems because they become manifest in the comparison with logical grammar. But of course they are in fact problems for the discipline concerned. Of its nature, contextual reasoning of any variety is not fully logical in its nature. Within empirical science, the processes of verification and induction have been discussed, in form or another, as logical problems since the time of Plato and Aristotle.

(c) A study of the difference, between various existential

approaches to reality—the scientific, the philosophic, the aesthetic, the religious, noting the nature of their theoretical concern, their methods, logical strength and logical problems.

(d) A study of logical formalization, i.e. of how techniques and language used within formal logic may be used to clarify and organize extra logical contexts. Thus, for example, the discipline called 'deontic logic' is a logical formalization of theoretical thinking on obligation *(deon* in Greek connoting 'that which is binding'), and the logic of preference is, similarly, an axiomatization of propositions about preference. There are no practical limits to the use that may be made of logical formalization. The study in applied logic is a general one with the presentation of some examples.

(e) A study of formal detachment: whether or not impersonal knowledge is a false ideal and even an impossibility.

Chapter-9

Logical Problems in Empirical Science

Chapter-9

I. INTRODUCTION

There are two main kinds of strictly logical problems in empirical science: (1) that which arises when a piece of reasoning is not, and cannot be, *completely* governed by any logical form, i.e. when the reasoning is contextual; (2) that which arises when reasoning is governed by a form which is not perfectly logical, i.e. not of its nature truth-transmitting—this occurs in verification and, more broadly, in the whole inductive development of science. These problems are inescapably part of the human condition: relatively little falls within reach of an absolute human proof. Thus they constitute a challenge to rational skill to compensate, as far as is possible, for the absence of reason's own basic logical forms. And they emphasize that rationality should not be identified with logicality: the ultimate universal challenge and duty with which life confronts us is being rational (which is always possible) rather than being logical (which is often not possible if one defines and relativizes that word to the forms of the existing science).

II. THE GENERAL PROBLEM OF CONTEXTUAL REASONING

Contextual reasoning occurs where the reasoning process is not purely logical, i.e. where the power of the evidence (compelling or unconvincing as the case may be) derives indissolubly from both the form of the argument and from experience of the concepts constituting the particular context.

The significant historical facts are: (a) Modern formal logic, being constructive and not abstractive, seeks transcendent, context free truths or laws and does not concern itself at all with contextual reasoning which is confined to applied logic. Within applied logic itself (which as we have see, is teamwork) the main analyses and classifications will be made, naturally, by contextual experts rather than by the formal logician. (b) Traditional logic which was abstractive examined contextual reasoning but produced no really deep systematic study of it; the examination was predominantly concerned with fallacies in reasoning and no general theory was ever achieved. Indeed it was commonly assumed that a complete classification of fallacies would be impossible; the modern logician, Augustus de Morgan, sums up the attitude (in his *Formal Logic*): 'There is no such thing as a classification of the ways in which men may arrive at an error: it is much to be doubted whether there ever can be.' (p.276)

For over two thousand years fallacies were discussed within the framework presented in Aristotle's *Sophistical Refutations* where he lists thirteen types of fallacies, sophisms or elenchs as they have been variously called. (The frame-work has been already described in the preparatory section, A, of this textbook.) Aristotle's other accounts, in the *Prior Analytics* and the *Rhetoric,* are briefer; they are concerned, respectively, with breaches of syllogistic law and with observations about arguments that are useful-for persuasive speech. The indications from the literature on fallacies (a vast amount of ancient and medieval writings have still to be edited, of course) is that this was a topic of recurrent interest in every century but that discussions were broadly the same and cramped themselves within the Aristotelian framework. Henry Aldrich in his *Artis Logicae Compendium* (1691) ends his conventional treatment as follows:

> These, then, are the thirteen kinds of fallacy familiar to the ancients and normally presented to Logic students as examples. The number could be cut down; for some seem to coincide and, moreover, three of them—Non-Cause, Begging the Question and Many Questions—are not fallacies properly so-called, that is, ill-formed syllogisms, but rather faults of the opponent. The number could also be increased; but since it satisfied Aristotle it has satisfied

all later logicians.

There are traditional logicians, like Peter Ramus in the sixteenth century, who anticipated the outlook of modern Mathematical Logic in holding that logic is a science of correct forms and should not concern itself with fallacies. And there were others who altered the framework somewhat. Francis Bacon's list of Idols (of the Tribe, the Den, the Market Place and the Theatre) is particularly psychological. He is interested in the human person reasoning and in the 'false appearances' imposed on him by the general nature of the human mind, by his own individual nature and history, by the very language in which he thinks, and by currently received philosophies and methods of demonstration.

No matter what context a person reasons in he cannot avoid being gravitated towards the invalid and the erroneous, if he lives and thinks under the government of 'false appearances.' The *Port Royal Logic* of 1662 (which was originally entitled *The Art of Thinking* and which was the prototype for text books on logic until mathematical logic succeeded in displacing the Rennaissance interpretation of Logic) continued Bacon's search for psychological classifications without anything substantial being added. And the efforts of Bentham, Whately and Mill to reclassify fallacies did not produce any substantial alteration either.

Finally, Arabian logic preserved the Aristotelian tradition and otherwise did not concern itself with fallacies. In Indian logic which developed independently of the West, there was a basic interest in inference and in theory of debate. The classical Indian text on logic was the Nyāya sūtra (written during the first three centuries A.D.) and commentaries over more than ten centuries elaborated its classification of fallacies and its subtleties of disputation. With the development, in the fourteenth century, of a new and more formal logic (by the Navya Nyāya, or New Nyāya School) disputation and fallacies were no longer considered within logic.

Thus traditionally, contextual reasoning has been treated in the very limiting area of disputation and, predominantly, within a framework of fallacies. Even within those terms of reference no systematic theory has been achieved. A modern study of contextual reasoning requires the cooperation of the formal logician and experts in the particular contexts. Their basic problem does not consist in discovering the presence or absence of logical form but in describing and assessing the influence of conceptual experience and contextual intuition on the reasoning. Thus the precise problem of contextual reasoning is mainly one for the contextual experts.

III. THE PROBLEM OF VERIFICATION

When a proposition is true a valid deductive process is, by its very nature, a logical certification that all the implications are true also. The deductive process simply unfolds the meaning of the original proposition and so is truth preserving, truth-transmitting. But when the original proposition is false a valid deductive process cannot over constitute a logical certification either of truth or of falsity. As the meaning is deductively unfolded there is no logical basis for sayińg at any point that there or is not correspondence with facts; it is thought is content that is implied, not correspondence or lack of correspondence with facts, and many elements implicit in what a false proposition says may happen to be true. Thus when an hypothesis is neither accepted as true nor rejected as false there is no *purely logical* basis for using the results of valid deduction as confirmation of it. In saying that verification is a logical problem, what one means is that the movement from evidence (truth of implications) to conclusion (truth of hypothesis) is not governed by logical form (i.e. the movement is not of its nature truth transmitting) and that this fact—to which logic draws attention—constitutes a problem wherever a verification procedure is used.

Quite clearly the type of rationality present when one accepts an hypothesis as being confirmed cannot be completely identified with logicality. By intution and experience one may judge it *unlikely* that *this implication* ('X was at the scene of the crime with a gun) would turn out to be true without the hypothesis ('X was the killer') being true. This is an extralogical basis of judgement: the thought content of the conclusion exists not in a framework of *objective logical necessitation* in the light of the evidence but in that of *subjective* rational belief because of the evidence. Judicial enquiries control and define this kind of belief (based on confirmation) when it may be expressed in the form of a court verdict: every effort is required of the defence to *falsify* the affirmations of prosecution or plaintiff (this includes cross-examination of witnesses and questioning their legal weight in the case) and the target of jury deliberations is defined as defined no more can never be required than certitude beyond reasonable doubt, and in civil cases judgement on the felt balance of probabilities may suffice. Thus the law admits a systematic procedure of confirmation only in identify the flasification and it does not identify the outcome of successful confirmation with absolute certitude.

In empirical science the scientist does not wait dependently on experience but confronts the world with conceptions from his own reason. One might say with Popper that science begins effectively with the imaginative proposal of hypotheses. Many logicians believe that in this heuristic movement of reason there is an invisible axiom present, an implicit faith that the world is of such a kind as to correspond with rational expectancies. Historically, this seems to enter into the traditional outlook of western science whether one describes it, logically, as an axiom or, psycho1ogically, as a faith. Science is a search for a plan by a faculty which has, itself the capacity to conceive plans.

Since the time of the Greeks the term, hypothesis, has come to have four distinct meanings:

(1) *a mere supposition*, a proposition set up to see what its implications are This movement of reason is behind many contemporary axiomatic systems. Riemann constructed his new

geometry on a basis of supposition and at a time when there was no use for it in prospect ; it was imensely useful to Einstein later on. Similarly, three-valued logic was worked out and then later used to axiomatize quantum mechanics. Historically, science would have been held back if there werenot people prepared to suppose and to work out consistent systems from suppositions, if everyone had as a governing criterion: is this likely to be true?

(2) *a proposition which is being tested* through investigations of its consequences. 'is virtue knowledge?' asks Socrates of meno. 'If virtue is knowledge it will be teachable.' But it soon appears that virtue is not teachable at all, at least in the way in which the arts and sciences are teachable. Physicsits today use the same procedure in testing mathematical systems for objectivity.

(3) *a fictional entity or proposition* which is not regarded as having objectivity and is never tested against consequences for objectivity but serves simply to unify and systematize a great amount of empirical data. This was a standard device in astronomy from the time of Ptolemy to Galileo. It is used often in the communication of scientific data to the general public diagrams and mechanical models often function in this way in public relations.

(4) nowadays the word, hypothesis, is being linked up with the study of creative thinking and is *often used with a predominantly psychological meaning* as a bold and penetrating conjecture on the part of some scientist.

Both the use of hypotheses and the method of verifying them vary from science to science, according as the character of the science happens to be purely empirical (e.g. the work of Darwin or Freud), or experimental (e.g.. the work of Harvey or Faraday) or a combination of experimentation with mathematical reasoning (e.g. the work of Galileo; Newton, Fourier). Not all scientific work is directed and controlled by hypothesis, but in the absence of well-formulated hypotheses, the research can hardly be better than exploration. In the field of mathematical physics and particularly in astronomy, the meaning of hypothesis is both extended and altered: a whole theory a complex system of proposition comes to be regarded as a single hypothesis.

The heuristic approach to the world, the approach by way of hypothesis, is given an empirical value, of course: it is kept under factual control by a process of experimental or observational verification. But quite clearly, in science great confidence is shown in the heuristic function of reason and in the objectivity of what appeals to reason. Where the discrimination cannot be made in experiment or observation, one theory is preferred to its rival if it is superior internally in consistency, mathematical simplicity or explanatory range. Indeed even when an hypothesis is falsified it may still be needed and be retained for rational, explanatory qualities it possesses, and for the way it fits into the existing body of laws.

An hypothesis can be subjected to processes of confirmation and falsification. It is confirmed in the degree to which implications of it are discovered to be true; it is falsified if any implication is discovered to be false. In the latter case we *deduce* its falsity, i.e. the falsity of the implication necessitates, logically, the falsity of the hypothesis and the movement of valid deduction formalizes and express this. In the former case no deduction is possible and the language used is that of corroboration. For Popper 'the non-verifiability of hypotheses is methodologically important'. (*The Logic of Scientific Discovery*, p.253) so important indeed that scientific testing must be structured primarily as a persevering search for negative, falsifying instances. Corroboration must be conceived as the degree to which an hypothesis has stood up to severe testing of this kind and thus proved its mettle:

> It is even quite misleading to regard every 'verification' of a prediction as something like a practical *corroboration* of the *explicans*: it would be more correct to say that only

> such verification of predictions which are 'unexpected' [without the theory under examination] may be regarded as corroborations of the *explicans*, and so the theory. This means that a prediction can be used to corroborate a theory only if its comparison with observations might be regarded as a serious attempt at testing the *explicians* a serious attempt at refuting it. A ['risky'] prediction of this kind may be called 'relevant to a test of the theory'. (*Objective knowledge: An Evolutioanry Approach*, pp. 353–4)

He quotes with approval the remark of Weyl: Once and for all I wish to record my unbounded admiration for the work of the experimenter in his struggle to wrest *interpretable facts* [interpretations being equivalent to hypotheses] from an unyielding Nature who knows so well how to meet our theories with a decisive No or with an inaudible Yes.'

Thus, if in scientific exploration one uses the compass of logic, the fact one must go by is that although hypotheses, being of an unrestrictedly general and empirical content, cannot be proved they can nevertheless be tested. The distinctive character of scientific ideas lies in the boldness of their empirical content, in how disprovable they are in what tests they attract and what discussions and predictions they stimulate. In guiding us rigorously to disprooof (and not supplying us with an instrument of positive proof) logic counsels a human empahsis on learning from mistakes. No one has set out so impressively as Popper the intellectual case for accepting, at the level of methodology, this familiar everyday consequence of the human condition. It is a pathway of disproof that logic lays down for the advance of science:

> The wrong view of science betrays itself in the craving to be right; for it is not his *possession* of knowledge, of irrefutable truth, that makes the man of science, but his persistent and recklessly critical *quest* for truth. (ibid., p.281)

Medawar put it:

> The exploratory process is a sort of dialogue between fact and fancy at least in the sense that it begins with an imaginative conjecture about what the world may be like, and proceeds from that point to, as far as possible, objective observation and criticism. Eventually one builds up a structure of beliefs about the natural world, which is never complete, never beyond the possibility of correction or emendation in some particular. So truth is really a direction in which one is moving: it is not something which one never finally achieves. One of the greatest strengths of Popper's philosophy is that it gives a plausible and helpful account of what goes on in the head of a scientist when he is actually engaged in the process of exploration...Popper's methodology has, among other great strengths the strength of completely abolishing... cultural distinction... By 'the tragedy of the two cultures' I mean the entirely erroneous belief that there is an enormous gap between people like artists and poets and writers, who work through the imagination, and scientists, who are, intellectually speaking, rude mechanicals...Both artists, in the conventional sense, and scientists turn out to rely primarily on the imagination for the generation of their ideas. Both are seekers after truth. (Broadcast on B.B.C., August 1972)

While keeping it responsible to observation and experience, Popper's presentation of scientific method places due emphasis on the understanding provided by hypotheses, on their explanatory power:

> I can therefore gladly admit that falsificationists like myself much prefer an attempt to solve an interesting problem by a bold conjecture, *even (and especially) if it soon turns out to be false*, to any recital of a sequence of irrelevant truisms. We prefer this because we believe that this is the way in which we can learn from our mistakes; and that in finding that our conjecture was false, we shall have learnt much about the truth, and shall have got nearer

to the truth.

> I therefore hold that both ideas the idea of truth, in the sense of correspondence with the facts, and the idea of content (which may be measured by the same measure as testability) play about equally important roles in our considerations, and that both can shed much light on the idea of progress in science. (*Conjectures and Refutations: The Growth of Scientific Knowledge*, p.231)

Rationality, when it cannot identify itself with logicality, knows how to define and control its own boldness:

> With the idol of certainty... there falls one of the defences of obscurantism which bar the way of scientific advance. For the worship of this idol hampers not only the boldness of our questions, but also the rigour and integrity of our tests... Sciences never pursues the illusory aim of making its answers final,or even probable. Its advance is rather towards an infinite yet attainable aim: that of ever discovering new, deeper and more general problems, and of subjecting our ever tentative answers to ever renewed and ever more rigorous tests. (*The Logic of Scientific Dicovery* p. 280-81).

IV. PROBABILITY VALUES AND TRUTH VALUES

Since scientific theories are not logically provable, is it a correct definition of the rationality of science to say that it aims to approximate truth in theories that have high probability value? It is true that as part of the general theory of additive function of sets, pure mathematics provides a calculus (neutral in itself) which can be used and interpreted in any domain or situation that is sufficiently formalized for calculation. Quite clearly science continously uses probability calculation in its routine work of conjecture, observation and experiment. Also one can take particular scientific hypotheses and, following one's conception of what corroboration is, use the mathematical calculus as a measure of the relative degree of corroboration; the resulting probability evaluation is a function not only, of course, of the abstract mathematical calculus (which is rigorously worked out) but also of the non-mathematical ideas and values which are needed to link the calculus with the particular context (its ideas and values being patient of definition and organization in more ways than one). Thus it is meaningful scientific practice to say both that certain empirical generalizations are very probable and that some hypotheses are more probable than others.

The problem is; how clear are the concepts, *probable* and *probablistic thinking* and what part have they in the rationality and aim of science?

On the clarity of the concept of probability, two observations are basic firstly, there is no accepted theory unifying all nuances of meaning in the common usage of the word, probable; secondly, within science and the philosophy of science, there is no accepted definition of probability: there is no provision of an axiomatic framework for the mathematical calculus, i.e. no agreement and formalization of basic facts within experience to which calculations precisely refer.

In common usage, to express our degree of confidence we use such terms as *probable, likely, plausible, credible, impossible, presumptive, improbable, unlikely*. We also say there is *a good chance*; the *chances* are 1 in 4 (*the odds* there are 1 to 3), there is a *reasonable prospect*, etc., etc; we say this will *perhaps* happen, or this *usually* happens. Probability statements often refer to the long run purporting to be based on a law of large numbers.' to give the logic of long runs' and 'large numbers'. The ordinary context for reference to probability is matters of fact, but a probability statement does not refer to any real individual event: it does not *say that* in the next 2 tosses of a penny one will be heads, the other tails. Thus it is neither proved nor disproved by the real outcome here; again it is not affected by past real outcomes; even if I have got 3 consecutive heads, the probability before the next toss is still ½. The common sesne conception of probability seems, generally, to be a very objective one, reflecting something out there, namely conditions that enable and favour some event, without ensuring its realization; ordinarily one looks to frequency of occurrence as the natural mode of verifying probability statements, but only a rudimentary language of probability values is used.

Theories of probability relativize its meaning, variously, to the mathematical calculus (probability being presented indefinitely as whatever can satisfy the axioms of mathematical theory), to empirical frequency (all agree that knowledge of frequencies can give rise, properly, to probability judgements), to justified degrees of belief, to evidence or warranted assertibility, or to degrees of reasonable confidence (which can vary from person to person without imputation of fault) Each of these theories is regarded as having merits and demerits, no single one being wholly satisfactory. Max Black comments:

> One reason may be that an acceptable philosophy of probability is called upon to perform a number of tasks that are hard to reconcile; to show why some probability judgements are *a priori* where as others are contingent; to provide a firm basis for a calculus of probability while recognizing probability judgements that are incorrigibly imprecise; to account for and to defend the connection between 'rationality' and specifiable degrees of confidence in conclusion following with probability from given premises; and, above all, to show how and why it is justifiable to act on probabilities...That all the theories can, with greater or less display of ingenuity, provide a basis for the calculus of chances testifies only to the remarkable economy and simplicity of the needed axioms. (*The Encyclopedia of Philosophy*, vol 6, pp.477–8).

Is it substantially accurate and significant to say that the content of science is what is probably so, and the aim of science is to approximate truth through achieving higher degrees of probability in its generalizations and theories?

Popper is emphatic here. When one uses the term, probability, in an absolute sense (as distinct from its relative sense in calculation which of course is a procedure used everywhere in life and science) one cannot relativize either the content or the aim of science to it. Beginning with a minimal description of probability as 'something that satisfies the laws of the calculus of probabilities' it is an elementary consequence of the general multiplication principle for probabilities that the more a statement asserts, the less probable it is:

> This may be expressed by saying that the logical probability of a sentence X on a given evidence Y decreases when the informative content of X increases. (*Conjectures and Refutations: The Growth of Scientific Knowledge*, p.286)

But scientists do not work by a rule of accepting the most probable hypothesis, the hypothesis which goes as little beyond the evidence as possible. On the contrary they care not for highly probable trivialities but for bold hypotheses with high content that can be more severely and more independently tested:

> This may sound paradoxical to some people but if high probability were an aim of science, then scientists should say as little as possible, and preferably utter tautologies only. But their aim is to 'advance' science, that is to *add to* its content. Yet this means lowering its probability. And in view of the high content of universal laws, it is neither surprising to find that their probability is zero, nor that those philosophers who believe that science must aim at high probabilities cannot do justice to facts such as these: that the formulation (and testing) *of universal laws* is considered their most important aim by most scientists: or that the intersubjective testability of science depends upon these laws [lie. the objectivity of scientific statements lies in the fact that having empirical content they can be intersubjectively tested] I. (Ibid., p. 286)

The kind of approach to truth that science makes is that through becoming more comprehensive in its theories, and this means as a rule progress through less familiar and less comfortable or plausible theories. The kind of verisimilitude sought is that based on richness of content,i.e. the similitude sought is to comprehensive truth; it is not a similitude defined by the diminution in it of the risk of being falsified (the limiting case being lack of content), by a high correlation between truth claim and evidence. Popper believes that a clear technical distinction should be drawn between *verisimilitude* (a quality of hypotheses which have proved their mettle in severe testing and which have high empirical content) and *probability* (a term which should be used exclusively in the sense laid down by the calculus of probability). In this language the aim of science would be described, of course, as progress towards truth in verisimilitudes.

Within the framework of this distinction of Popper's, probability language could take on very definite and clear cut meanings in ordinary life and technically. For probabilistic thinking is a clear example of model thinking (handling the complex world from a rational position of less complexity, as when, e.g. one uses a machine model one's thinking about living things and living functions or models for thinking about industrial relations from the conception of factories as small societies of people). The model used here is an abstract mathematical one. Probabilistic thinking consists firstly in working out a mathematical system with elements to which are assigned, *a priori*, probabilities. The only law is that these probabilities sum into unity (=1). There may be many systems or models depending on the number of elements and the probabilities assigned to them. Whether any of these systems may or may not relate to the real world is not a mathematical-question. How does one choose to operate this or that mathematical model in real life or in science? The system which consists of two elements each with equal probabilities is found to be suitable for predicting the tosses of a coin. It works. In other situations (e.g. the weather over the next four years) one may take a good sample work out probabilities on the basis of frequency ratios in this sample and use the mathematical model which has the same number of elements and the probabilities than one has worked out.

There may be great difficulty in determining the mathematical model one should use (random sampling is the general technique) but finally in probabilistic thinking there is (1) a model and (2) the real complex world one is investgates. One takes readings of the model which the mathematician provides (he knows the model throughly, is *certain* about its features) and one projects these into the real world (predicts they will be true of its to a useful approximation any how). Thus a probability statement purports to be accurate reading of a chosen mathematical model in this respect it may be true or false. It is also a projection of this reading into the real world and a heuristic conception of events in terms of it in this respect it may be successful or unsuccessful. De facto, mathematical calculation underlines the prospect of the reading as being better with things taken in the mass and with long runs.

It is argued that probabilistic thinking makes presuppositions about the world that the world intelligible, conforming to human models, that its plan can be represented in samples. In *probability and Induction*, William Kneale writes:

> The thesis which I wish to dispute [is that]...probability rules concerning transcendent objects such as electrons are ultimate and presuppose no principles of necessity or impossibility whatsoever. When the notion of probability has become as important as it now is in physical science, the need for a satisfactory definition is urgent...But what is the definition adopted by those who try to treat probability rules as ultimate? Clearly they cannot hold any form of the subjectivist theory, and they are debarred from defining probability by reference to ranges or fields of possibility, because they have denied that there can be

> truths of principle in this domain. They must therefore be committed to the frequency definition, and this by itself is enough to condemn their view. For they are after all assuming laws, but laws of the wildest kind about the convergence of frequency series to limits... So long as we believe that there are or may be principles of necessity or impossibility, we have good reason for conjecturing probability rules, whereas without that belief we should have no reason. (pp: 255–6)

V. THE PROBLEM OF INDUCTION

The problems of verification and probability evaluation reflect the difficulty of integrating the empirical and the rational in logical evidence conclusion structures. Such an integration takes place, however imperfectly, every time one subjects an imaginative hypothesis to the control of empirical evidence; also when one reaches a generalization on the basis of limited experience. This latter form of the integration gives rise to the traditional problem of induction. It goes back to the time of Aristotle and has, indeed, been the main logical problem in science for those who have believed that scientific method starts from observation and experiment and proceeds, gradually, to generalization: there is first, in this narrow Baconian view, the industrious gathering of the 'countless grapes, ripe and in season' from which the wine of science then flows.

Although Aristotle's meaning of the term, *induction*, was more general, it came to mean 'coming to see or believe a general truth through the contemplation of particular instances'. There are three kinds of induction and they are all mentioned by Aristotle:

(1) The process by which we become aware of a particular instance as exemplifying a general truth. For instance in the apprehension of this red patch as being darker than that pink patch we may see that any red patch is darker than any pink patch. Here there is no indeference no relationship of evidence and conclusion; rather the sense experience is such as to

facilitate an act of direct insight into a general truth This kind of induction is called intuitive induction.

(2) The process by which we see the truth a general proposition by showing that it holds of every instance that is said to fall under it. This process has usually been known as 'induction by complete enumeration', 'perfect induction', 'complete' induction'. Another suggested name is 'summary induction' and this brings out the fact that it is not a conclusion from evidence, but rather a shorthand formulation.

(3) A process of reasoning in which we generalize from particular instances. This is called 'induction by incomplete enumeration' or 'induction by simple enumeration'. But it is not to be regarded as a process simply of counting; it is a counting of instances recognized as having certain properties in common:

> Everyone makes inferences by simple enumeration. Having met half a dozen Scotsmen all of whom are somewhat lacking in humour, we conclude that no Scotsman can see a joke. This precarious generalization is liable to be upset by the next Scotsman we meet; it could not survive a reading of the works of David Hume. The appearance of a single contradictory instance disproves the conclusion. It is obvious that if the number of observed instances are few in comparison with those that have not been observed, there is considerable likelihood that contradictory instances may be found among the latter. An example of simple enumeration, found in every elementary book of logic, has become famous because contradictory instances were discovered. The conclusion *all swans are white* was derived by many people from their observation of swans in Europe all of which happened to be white. On the discovery of Australia black swans were discovered. (Stebbing, *A Modern* Introduction to *Logic,* p.247)

The historical problem of induction arises with the third kind of induction. It arises when we say we can draw general conclusions about the universe, and when we try to justify as strict proof the scientific procedures which end in such conclusions. For it seems, at first sight anyway, that no general conclusion about the universe could be *logically necessitated* by partial experience of it, that evidence covering only some instances could never *implicate* a conclusion about all instances, past, present and future.

Von Wright points out that logically an inductive inference can take place without the conclusion being a generalization:

> By an inductive inference we mean roughly this: From the fact that something is true of a certain number of members of a class, we conclude that the same thing will be true of unknown members of that class also. If this conclusion applies to an unlimited number of unexamined members of the class, we say that the induction has led to the establishment of generalization. As this is the most important type of inductive inference, induction is often defined as the process by which we proceed from particular to general, or from less general to more general propositions.
>
> It is, however, not necessary that an inductive inference should lead to a generalization. We may also extend the conclusion to a limited number of unknown members of the class, e.g., to the next member which turns up, thus proceeding from particulars to a new particular. Both cases of inductive inference, that from particulars to universals and that from particulars to particulars, are covered by the definition of induction as reasoning from the known to the unknown. This definition also includes induction as reasoning from the past to the future. It must be observed that this time characteristic of inductive inference, which is sometimes mentioned in the definition of it, is of no essential importance, and that induction may also proceed from past cases to other unexamined instances belonging to the past. (*The Logical Problem of Induction*, p.1)

From the time of Francis Bacon many logicians have tried to validate as proof a process of reasoning from particulars to a universal.

Since medieval times logicians have emphasized that a principle such as the uniformity of nature functions in all inductive reasoning. This strengthens the evidential force of particular instances. For some (e.g. many Scholastics, Newton, Mill and some Neo-Scholastics) it has meant that inductive argumentation is, on ultimate analysis, syllogistic. W. E. Johnson in his (*Logic* part II, ch. X and XI) maintains that there is a kind of induction that is syllogistic in form and a kind that is not; the former is called formal or demonstrative induction, the latter is called pure or problematic induction. He gives as an example of formal or demonstrative induction: 'Every specimen of argon has the same atomic weight as this specimen of argon; but this specimen has the atomic weight 39.9; therefore every specimen has the atomic weight 39.9.' Here the conclusion follows of necessity from the premises but it is only probably -true since the major premises rests on a problematic induction. 'This species of induction I have called problematic, because in my view, the universal proposition which it establishes must be regarded, not as absolutely certified, but as accepted only with a higher or lower degree of probability depending upon the collective character of the instances enumerated.' (pp.240, 241)

John Stuart Mill's justification of induction consists essentially in presenting it as a process of analysis. We can never be sure of a generalization for there is always the possibility of an unfavourable instance coming to our knowledge. But the inductive process is not a generalization form particulars, it is a process of analysing particulars. Inconsistently with his extreme Empiricism he assumes that the reality underlying experience is machine like, and that every phenomenon is the carrying into effect of a set of underlying tendencies. Thus the work of proving a law of nature consists in analysing particulars, identifying tendencies in A and then effects in B.

This work is possible granted two theoretical assumptions

and two practical ones. The theroretical assumptions are, firstly 'the whole of the present facts are in the infallible results of all the facts which existed at the moment previous', and secondly that each moment in the present set of facts is related by casual law to some element in the antecedent set. The two practical assumptions are that we can exhaustively describe the context of a particular phenomenon and that we can decompose this context into its constituents facts. Mill's experimental methods (of Agreement, Difference etc) are then applied to prove in regard to all but one of these facts that it cannot be the cause of the given effect.

The essential criticism if this theory of induction is its unreality. 'For Mill the universe is already neatly arranged in piles of universals. consequently the only problem involved in scientific discovery, as he sees it, is the problem of sorting out connections between universals', (Anschutz, *The Philosophy of J.S. Mill*, p. 110) He held that all inductive investigation is a search for causes—there is 'no other uniformity in the events of nature than that which arises from the law of causation.' (A *system of Logic*, Bk. III, ch. XXI, p.4, note) But his experimental methods are not really procedures or techniques for determining cause and effect. Rather they formulate separately and conventionally conditions which a cause fulfils: the cause of any effect is so related to it as to occur whenever the effect occurs, and never when it does not, and to vary or be constant as the effect varies or is constant, when susceptible of variations in quantity or degree. Quite clearly if one can reduce a phenomenon to these terms one can identify the members of a causal relationship but Mill's Methods are not procedures helping the scientist to reduce phenomena to these terms. They are pre-scientific, presupposing a situation that can be solved by common sense.

Modern logicians are satisfied that induction cannot be reduced to deduction. It is not governed by implication and theories which aimed at presenting it as a form of strict logical proof have now become pointless. If particular inductive conclusions are to be evaluated it can only be by a use of the calculus of probabilities. However as Von Wright most acutely points out: Induction is self-justifying as a reasoned policy for purposes of prediction and generalization'; in fact he points out, there is a tautology here: for the criterion by which we judge a policy of reasoning about the unknown to be a *reasoned* policy can only be that it is grounded in the known, in consummated experience; this is equivalently to *require* that it be an inductive policy. Although Hume was fundamentally right and convincing in all he said about it being impossible to adduce any special fact of nature on which we could ground confidence in inductive inference, he failed to see that the meaning of words 'unknown', 'human faculties', 'reasoned policy', 'inductive policy', make that kind of grounding impossible, irrelevant and unnecessary. The demand for his type of justification of inductive inference, and the problem of a resulting scepticism are solved by an analysis of the contextual language. Von Wright sums up his solution to Hume's problem', occasioned by Hume pointing out the impossibility of guaranteeing the truth of any synthetical assertion concerning things outside the domain of our actual or recorded experience:

> Our examination of policies for predicting and generalizing has thus led us to the conclusion that the truth contained in the idea that induction is the best mode of reasoning about the unknown is a disguised tautology. It is not that the inductive method possesses some features, *besides being inductive*, which give it a superiority over other policies. Its superiority is rooted in the fact that the inductive character of a policy is the very criterion by means of which we judge its goodness. The superiority of induction, in other words, is concealed in the *meaning* of a policy's goodness. (*The Logical Problem of Induction*, p.175)

The conception of induction as a policy is recent. It appears also in Kneale, Braithwaite, Reichenbach and Wisdom. Von Wright points out that with this conception.

> the problem of the justification of induction may be said to have under gone a transformation. From having been a problem of ascertaining the conditions of truth or of probability in single inductive conclusions, it has become a problem of showing the superiority of the inductive policy, *as such,* over rival policies. (lbid., p.224)

A new modern problem of induction has, however, arisen: whether it is possible to assign any probability to the particular inductive conclusions of empirical science without making certain assumptions about the world in which we live. In *Human Knowledge: Its Scope and Limits,* Bertrand Russell says:

> From the time of Laplace onwards, various attempts have been made to show that the probable truth of an inductive inference follows from the mathematical theory of probability. It is now generally agreed that these attempts were all unsuccessful, and that, if inductive arguments are to be valid, it must be in virtue of some extra-logical characteristics of the actual world, as opposed to the various logically possible worlds that may be contemplated by the logician. (p.*425)*

J. M. Keynes has formulated these extra-logical characteristics which must be assumed, in two principle & s:a *Principle of Limited Independent Variety* ('the objects in the field , over which our generalizations extend, do not have an infinite number of independent qualities; that, in other words, their characteristics. however numerous, cohere together in groups of invariable connexion, which are finite in number') and a *principle of Atomic Uniformity* (that natural occurrences can be regarded as compounded of small changes taking place in accordance with enduring mathematical laws). If these principles are false or not justifiable there is no logical ground, it is argued, that any generalization with regard to the existent world is more likely to be true than false. These principles which are not established by science itself, constitute, for the scientist, a faith.

And indeed the scientist is distinguished for his antecedent belief, even passionate' belief, in the rationality of what he investigates. Even human pathology is made the subject of science, understanding and therapy. As a lived option 'the real is rational represents. logically, a strong enduring faith on which the human mind has been growing throughout the history of science. Jacques Monod puts it that

> in order to construct knowledge you have got to make a value judgement to begin with...[And this] is exactly what Popper says in the last chapter of his book *The Open Society*...Popper doesn't talk about objective versus non-objective knowledge. He talks about the rational versus the irrational attitude. And he admits, as I do, that to choose the rational versus the irrational attitude. And he admits, as I do, that to choose the rational rather than the irrational attitude is a value judgement it's not a judgement of knowledge. And therefore it's the basis for an ethic (B.B.C. Broadcast, July 1972)

Thus the life of science and of scientific education is more than the increase of knowledge: the logical meaning of being a scientist is that one's whole person is involved in a fundamental, magnanimous option.

Nelson Goodman goes so far as to say that, technically speaking, the traditional problem of inductive generalization is a distorted formulation of the really predominant human problem which is one of verification. We should begin with the fact that our mental approach to the world is rational, heuristic and projective; accordingly, our problem should be situated within a theory of projection:

> The reorientation of our problem may be portrayed in ... figurative language. Hume thought of the mind as being set in motion making predictions by, and in accordance with, regularities in what it observed. This left him with the problem of differentiating between the regularities that do and those that do not thus set the mind in motion.

> We, on the contrary, regard the mind as in motion from the start, striking out with spontaneous predictions in dozens of directions, and gradually rectifying and channelling its predictive processes. We ask not how predictions come to be made, but how ... they come to be sorted out as valid and invalid. Literally, of course, we are not cocerned with describing how the mind works but rather with describing or defining the distinction it makes between valid and invalid projections. (*Fact, Fiction and Forecast*, p.87)

The argument that inductive inference is the best rational approach to the unknown received a substantial corroboration from Peirce. In the *collected papers* (vol. II, p.455 seq.) he speaks of the 'constant tendency of the inductive process to correct itself' as the 'essence' and 'the marvel' of induction. When consistently employed it is, of its nature, self-correcting giving better indications, as it grows, of what a true generalization a true hypothesis would be. He says (ibid., p.501):

> the validity of an inductive argument consists, then, in the fact that it pursues a method which if duly persisted in, must, in the very nature of things, lead to a result indefinitely approximating to the truth in the long run.

Reichenbach's Method of Correction reiterates and strengthens Peirce's presentation of induction as an indefinite and. self-correcting approximation to the truth.

A minority view held by Donald Williams (*The Ground of induction* Harvard University Press, 1947), and Roy Harrod (*Foundations of Inductive Logic*, Macmillan, London, 1956) maintains that the probability of an inductive conclusion is of logical consequence from the inductive procedure itself. Harrod (who wrote his book some years after Williams saying: 'He alone in the present age believes that the validity of induction can be demonstrated without prior assumptions. I am in complete accord'.) points out:

> The task before us is simple, but arduous. It is required to

> show that there can be valid inductions about nature without any prior assumptions about the characteristics of nature whatever. There must be no prior assumption that nature is uniform in whole or in part, or that causes operate. The Principle of Indifference must not be used in any form whatever. No initial prior probabilities must be postulated. We must remain totally open minded until the accumulation of evidence from experience begins to give guidance. The trouble is that so far logicians have been unable to specify any valid principle or principles justifying argument directly from experience without the aid of some prior assumption. (P. 23)

For Williams there is a principle which justifies, logically and fully, the probability of inductive conclusions about the world. This principle is not a statement about the world. It is a statement about the relationship of any sample to the whole of which it is a sample. What is this statement? 'Given a fair-sized sample, then, from any population. with no further material information, we know logically that it very probably is one of those which match the population, and hence that very probably the population has a composition similar to that which we: discern in the sample. This is the logical justification of induction.' (p- 97)

Taking this statement, it may be argued against Williams that the material information from which one proceeds to ascertain the probability of matching—'given' a 'sample', 'fair-sized', from a 'population'—involves some general assumptions about the world, namely that it too is rational, characterized by continuity (so that there is continuity between what is within and what is outside our sense experience), by repetition and by simplicity (it can be represented in human sampling). Harrod indeed seems to make important concessions to this viewpoint on pp- 253 and 261 of his book.

VI. A GENERAL CONCLUSION

A twofold concern must characterize the search for true knowledge: a concern to have true propositions as starting points and a concern to have sound theoretic processes for drawing conclusions which must also be true. In purely deductive systems or deductive procedures of science the theoretic processes used translate logical laws, as we have seen; the methodological problem lies in acquiring true or acceptable propositions as starting points.

In empirical science, however, logical problems are created by the theoretic processes used At first sight the main problem associated with scientific investigation—the problem of verification—may appear different from the main problem associated with science when it is organized into a system of propositions—the problem of inductive generalization. But they are both essentially the problem of integrating the empirical and the rational in a logical evidence conclusion structure. A scientist in giving some new conclusion to the world may not present it according to his actual method of discovery (e.g. hypothesis, deduction of implications, setting up appropriate experiments to verify these). Rather he often chooses to present his data and experiment first, proceeding then to interpret and generalize them into results. Thus a method that is hypothetico deductive may be translated as an inductive process where the empirical evidence comes first and the generalization last.

The problems of verification, probability and induction must be examined both as deriving from an absence of logical form and as manifesting the presence of rational skill and of living magnanimous faith in rationality.

Chapter-10

Theoretical Thought outside the Empirical Sciences

Chapter-10

1. INTRODUCTION

The empirical sciences develop a world-picture on the basis of a metrical approach to reality (the term *world-picture* including, as in modern microphysics, a symbolic representation of atomic process that are in principle inaccessible to sense-perception and imagination). Other approaches to reality also issue in an understanding of it, for instance the philosophic, the aesthetic the purely mathematical the religious and of course every discipline and life itself is an historic process and admits of an enquiry into its history. Each of these approaches has developed its own method and cutting edge; each enriches human experience each includes the evidence-conclusion structure.

Evidence, inference, conclusion: these terms are used over a vast area of human living; they apply wherever there is a desire for a reasoned approximation to reality. Evidence includes not only the observations and experiments of the physicist, but the documentation of the historian, the statistics of the sociologist, the case histories of the clinical psychiatrist, the testimonies in a court of enquiry, the intuitions of the poet. Similarly, inference can refer to the rigorous deductive processes of a mathematician; to the due process of law (which however can deliberately sacrifice some aids to the reasoning out of truth in order to serve what are deemed to be more ultimate social values); to clinical reasoning that is based on rapid cross-checking of various models in which different modes of knowledge have found condensation (e.g. models of anatomy, of physiological functioning of body parts, of pathological processes underlying mental neuroses functioning of body parts, of pathological processes underlying mental neuroses and psychoses); and to the less formal inferences in everyday life. Conclusions, correspondingly, are as diverse in form as the hypotheses of an Einstein, the verdict of a court, the average decisions of life, the diagnosis of psychiatrist, the poetic vision of Teilhard de Chardin, the historical explanation of a Toynbee.

One fact that emerges from the whole array of human reasonings is how extremely difficult it is to achieve certitude. Within any given system, on the basis of accepted viewpoints or principles, confidence develops easily as the main issue is the logical soundness of inference. But certitude becomes more difficult according as less can be assumed. Where questions demand the utmost rigour proof may not be feasible; the realistic objective may consist in discerning where the weight of rationality lies. Since the life we are fitted to live is neither more nor less than a rational free life, human life is not attenuated by the absence of full logical proof, provided that among various alternatives rational choices are clearly discernible.

II. THEORETICAL REASONING THAT IS NOT SUBJECT TO CONTROL AND EVALUATION BY EITHER OBSERVATION OR EXPERIMENT

The logical structure of mathematics has been made very explicit over the last hundred years.This has been a primary and constant objective in the development of modern mathematical logic which indeed has tended to be content with a language from that could accommodate and formalize mathematical reasoning. since the time of Boole, the new logicians looked particularly to Mathematics as to the most general and transparent context of human reasoning, developing without reference to our particular world, functioning independently of sense experience and away from any controlling reference to observed facts. This was true whether or not one held the further logistic view that it was a deductive connection with logic itself which guaranteed the rational and objective force of mathematical calculation. Mathematical science was valued for its intrinsic rationality; and, for all who shared the scientists faith in the rationality of the universe, this grounded a hope in its ultimate utility even though it developed away from the control of observation and experiment.

There have been two different formal ways in which mathematical reasoning and mathematical science (as a body of propositions) have been presented. In the tradition of Frege, Russell and Hilbert the logic implicit in mathematics was displayed best by elaborating mathematics as an axiomatic system. For Gentzen this kind of formalization did not all express the kind of inferential procedures which mathematicians practise in their proofs, and considerable formal advantages would be obtained if one could do this: 'So I wanted for one thing to establish a formalism which would approximate as far as possible to actual inference. Thus arose a calculus of natural inference.' Thus with Gentzen, one of its two pioneers, the natural deduction approach began as a method of formalizing procedures that are fundamental but informal within mathematics.

With regard to Jakowski, the other and independent originator, the new approach was a reduction to system of the method of suppositions used in mathematics (and indeed in all reasoning where we prove an implication by making an assumption and obtaining a conclusion). In his paper of 1934, Jaskowski writes:

> In 1926 Professor J. Lukasiewicz called attention to the fact that mathematicians in their proofs do not appeal to the theses of the theory of deduction, but make use of other methods of reasoning. The chief means employed in their method is that of an arbitrary supposition. The problem raised by Mr Lukasiewicz was to put those methods under the from of structural rules and to analyse their relation to the theory of deduction. The present paper contains the solution of that problem.

Prescinding from the problem of the precise nature of mathematical science as *knowledge*, and also from all problems raised by the study of the foundations of mathematics, one might summarize the contribution which modern logic makes to the understanding of mathematical reasoning and system as follows: mathematics is the primary existential context in which the grammar of logic is exercised, and there are so many points of similarly between mathematical systems and logical systems that many metalogical insights coincide with mathematical ones.

With regard to religious doctrines, it is in their nature to be highly axiomatized when they present themselves as based on revealed truths that transcend human experience. Their transcendent character makes it logical that they develop through maintaining continuous deductive contact with their revelation. For a person who transcends the universe in belief or in searching, an inner clarity and consistency is an important logical certification of the worth of religious doctrine. Of course a concrete religious system may also contain an ethics and other theoretical components that are natural and therefore, logically, subject to rational experiential analysis and testing.

Transcending the world in order to explain it is a movement of reason and is not at all discontinuous with the scientific process. The latter proceeds—on the basis that the world is knowable and that there is an explanatory answer for every intelligible question—to frame hypotheses concerning what is unknown about the world. The movement of a natural theology proceeds—on the basis that to exist is to be intelligible, this world being intelligible in virtue simply of being existential—to conclude that the world is not total being (since it does not explain itself completely) and to commit itself to belief in divine creative being. Not to proceed to this commitment is seen theologically, as an exercise of preference for loss or attenuation of meaning—a type of preference that is not normal in scientific. contexts. Thus the movement of transcending is a genuine theoretical effort of understanding with a resultant explanation which science itself is neither called up to accept nor to oppose. What this movement can mean to the person and what it requires of the person are, of course, questions which concern not the logic of religious faith but the study of its vitality.

III. THE LOGICAL STRUCTURE OF PHILOSOPHY AND OF PHILOSOPHIZING

As one moves from the empirical sciences and mathematics to describe the content and method of philosophy, two basic facts have to be kept in mind.

(1) One of the main tasks of philosophy is to achieve a clear understanding of itself. This requires an appreciation of the difference between it and other disciplines especially the physical sciences and scientific psychology. However, in the two-thousand-year-old tradition of western philosophy these disciplines were not separate and independent until the last century. A variety of problems and bodies of knowledge were, from time to time, called philosophical that are seen now to be scientific. Further, today there is not consensus on the range of the term 'philosophy' and 'philosophizing' and so even contemporary philosophy may not be totally acceptable as philosophy in the future. The consequence of this lack of precision and self clarification within the tradition is that the task of describing philosophy must confine itself to the central core. (2) Difficulties arising out of attempts to solve philosophical problems rather than the problems themselves can become central. Thus at any particular time, philosophical method can become a dominant preoccupation and controversy and indeed, in one view, philosophy is conceived best in terms of method or activity rather than of content.

One can discern the general location of philosophic interest and enquiry by considering the logical organization of other disciplines. In each case there is a basis from which one begins, effectively, to demonstrate—there is primitive language and basic truths or axioms. Thus when knowledge is axiomatized—as it is in the empirical sciences, in mathematics, in religious doctrines one may ask whether (a) primitive language and (b) basic axioms generate a Problematique of their own: do they open on to an area of presupposition which, while not exercising any deductive force within axiomatic systems, is logically part of their total meaningfulness and rationality? Is axiomatized knowledge a well constructed raft floating on waters of supposition? Kant developed his philosophy in reaction to the disturbing puzzle of geometry as a body of propositions which, independently of experience, were clear and transparently true and also were confidently and successfully applied to the real world—how was that possible? It is certainly true that the area of human presupposition is also the area of philosophical investigation:

(a) Concepts and terms employed in familiar and scientific explanation such as 'reality', 'knowledge', 'truth', 'freedom', 'obligation', 'objectivity',—have been subjects for profound wonder and critical enquiry to philosophers. They have been highly controversial too, resistant to any agreed philosophical analysis into unproblematic terms. It was Socrates who first defined and analysed the philosophical function of elucidating concept. Asked questions about what particular things are right, he moved the enquiry to the more fundamental level it presupposed, asking 'But what is rightness?' This type of fundamental questioning was described by Plato as the mark of the true dialectical philosopher. Aristotle moved the questioning to the most general term of all asking 'what is it to-be-something?' Since then conceptual questions of this kind have been accepted as central in philosophy. They are second-order question and their treatment, of its nature, combines conceptual intuition and analysis.

(b) It has always been a function of philosophic enquiry to elucidate ultimate presuppositions in human life, rational investigation and explanatory systems (e.g. what is a *fact* what can we say about *being real,* as such? what exactly is *knowledge as a* reality *in* itself? what does it mean to say that human knowledge is *objective?* do our sensations *and* thoughts disclose a separate external existence of their objects? are there reasons for faith in the human intelligibility of the world?). Traditionally philosophy has also sought to discover what is most basic about the human subject in life (are human beings completely organic or is their vitality spiritual also? what does an analysis of present human life at its highest, i.e. of personal, intelligent, free living, reveal about the possibility that the grave is not the end of a person's life?). And it has enquired into the purpose or lack of it that makes life ultimately meaningful or meaningless, and into the presence of objective values or imperatives in human life (this dimension has given rise to theistic and atheistic doctrine and to varieties of ethical theory).

Of course it must be borne in mind that a good deal of the psychological and ethical content of traditional and contemporary philosophy may, at some future time, be seen as formally belonging to scientific psychology and social science. It has been a recurring feature in the history of philosophy that it recognize sections of its enquiry as belonging to the advancing rationality and axiomatizing range of science. Philosophizing seems to require indeed an attitude of understanding, affirming and valuing the axiomatic power of science while recognizing that it itself works at an underlying level, uncovering and elucidating presuppositions and warrants that, however, do not do logically function as axioms for the deduction of theorems. Readjustment of the boundaries of philosophy and science can be, then, a normal continuing feature of the historical development of the two disciplines

When one looks at the central core of philosophical problems which lie at the roots of objective thought, subjective life and human destiny, and at the variety of philosophical views that have been elaborated in history, it becomes quite clear, firstly, that philosophy is quite different from science in not being a metrical experimental discipline and in not structuring into an axiomatic system. Secondly, while an understanding of how language works is essential, philosophical problems cannot be solved completely and positively by becoming clearer about the way in which an expression is made, by removing ambiguity and unravelling knotted thought. For philosophy is more than problem solving, than the elucidating of presuppositions and basic concepts. The great philosophies have derived from heuristic intuitions of what might be a true perspective on reality and might bring us a deeper understanding of human rationality and human hopes. Philosophizing in its fullest sense seems to consist. in asking ultimate questions of life in a profound silence of inner contemplation and in methodically objectifying such personal reflection, bringing it within the each of critical discussion.

Critical discussion is the aspect of philosophical method that is emphasized today. This is quite understandable. There is no public experiment or objective decision procedure for discriminating between opposing philosophical views. Critical discussion is the medium in which a philosopher experiences the testing of his view and a medium too which stimulates, wakes and energizes others to personal evolution and, possibly, individual appropriation of it. Philosophers in the past have seen philosophical method in aspects that were not overtly socializing: For Plato and Hegell it is dialectical; for Aquinas it consists primarily of conceptual analysis and resolution; for Bergson it is intuitive; for Wittgenstein it is the uncovering of nonsense, for Husserl it is phenomenological description. There are modern thinkers who feel that 'the world' is to be left to the scientis and that philosophical problems must be seen and discussed as problems situated in the language which we use to describe the world; this is somewhat of an extreme from those philosophers, in the past, who believed that philosophy should imitate science—using experimental enquiry (as Hume advocated), axiomatizing like geometry (as Spinoza did) or seeing itself as unified science (as Herbert Spencer felt).

For much of this century, arising from the work of Boole, Frege, Russell and the early Wittgenstein, a consistently held hope and belief was that there is a universal grammer for human thought and communication and that it is possible to master and formalize this grammar and thus bring about a mutation in the quality, clarity and range of philosophical thought. As a case in point, many Polish logicians never lost sight of the fact that their technical work in logic grew out of philosophical concerns and retained their objective of using the new analytic tools to further philosophical enquiry. Indeed Lukasiewicz believed that philosophy must be refashioned and acquire the structure and language that characterize formal logical systems. Since this was generally held, in Poland, to be an impossible development he was called an 'anti-philosopher' there.

Friedrich Waismann indeed argues that the conception of a whole philosophical view is never a matter of logical steps, and being conceived it can neither be proved nor disproved by strictly logical reasoning. What is essential to philosophy is the breaking through to a deeper insight which cannot be lodged in a theorem and cannot therefore be demonstrated.

> Philosophical arguments are none of them logically *compelling...* [They] are not deductive; therefore they are not rigorous; and therefore they don't prove anything ... No philosophical argument ends with a Q.E.D. However forceful it never forces. There is no bullying in philosophy, neither with the stick of logic nor with the stick of language... Yet they [philosophic arguments] have force...they really screen what actually happens—the quiet and patient undermining of categories over the whole field of thought. Their purpose is to open our eyes, to bring us to see things in a new way—from a wider standpoint unobstructed by misunderstandings... considerations such as these make us see what is already apparent in the use of rational that this term has a wider range of application than what can be established deductively. To say that an argument can be rational and yet not deductive is not a sort of contradiction as it would inevitably be in the opposite case, namely, of saying that a deductive argument need not be rational. (*Contemporary British Philosophy: Personal Statements* pp.470, 471,480)

On the whole it seems clear that in view of the peculiar nature of philosophizing, the philosopher must be free of a general dogmatic approach to method, above all from a 'dogmatism of precision'. At the same time one may note various forms of reasoning and refutation which by frequent recurrence demonstrate their distinctive efficiency within philosophy:

The infinite regress argument shows up an unsatisfactory explanation as possessing the crucial obscurity it purports to dissolve. A brief example is an argument of Wittgenstein's in *Philosophical Investigations:*

> How is he to know what colour he is to pick out when he hears 'red'? Quite simple: he is to take the colour whose image occurs to him when he hears the word. But how is he to know which colour it is 'whose image occurs to him'? Is a further criterion needed for that? (§ 239)

An infinite regress in needed criteria means that no criterion is really provided.

Model reasoning is familiar in philosophy. Choosing and working through the details of an analogy is often indispensable for articulating the details of one's view. And rigorously examining analogies is a method of refutation. Berkeley uses it in his *Principles of Human Knowledge:*

> It is said extension is a mode or accident of Matter and that Matter is the *substratum* that supports it. Now I desire that you would explain to me what is meant by Matter's *supporting* extension... It is evident *support* cannot here be taken in its usual or literal sense, as when we say that pillars support a building In what sense, therefore, must it be taken? For my part I am not able to discover any sense at all that can be applicable to it. (Part I, par. 16)

Ryle's use of the analogy, 'the ghost in the machine', is a powerful way of focusing the argument against mind-body dualism. In general, analogies play an important part in philosophical reasoning and self-explanation, as the living centre is frequently a broad vision of things.

Criticism that a philosophical view is inconsistent (and therefore false) or self-refuting (and therefore unacceptable) is frequent also; not surprisingly for when one theorizes at the limits of justification one may easily find one's theory subjected to one's own strictures. Thus it was argued that Logical Positivism was self-refuting because its theory of meaning rendered itself meaningless. It is argued similarly that total scepticism is self-refuting.

As a summary one can say that in elucidating concepts and propositions that constitute their concern philosophers describe, divide, define, analyse, make category distinctions and communicate to others by paradigm cases; in reasoning structures they show, by their example, that their discipline cannot impose a dogmatism of precision and there are philosophic views with a formalistic structure, and others structured quite informally. In its history philosophy has accommodated all forms of argumentation Popper puts it: 'Philosophers are as free as others to use any method in searching for the truth.'

Philosophy is a limited human enterprise. The fact that it rases ultimate questions does not guarantee it any measure of success in answering them; it is simply its business to formulate such questions and to try to answer them by a purely human investigation. Further the fact that philosophical views are not amenable to experimental confirmation or falsification has, as a practical consequence, that no philosophical view is ever definitely eliminated and a linear development of philosophical insights has proved utopian. Essentially, philosophy takes a more generalized approach to reality than the sciences. and a non-metrical one. Conceptual analysis is the cutting edge in its investigations, and the ability to display a doctrine analytically, as a development out of accepted concepts and intuitions, is the main test of philosophical rectitude.

IV. THE USE OF LOGICAL TECHNIQUES IN FORMAL ANALYSES

Organizing knowledge into formal systems & becoming standard procedure in life and in science. Educated people want to see in explicit fashion the primitive terms, postulates and rules of inference in every body of doctrine. They want to force out inconsistencies and vagueness by conceptual improvement and to expose the quality of argument. Further, the widespread use of computers is forcing people to be very analytic and formal as a prerequisite for programming machines. However one may easily fail to distinguish between organizing propositions into a formal system and proving a particular point; as a consequence, one may think one is proving a proposition when all one is doing is situating it in the wider context of one's own formal system. Where the latter is not shared or acceptable, the argument will have little force. Thus while the expert must have a good formal grasp of his subject matter. He needs also the skill of communicating with people to whom his formal system is unfamiliar or even, perhaps, unacceptable. While it relates propositions that the total intelligibility is organized and transparent, it does not represent the way that individual propositions are actually discovered or the basis on which others will necessarily believe them.

One technique that can be used in formal analysis and exposition is the application of a certain amount of the conceptual apparatus of mathematical logic (e.g. the notation of propositional logic, predicate logic, class logic, modal logic) and of its methods. In 1926, L. Bloomfield advocating the use of the axiomatic method in linguisitics and especially in phonology, wrote:

> The method of postulates (that is assumptions or axioms) and definitions is fully adequate to mathematics as for other sciences, the more complex their subject matter, the less amenable are they to this method, since, under it, every descriptive or historical fact becomes the subject of a new postulate.

> Nevertheless the postulational method can further the study of language, because it forces us to state explicit whatever we assume, to define our terms and to decide what things may exist independently and what things are interdependent.
>
> Certain errors can be avoided or corrected by examining and formulating our (at present tacit) assumptions and defining our (often undefined) terms.
>
> Also, the postulational method saves discussion, because it limits our statements to a defined terminology; in particular, it cuts us off from psychological dispute Discussion of the fundamentals of our science seems to consist one half of obvious truisms, and one half of metaphysics; this is characteristic of matters which form no real part of a subject. they should properly be disposed of by merely naming certain concepts as belonging to the domain of other sciences. ('A Set of Postulates for the Sciences', *Language,* 1926, pp. 153-4)

Since then much work has been done in linguistics on the logical reconstruction of theories. The literature of applied logic also includes the analysis of well-known paradoxes and such famous arguments as St Anselm's Ontological Argument. More importantly, a Temporal Logic (or Logic of Tense) provides the linguistic and inferential apparatus for reasoning that is grounded in change through time; there has been the development of a Deontic Logic-a logic of normative concepts, especially of obligation; and there are logics of preference and of commands symbolizing conceptual aspects Of these entities and formalizing the relationships (especially of implication) which obtain between statements that express them.

Contemporary deontic logic provides a clear and substantial example of the application of logical apparatus and method to theoretical thought. It was initiated by G.H. von Wright whose paper, *Deontic Logic* (1951) and subsequent writings have shaped the contemporary discussions. There were some anticipations of this development: medieval logicians were alive to the possibility of a logic of obligation based on modal logic: in 1926 Ernst Mally, a student of Alexius Meinong, published an axiom system for the notion of *ought*. In *An Essay in Deontic Logic and the General Theory of Action* (1968), von Wright provides perspective on the development over nearly twenty years:

> Deontic Logic, in its modern form, was born as an off shoot of modal logic, its point of departure was the observation of a formal analogy between the concepts of possibility, impossibility and necessity on the one hand and the notions of permission, prohibition and obligation on the other hand.
>
> I soon realized that a deontic logic analgous to a propositional modal logic is inadequate as a proposed formalization of norms (rules) of action. It does not permit expression of the distinction, for example, between an obligation to destroy a certain state of affairs and a prohibition against producing this same state. In order to express this distinction, symbolic means for differentiating between the 'active' and the 'passive' mood of behaviour have to be created. This, in turn requires means of expressing that a state of affairs comes into being, continues or passes away. What is required is thus a Logic of Action founded upon a Logic of Change.
>
> In *Norm and Action* (1963) I tried to meet these requirements. The rudiments of a formal theory of change and of action were developed and used as a basis for deontic logic. The new fabric presented a rather different look from the original one. In particular, the close analogy with modal logic threatened to break down. As a consequence, the building of a deontic logic came to appear to me as 'a much more radical departure from existing logical theory than I at first realized ...
>
> It was not without surprise that I found that the

analogy between deontic and modal logic which in *Norm and Action* had seemed to me to break down, was restored when the formal theory of action was given a more accomplished shape. Deontic logic, as I see the subject now, is essentially a branch or facet of modal logic. *Permissibility* as deontic possibility of acting closely parallels *ability* as human (and naturalistic) possibility of doing things.The various conditional permission concepts, moreover, suggest as their analogues a variety of relative modalities. If these suggestions turned out to be fruitful for the study of modal concepts, one could perhaps say that deontic logic had paid off the debt it owes to modal logic for its birth.

The applications of deontic logic are in ethics and the philosophy of law. It would seem that applications to ethics require, in order to be a fruitful, a complement in the form of a logic of value concepts. The applications to legal theory are, I believe of a more direct nature. Two problems for the treatment of which deontic logic seems to provide a useful basis, are those of *completeness* of normative (legal) systems and of the *hierarchy* of norms of legal order. (3-5)

Much work has been done in devising an appropriate semantical basis. At first von Wright applied deontic operators (the Greek *deon* means that which is binding) to action describing sentences only. In *Norm and Action* he constructs such sentences in this way: *pTq* expresses the transformation of a state of affairs *p* into a state of affairs *q; d* (*pTq*) expresses the bringing about of this transformation, and *f* (*pTq*) expresses the forbearing from bringing it about. Deontic operators such as *O* (obligation) and *P*(permissibility) are attached to such *df*-sentences. His system was strictly speaking a logic of act-names rather than of propositions, the notion of truth-value being replaced by that of *performace-value*. Since then he has accepted a wider application of deontic operators, namely to closed and open sentences which can be descriptions of states of affairs or statements about act-individuals.

The notion of permission is the primitive deontic operator, obligation being defined by it:

$$Op \equiv \sim P \sim p$$

There are three principles or axioms: a principle of permission, that for any act *p*, either *p* or ~*p* is permitted:

$$Pp \vee P \sim p.$$

The second principle is one of deontic distribution:

$$P\,(p \vee q) \equiv Pp \vee Pq.$$

There is a principle of deontic contingency, stating that

$O(p \vee \sim p)$ and $\sim P(p \;\&\; \sim p)$ are not valid.

The rules of inference of propositional logic are used along with *a rule of extensionality:*

If *p* and *q* are logically equivalent, *Pp and Pq* are logically equivalent. The validity of deontic formulae can be determined by a truth-table method; thus the system is a decidable one.

A. R. Anderson sought to simplify and reduce deontic logic by translating 'It is obligatory that *p*' into 'If *p* is not done then—necessarily some sanction or penalty will be applied.' Sören Hallden has developed a deontic system in which the basic type of sentence is 'it is better if *p* than if *q*'; he defines 'it ought to be the case that *p*' as 'it is better if *p* than if not-*p*.' These approaches fail to include and formalize the notion of moral commitment which von Wright, Nicholas Rescher and other logicians regard as essential for a deontic system. The difference in approach underlines the fact that a formal system, achieving an intelligibility that is intrinsic in basis, cannot determine its own applicability.

Concerning the axiomatic work that was done, R. Hilpinen observes:

> In this approach, plausible looking candidates for logical truth are selected as axioms for the notion studied, a sample of consequences (or theorems) is derived from these axioms, and the adequacy of the axiom system is decided by

> considering these consequences. Deontic formulate are normally interpreted simply by translating them to sentences of ordinary language. The plausibility of putative theorems is judged on the basis of the intuitive plausibility of their ordinary-language counterparts...The formulation of our intutions concerning deontic notions in ordinary language often involves ambiguous expressions such as 'implies', 'requires', etc... Recent studies by Stig Kanger, Saul A. Kripke, Jaakko Hintikka, Richard Montague, W.H. Hanson and others indicate that the application of modern semantical methods (model theory) to deontic logic gives a more fruitful basis for understanding deontic formulae and judging their acceptability. (*Deontic Logic: Introductory and Systematic Readings*, pp. 15-16)

Jaakko Hintikka points out the basic formal importance of distinguishing deontic consequence and logical consequence:

> What does the validity of a statement of the form ($p \supset q$) mean? According to our definitions above it means that the statement ($p \& {\sim} q$) is not satisfable. The intuitive meaning of this fact can be expressed by saying *that p cannot* be realized without *ipso facto* realizing *q*, too. When we are thinking of or discussing normative matters, we often—unwittingly—slip into discussing something else. Without noticing it, we concentrate our attention, not on what can or cannot be realized, but rather on what can or cannot be realized *without violating any obligations.* In the case at hand, we are tacitly considering whether *p* can be realized without realizing *q while all norms are satisfied.* In other words, we are interested in whether ($p \& {\sim} q$) can be true, not in any old possible world, but in a *deontically perfect* world. This means that we are considering, not the satisfiability of $P(p \& {\sim} q)$, but the satisfiability of $P(p \& {\sim} q)$, in other words, not the validity of ($P \supset$ q), but the: validity of $O(p \supset q)$. *(Deontic Logic: Introductory and Systematic Readings,* p.78)

In $p \supset q$ we state that the realization of *p* involves *q* as a logical consequence and therefore in any arbitrary world; in $O(p \supset q)$ we state that as the force of a norm (in a world where all norms are fulfilled) the realization of p involves q. In the latter case q is a deontic consequence rather than a logical consequence of p. A System of purely deontic consequences does not provide an adequate basis for solving the ethical problems of actual human living, many of which arise because previous obligations have been neglected. Further fallacies arise when the distinction between logical consequence and deontic consequence is not observed in the first addition of his *Formal Logic*, Prior put forward as an evident truth of logic: if we are obliged to do *A*, then if our doing *A* implies that we ought to do *B*, we are obliged to *B*.' However the obligation of doing *B* arises *as a consequence because* not only are we oblidged to do *A* but also we are in a world where, all norms being satisfied, we actually do *A*. if we did not do *A* the basis for concluding that we are obliged to do *B* would be gone.

It seems that the formal problems encountered by deontic logic clarify the nature and difficulties of ethical thought itself. In summary one may say that in constructing a deontic logic one encounters difficulty in devising satisfactory linguistic forms for deontic content: in reaching a set of axioms whose derivatives are at no point in conflict with moral intution, or alternatively, in establishing an independent decision procedure for deontic statements which claim to be formally true but are not simply instances or application of truths in formal logic.

This section on the application of logical techniques must, finally, give due prominence to the fact that at the present time formal analyses and expositions of all kinds make as much use as possible, in inference, of the *formalistic method* which is based on the fact that one may deal with words in two entirely different ways: one may be concerned with them materially (as a set of waves in the air, or as a series of ink marks, governed by *syntactical* rules which refer exclusively to their material form and never to their meaning) or one may be concerned with them as having meaning (and as coming therefore under the rules of semantics). One of the most important achievements of modern methodology is the realization that operating with language on the syntactic level can make the work of thought considerably easier. Such a method is called *formalism.* It consists in ignoring every meaning of the signs employed and considering the signs exclusively according to their written form. The method is based on the clear distinction between a language in itself with its purely syntactic rules and the giving of meaning to this language. It would be easy to construct a language without attaching any meaning to it and different interpretations could be assigned to the same formalized language. Indeed formalism consists essentially in the extension of a method known for centuries, namely that of calculation which occurs in the language of numbers.

Thus a sign may be said to have a twofold meaning:

(I) it has *an operational meaning* for us if we know how to use it, know the syntactical rules which are applicable to it;

(2) it has an *eidetic meaning* for us if we know what it refers to and connotes. When an eidetic meaning is given, an operational meaning is always given along with it but not vice versa. Bochenski notes: 'There are two extreme positions in philosophy today: on the one hand it is held that human knowledge is limited to eidetic meanings, and on the other that it is limited to the purely operational. In the first case all formalism is excluded, or at any rate systems which cannot be fully interpreted are rejected. On the other side, it is maintained that there is no such thing as eidetic meaning, and that only operational meaning is at our disposal. Both views are erroneous. It is perfectly clear that in certain cases there is an eidetic meaning. On the other hand, however, there seems to be parts of mathematics, physics, astronomy, etc. which cannot be given any eidetic meaning, although on the whole they lead to consequences which it is possible to interpret eidetically.' (*The Methods of Contemporary Thought, p.39*)

Formalism is used in many spheres of modern research, including Logic. It has been humoursly put that in formalism one does not know what one is saying, nor whether what one is saying is true. But Bochenski notes:

(1) The goal of formalism is always knowledge. A formalistic system only fulfils its task. Therefore, if it is ultimately possible to interpret its results eidetically.

(2) The rules governing formalistic operations must make sense eidetically. They prescribe what we are to do and it must be possible to understand them, ultimately.

(3) In practice, formalized systems are nearly always developed by first establishing meaningful signs, then abstracting from their meaning and building up the system formalistically and finally giving a full interpretation to the finished system. (This holds in particular for logic)

(4) Although it would not be impossible to have a science whose system had no meaning except a syntactic one, this cannot be the case logic. For logic has to provide rules of deduction for all indirect thinking and if its rules werenot eidetically meaningful no deduction could be carried out. Accordingly most contemporary logicians hold that systems which do not permit any known eidetic interpretation are not really logic.

Formalism is a very useful method to use in conjunction with other methods, for the following reasons:

(a) in very complicated matters our eidetic understanding may break down and be helped on by formalistic processes;

(b) the use of formalism (which handles signs according to their written shape) helps to exclude tacit presuppositions about objects;

(c) the process of formalistic deduction is suitable for delimiting and clarifying primitive concept or terms;

(d) a system that is developed purely formalistically may permit of many interpretations and therefore of many uses.

It is important to note that while the extensive use of artificial symbols has occurred at the same time as the development of formalism, artificial symbols need not be regarded formalistically. For example, the primitive parts of the language of mathematical logic are usually not regarded, formalistically.

Chapter-11

Formal Detachment: Ideal or Myth?

Chapter-11

I. INTRODUCTION

The sense in which our knowledge may be said to be objective is a matter of great contemporary discussion in both science and philosophy. Added to this interest is an unprecedented grasp and power of formalization which has created a technology of computerization. Against this background the contemporary writings of Michael Polanyi and (from the last century) the *Grammar of Assent* of John Henry Newman are particularly important for their argument that human knowing is *basically* informal, that it is not true to say either that, ideally, human knowledge should be purely formal or that, factually, One could know in a completely formal way. In contrast, objectivist writings are concerned with scientific knowledge as something which, being stated and formalized in human language, is no longer part of ourselves, and grow through being subject to universal criticism. All these writings are valuable for development an overall perspective. They are not in direct conflict and indeed it may emerge that they combine in any full account of knowledge:, both formal and informal

II. MICHAEL POLANYI

In 1958 Michael Polanyi, a distinguished physical chemist, published his Gifford Lectures (1951-2) as *Personal Knowledge: Towards a Post Critical Philosophy.* He wrote:

> I start by rejecting the ideal of scientific detachment. In the exact sciences, this false ideal is perhaps harmless, for is in fact disregarded there by scientists. But we shall see that it exercises a destructive influence in biology, psychology and sociology, and falsifies our whole outlook far beyond the domain of science. I want to establish an alternative ideal of knowledge, quite generally.

> Hence the wide scope of this book and hence also the coining of the new term I have used for my title: Personal Knowledge. The two words may seem to contradict each other: for true knowledge is deemed impersonal, universally established, objective But the seeming contradiction is resolved by modifying the conception of knowing.
>
> [Personal participation of the knower in all acts of understanding] does not make our understanding subjective. Comprehension is neither an arbitrary act nor a passive experience, but a responsible act claiming universal validity. Such knowing is indeed objective in the sense of establishing contact with a hidden reality; a contact that is defined as the condition for anticipating an indeterminate range of yet known (and perhaps yet inconceivable) true implications. It seems reasonable to describe this fusion of the personal and the objective as Personal Knowledge. (Preface)

In this and subsequent writings Polanyi argues that the urge to have an impersonal knowledge has made science disjoin subjectivity and objectivity, has made it seek a quality of total exteriority which is impossible for human understanding and has made prediction rather than understanding its central criterion.

In his view, with regard to all explicit formalized knowledge there is always a tacit dimension—unformalized knowing. Tacit thought is an indispensable part of all knowledge, and the ideal of eliminating all unformalized elements from scientific knowing and establishing a strictly detached, objective knowledge never was realized and could not be:

> I think I can show that the process of formalizing all knowledge to the exclusion of any tacit knowing is self-defeating. For, in order that we may formalize the relations that constitute a comprehensive entity, for example, the relations that constitute a frog, this entity, i.e. the frog, must be first identified informally by tacit knowing; and,

> indeed, the meaning of a mathematical theory of the frog lies in its continued bearing on this still tactitly known frog. Moreover, the act of bringing a mathematical theory to bear on its subject is itself a tacit integration of the kind we have recognized in the use of a denotative word for designating its object. And we have seen also that a true knowledge of a theory can be established only after it has been interiorized and extensively used to interpret experience. Therefore a mathematical theory can be constructed only by relying on *prior* tacit knowing and can function as a theory only *within* an act of tacit knowing, which consists in our attending *from* it to the previously established experience on which it bears. Thus the ideal of a comprehensive mathematical theory of experience which would eliminate all tacit knowing is proved to be self-contradictory and logically unsound. (*The Tacit Dimension*, pp. 20-21)

Formalized knowledge has the great value of being patient of critical reflection; it is an external, explicit, articulate system and we can examine its derivation from specifiable premisses according to clear rules of inference. This is its logical difference from knowledge which being acquired and held tacitly, is *a critical.* It does not follow, however, that the ideal is a completely precise and strictly logical representation of knowledge and that the presence of tacit thought is a flaw to be eliminated. For tacit operations are of their nature necessary for the production and the renewal of articulate frameworks. Further, formulating our knowledge not only makes us better informed, it also increases our mental power to re organize, tacitly, our knowledge from ever new points of view; thus it maintains the supremacy of our tacit powers:

> In the last few thousand years human beings have enormously increased the range of comprehension by equipping our tacit powers with a cultural machinery of language and writing. Immersed in this cultural milieu, we now respond to a much increased range of potential thought.

(*The Tacit Dimension,* p.91)

Humanly we can only see the universe from a centre within ourselves and we must give existence to our vision in the imitation, the medium, of human language. Human perspective cannot be eliminated from human knowledge or human expression:

> In the Ptolemaic system, as in the cosmogony of the Bible, man was assigned a central position in the universe, from which position he was ousted by Copernicus. Ever since, writers eager to drive the lesson home have urged us, resolutely and repeatedly, to abandon all sentimental egoism, and to see ourselves objectively in the true perspective of time and space.
>
> What is the true lesson of the Copernican revolution? Why did Copernicus exchange his actual terrestrial station for an imaginary solar stand-point? The only justification for this lay in the greater intellectual satisfaction he derived from the celestial panorama as seen from the sun instead of the earth. Copernicus gave preference to man's delight in abstract theory, at the price of rejecting the evidence of our senses, which present us with the irresistible fact of the sun, the moon and the stars rising daily in the east to travel across the sky towards their setting in the west. In a literal sense, therefore, the new Copernican system was as anthropocentirc as the Ptolemaic view, the difference being merely that it preferred to satisfy a different human affection. (*Personal Knowledge: Towards a Post Critical Philosophy*, pp. 3-4)

Thus in considering theoretical knowledge to be superior to immediate experience we are not ceasing to be anthropocentric: what we are doing is favouring an anthropocentrism of our reason, believing that rationality commands universal acceptance by rational creatures everywhere, and enables us to make even prophetic contact with reality: 'In this whole indeterminate scope of its true implications lies the deepest sense in which objectivity is attributed to scientific theory.' (Ibid., p.5) The prophetic power inherent in abstract theory has been shrunk and distorted into the concept of scientific theory as 'a convenient contrivance, a device for recording events and computing their future course' whereas the true nature and core of theory is the *understanding* that it gives:

> To say that the discovery of objective truth in science consists in the apprehension of a rationality which commands our respect and arouses our contemplative admiration; that such discovery, while using the experience of our sense as clues, transcends this experience by embracing the vision of a reality beyond the impressions of our senses, a vision which speaks for itself in guiding us to an ever deeper understanding of reality—such an account of scientific procedure would be generally shrugged aside as out dated Platonism: a piece of mystery-mongering unworthy of an enlightened age. Yet it is precisely on this conception of objectivity that I wish to insist. (Ibid., pp. 5-6)

Further, intellectual passion is a reality *in* science: it has a logical function within scientific understanding, serving as a guide to what is precious to science, to what is of higher and what of lesser interest:

> Scientific discovery reveals new knowledge, but the new vision which accompanies it is not knowledge. It is less than knowledge, for it is a guess; but it is more than knowledge, for it is a foreknowledge of things yet unknwon and at present perhaps inconceivable. Our vision of the general nature of things is our guide for the interpretation of all future experience. Such guidance is indispensable. Theories of the scientific method which try to explain the establishment of scientific truth by any purely objective formal procedure are doomed to failure. Any process of enquiry unguided by intellectual passions would inevitably spread out into a desert of trivialities. Our vision of reality, to which our sense of scientific beauty responds, must

> suggest to us the kind of questions that it should be reasonable and interesting to explore. It should recommend the kind of conceptions and empirical relations that are intrinsically plausible and which should therefore be upheld, even when some evidence seems to contradict them, and tell us also, on the other hand, what empirical connections to reject as specious, even though there is evidence for them—evidence that we may as yet be unable to account for on any other assumptions. In fact, without a scale of interest and plausibility based on a vision of reality, nothing can be discovered that is of value to science; and only our grasp of scientific beauty, responding to the evidence of our senses, can evoke this vision. (Ibid., p.135)

A problem arises when we acknowledge the participation of the knower in shaping his knowledge and accept personal rather than impersonal knowledge as the ideal: is knowledge then something that we could determine at will, as we think fit?':

> I have argued that personal knowledge is fully determined, provided that it is pursued with unwavering universal intent. I have expounded the belief that the capacity of our minds to make contact with reality and the intellectual passion which impels us towards this contact will always suffice so to guide our personal judgement that it will achieve the full measure of truth that lies within the scope of our particular calling. (*The Study of Man*, p.27)

The existence, in every act of knowing, of a tacit and passionate contribution of the person, means that in knowing we exercise commitment and responsibility:

> Within its commitments the mind is warranted to exercise much ampler powers than those by which it is supposed to operate under objectivism; but by the very fact of assuming this new freedom it submits to a higher power to which it had hitherto refused recognition. Objectivism

> seeks to relieve us from all responsibility for the holding of our beliefs. That is why it can be logically expanded to systems of thought in which the responsibility of the human person is eliminated from the life and society of man. In recoiling from objectivism, we would acquire a nihilistic freedom of action but for the fact that our protest is made in the name of higher allegiances. We cast off the limitations of objectivism in order to fulfil our calling, which bids us to make up our minds about the whole range of matters with which man is properly concerned. (*Personal Knowledge: Towards a Post-Critical Philosophy*, pp. 323-4)

Once one acknowledges understanding rather than prediction as the core of knowledge the whole range of disciplines from Physics to the fine arts are seen to arise from the same tacit powers. Rationality in science is akin to rationality in ethics, in politics, in jurisprudence and law. Creative thinking in science is akin to intution in art and literature. As formal intellectual beauty is criterion of truth in science so is it a criterion of excellence in aesthetics. And science resembles religion, too, in resting on belief that leads to understanding:

> We must now recognize belief once more as the source of all knowledge. Tacit assent and intellectual passions, the sharing of an idiom and of a cultural heritage, affiliation to a like-minded community: such are the impulses which shape our vision of the nature of things on which we rely for our mastery of things. No intelligence, however critical or original, can operate outside such a fiduciary framework. (*Personal Knowledge; Towards a Post Critical Philosophy*, p.266).

So closely linked is the formal explicit rationality of science with its sources that Polanyi speaks of it as 'dwelling in' them as we are said to dwell in our own bodies:

> I suggest now that the supposed pre-suppositions of science are so futile because the actual foundation of our

> scientific beliefs cannot be asserted at all. When we accept a certain set of pre-suppositions and use them as our interpretative framework, we may be said to dwell in them as we do in our own body. Their uncritical acceptance for the time being consists in a process of assimilation by which we identify ourselves with them. They are not asserted and cannot be asserted, for assertion can be made only within a framework with which we have identified ourselves for the time being; as they are themselves our ultimate framework, they are essentially inarticulable.
>
> It is by his assimilation of the framework of science that the scientist makes sense of experience.This making sense of experience is a skilful act which impresses the personal participation of the scientist on the resultant knowledge. (Ibid., p. 60)

Through their common personal involvement there is an inescapable solidarity of science with all other cultural provinces.

At this point one may cite as support another contemporary scientist, C.H. Waddington, who argues that art absorbs central insights and concerns of science not through formal learning but by a kind of empathy which has important effects on the ways in which painters have worked. In his book, *Behind Appearance; A study of the relations between painting and the natural sciences in this century*, he points out that both art and science have, at times dealt with tangible objects and familiar experiences; together they have also engaged in dissolving familiar reality, in fusing space an time into a single continuum; they have responded to the impossibility of a single unified description of nature by complementary approaches at various levels and now artists like scientists are becoming preoccupied with the nature of their own activities and materials. Art and science now consciously share the same epistemological foundation: 'The observer does not wholly make what he observes, but his intrinstic character colours it.There is no strict objective-subjective dichotomy. The painter is *in* his painting, the scientist *in* his science.' (p.240) Examining the common tendency of twentieth-century painting and science towards probing behind appearances and their relationships at levels of conscious connections and unconscious reflections, Waddington concludes:

> The scientist does not go to the painter for a representation of scientific objects, but for the enrichment and deepening of his consciousness which comes when he finds a painter in whom the climate of scientific thought has penetrated into the spirit, leading to the production of works in which some of the deeper less easily expressible features of the scientific outlook are 'shown forth'. (p.155)

It may well be that one of the greatest recurring mistakes in history has been to take philosohic systems and scientific systems as the paradigm case of knowledge, assuming a simple identity between perfect knowledge and wholly explicit truth. Polanyi insists that it is in the very nature of human knowing to be a kind of groping that combines both *focal* and *subsidiary* awareness, that knows, in a specifiable way, that which we attend to and, in an unformalized way, that which we are relying upon: no knowledge is, or can be, wholly focal. Essentially this means that knowledge is studied best within a theory of life (indeed of evolving life) rather than within a theory of form or system.

Impersonalized knowledge exists only in the netural process of transference; in the sender it arises out of a living process, in the receiver it returns to a living process—that of another centre, another subjectivity. Marjorie Grene puts it as follows:

> ....only the explicit, formulable core of knowledge can be transferred. Neutrally, from person to person. Its implicit base (since it is not verbalized and cannot be formulated and so impersonalized) must be the groping *of someone*.
>
> But while personal, the subsidiary, or tacit, root of knowing is primarily directed away *from* the inner core of my being *to* the focal centre of my attention. All knowledge

consists in a *form-to relation.* Of course, subsidiary knowledge is mine: indeed, it is what relevantly to the present focal point of my attention, I have assimilated to my very self: it is what, out of my being in the world, I have interiorized to the point where I can rely on it to guide me towards a distally located goal. All knowing—whether tacit, as in perception or in skills, or explicit (though never totally so), as in the mastery of an intellectual discipline—displays this dual structure. I attend from a proximal pole, which is an aspect of my being, to a distal pole, which, by attending to it, I place at a distance from myself. All knowing, we could say, in other words, is orientation. The organism's placing of itself in its environment the dinoflagellate in the plankton, the salmon in its stream or the fox in its lair, prefigures the process by which we both shape and are shaped by our world, reaching out from what we have assimilated to what we seek.

Unlike the traditional ideal of a wholly explicit, self-guaranteeing truth, from-to knowledge cannot be instantaneous, it is a stretch, not only of attention, but of effort, effort must be lived, and living takes time. Knowledge, therefore, is imbedded both in living process (as Piaget, too, has argued in *Biologic et Connaissance* and as Suzanne Langer is arguing in her study of *Mind*) and in the uniquely human form of living process: in history. (*Knowing and Being*, Introduction, pp. x-xi)

The human living process must be seen not as automatic, not as arbitrary but as responsible. Responsibility is part of the human hope of achievement: the human way of being an active centre is characterized by a sense of calling and by a responsibility.

Situating his view within contemporary thinking, Polanyi concludes that while it diverges from the common analyses of science, it does respond to many facets of general scientific thought and to what Merleau-Ponty has called 'the philosophical mission of the twentieth-century'—'to explore the irrational and to integrate it into an enlarged reason'.

> [The common analysis of science] assumes that the logical foundation of empirical knowledge must be capable of definition by explicit rules. While the difficulties of this enterprise have not gone unnoticed, the reluctance to abandon it in principle still seems universal. My own attempts to acknowledge tacit powers of personal judgement as the decisive organon of discovery and the ultimate criterion of scientific truth, have been opposed by describing these agencies as psychological, not logical, in character. But this distinction is not explained by my critics. Is an act of perception which sees an object in a way that assimilates it to past instances of the same kind, a psychological process or a logical inference? We have seen that it can be mistaken and its results be false; and it certainly has a considerable likelihood of being true. To me this suggests that it is a logical process of inference even though it is not explicit. In any case, to perceive things rightly is certainly part of the process of scientific inquiry and to hold perceptions to be right underlies the holding of scientific propositions to be true. And if in consequence, we must accept the veridical powers of perception as the roots of empirical science, we cannot reasonably refuse to accept other tacit veridical processes having a similar structure. This is what I have been urging all along since I first wrote '...that the capacity of scientists to guess the presence of shapes as tokens of reality, differs from the capacity of our ordinary perception only by the fact that it can integrate shapes presented to it in terms which the perception of ordinary people cannot readily handle'. ('Tacit Knowing: Its Bearing on Some Problems of Philosophy' in *Knowing and Being*, pp. 172–3)

Current writings on the history of science have confirmed the view I put forward years ago that the pursuit of science is determined at every stage by unspecifiable

> powers of thought, and I have shown here how this fact forms my starting point for developing a theory of non-explicit thought. You may call such a theory—using a term coined by Gilber Ryle-an informal logic of science and of knowledge in general. Alternatively, you may call it a phenomenonlogy of science and knowledge, by reference to Husserl and Merleau-Ponty. This would correctly relate my enterprise both to analytic philosophy and to phenomenonlogy and exitertialims. ('The Logic of Tacit Inference', in *Knowing and Being*, p.155)

III. JOHN HENRY NEWMAN (1801-90)

Reading Newman's classic *Essay in aid of a Grammar of Assent*, one cannot fail to be struck by the fact that in its treatment of inference, it is in complete accord with Polanyi's *Personal Knowledge*. Although the language is that of an Illative Sense rather than of tacit and focal awareness the perspective, substance and emphases are the same.

For Newman it is fundamental that everyone who reasons is his own centre and that no development of logic can reverse this truth:

> The authoritative oracle, which is to decide our path, is something more searching and manifold than such jejune generalizations as treatises can give, which are most distinct and clear when we least need them. It is seated in the mind of the individual, who is thus his own law, his own teacher, and his own judge in those special cases of duty which are personal to him. It comes of an acquired habit, though it has its first origin in nature itself; and it is formed and matured by practice and experience; and it manifests itself; not in any breadth of view, any philosophical comprehension of the mutual relations of duty towards duty, or any consistency in its teachings, but it is a capacity sufficient for the occasion, deciding what ought to be done here and now, by this given person, under these given circumstances. It decides nothing

> hypothetical, it does not determine what a man should do ten years hence, or what another should do at this time. It may indeed happen to decide—ten years hence as it does now, and to decide a second case now as it now decides a first; still its present act is for the present, not for the distant or the future. (pp. 354-5)

Newman is concerned here with reasoning in concrete life. Reasoning may also be brought to bear on notions. In one important aspect, the nature of reasoning is determined by its constituent propositions. A proposition may be expressive of things, our apprehension of such a proposition being called *real* and our assent and belief real also; or it may be expressive to us of notions, our assent and belief being described as notional also. It is a paradoxy: that while assent most perfect when it is a *real* one, inference is *clearest* when it is exercised on notions—and ends, therefore, in a conclusion to which we give notional assent. One can see therefore an inescapable limitation in the method of logical inference which pursues the objective of public clarity as a common measure between mind and mind, as a means of joint investigation and as a recognized intellectual standard:

> What we desiderate [in the method of logical inference] is some thing which may supersede the need of personal gifts by a far-reaching and infallible rule. Now, without external symbols to mark out and to steady its course, the intellect runs wild; but with the aid of symbols, as in algebra, it advances with precision and effect. Let then our symbols be words: let all thought be arrested and embodied in words. let language have a monopoly of thought; and thought go for only so much as it can show itself to be worth in language. Let every prompting of the intellect be ignored, every momentum of argument be disowned, which is un provided with an equivalent wording, as its ticket for sharing in the common search after truth. Let the authority of nature, commonsense, experience, genius, go for nothing. Ratiocination, thus restricted and put into grooves, is what

I have called Inference, and the science, which is its regulating principle, is Logic. *(p.263)*

In practice, logic can succeed only insofar as words can in fact be found for representing 'the countless varieties and subtleties of human thought'; this means that it must fail, for it is not true that whatever can be thought can be adequately expressed in words:

> Even when argument is the most direct and severe of its kind, there must be those assumptions in the process which resolve themselves into the conditions of human nature; but how many more assumptions does that process in ordinary concrete matters involve, subtle assumptions not directly arising out of these primary conditions, but accompanying the course of reasoning, step by step, and traceable to the sentiments of the age, country, religion, social habits and ideas, of the particular inquirers or disputants, and passing current without detection, because admitted equally on all hands! And to these must be added the assumptions which are made from the necessity of the case, in consequence of the prolixity and elaborateness of any argument which should faithfully note down all the propositions which go to make it up. We recognize this tediousness even in the case of the theorems of Euclid, though mathematical proof is comparatively simple.
>
> Logic then does not really prove; it enables us to join issue with others; it suggests ideas; it opens views; it maps out for us the lines of thought; it verifies negatively; it determines when differences of opinion are hopeless; and when and how far conclusions are probable; but for genuine proof in concrete matter we require an *organon* more delicate, versatile and elastic than verbal argumentation. (pp. 270—71)

The simplicity and exactness of science, generally, makes it impossible for it to be ever a measure of fact, and so it is in the nature of things that the particular Science of logic can never contain or properly represent real inference in its formulas:

> As to Logic, its chain of conclusion hangs loose at both ends; both the point from which the proof should start, and the points at which it should arrive, are beyond its reach; it comes short both of first principles and of concrete issues. Even its most elaborate exhibitions fail to represent adequately the sum-total of considerations by which an individual mind is determined in its judgement of things: even its most careful combinations made to bear on a conclusion want that steadiness of aim which is necessary for hitting it. As I said when I began, thought is too keen and manifold, its sources are too remote and hidden, its path too personal, delicate and circuitous, its subject matter too various and intricate to admit of the trammels of any language, of whatever subtlety and of whatever compass. (p.284).

The method by which we become certain of what is concrete is a multiform and intricate process of ratiocination:

> First it does not supersede the logical form of inference, but is one and the same with it; it is no longer an abstraction, but carried out into the realities of life, its premisses being instinct with the substance and the momentum of that mass of probabilities, which, acting upon each other in correction and confirmation, carry it home definitely to the individual case, which is its original scope.
>
> Next, from what has been said it is plain, that such a process of reasoning is more or less implicit, and without the direct and full advertence of the mind exercising it... [The mind is] unequal to a complete analysis of the motives which carry it on to a particular conclusion, and is swayed and determined by a body of proof, which it recognizes only as a body, and not in its constituent parts. (p.292)

It seems to be a law of our minds that we recognize that certitude can correlate with an argument that is implicit, tacit, baffling our powers of analysis and incapable of being brought under logical rule:

> ...the processes of reasoning which legitimately lead to assent, to action, to certitude, are in fact too multiform, subtle, omnigenous too implicit, to allow of being measured by rule, that they are after all personal—verbal argumentation being useful only in subordination to a higher logic. (P. 303)

Methodical processes of inference are only instruments of the mind; the complete, living *organon* of resoning must be a person and not a mere method or calculus. Further the personal dimension includes such elements as a sober purpose of discovering truth, a moral earnestness and patience, with freedom from attachment to system:

> Thus a proof, except in abstract demonstration, has always in it, more or less, an element of the personal because 'prudence' is not a constituent part of our nature, but a personal endowment ... [Our language frequently signifies] that we have arrived at these conclusions—not *ex opere operato,* by a scientific necessity independent of ourselves—but by the action of our own minds, by our own individual perception of the truth in question, under a sense of duty to those conclusions and with an intellectual conscientiousness. (pp. 317-18)

Thus it is the mind that reasons and controls its own reasonings responsibly, the ultimate test of truth being the testimony borne to truth by the mind itself. Newman gives the name illative sense, to our living, spontaneous energy of judging and concluding, when it develops fully into an intellectual mastery of some particular field of enquiry:

> It is the mind that reasons, and that controls, its own reasonings, not any technical apparatus of words and propositions. This power of judging and concluding, when in its perfection, I call the Illative Sense...In no class of concrete reasonings, whether in experimental science,

> historical research, or theology is there any ultimate test of truth and error in our inferences besides the trust worthiness of the Illative Sense that gives them its sanction; just as there is no sufficient test of poetical excellence, heroic action, or gentleman-like conduct, other than the particular mental sense, be it genius, taste, sense of propriety, or the moral sense, to which those subject-matters are severally committed. Our duty in each of these is to strengthen and perfect the special faculty which is its living rule, and in every case as it comes to do our best. And such also is our duty and our necessity, as regards the Illative Sense. (pp. 353, 359)

IV. CONCLUSION

In *The Physicist's Conception of Nature* Werner Heisenberg writes:

> When we speak of the picture of nature in the exact science of our age, we do not mean a picture Of nature so much as a *picture of our relationship with nature.* The old division of the world into objective processes in space and time and the mind in which these processes are mirrored—in other words, the Cartesian difference between *res cogitans* and *res extensa*—is no longer a suitable starting point for our understanding of modern science. Science, we find, is now focused on the network of relationships between man and nature, on the framework which makes us as living beings dependent parts of nature, and which we as human beings have simultaneously made the object of our thoughts and actions. Science no longer confronts nature as an objective observer, but sees itself as an actor in this interplay between man and nature.

It seems clear that in this interplay an understanding is humanly developed which is in part a tacit mental vitality, in part an explicit objective account. Until now applied logic has been objectivist in confining itself to determining the logical status of explicit accounts. This is an inevitable result of an historical development which assigns to a logic of statesmants the basic position in the science, and which, indeed, technically, and fully justifies that assignation in respect of the other sections of existing logic. But a question arises now: what is the logical status of scientific understanding viewed, totally, in both tacit and explicit dimensions? What are the limits of logical clarification and explication here? And a further question develops: is there a section of logic more basic than the logic of propositions—a 'system logic' in which statements are no longer disjoined (simply something else in the world) but are symbolized as the world interiorized with a unique personal *weltanshauung*? Against the background of scientific relativity and of social personalism, must a grammar of rationality not acknowledge and—to the extent possible—formalize as rules the exercise of rational vitality at its personal depth? The interest in theory comparison within science, the contemporary development (for scientific purposes) of a new logic of framework transpositions, the conception (presented in the philosophy of logic section of this book) of metaformalism rather than formalism as the logical ideal for human living—there are positive indications of the value of considering the technical possibility of such a development within formal logic.

Chapter 12

Computational Process Theories

Chapter-12

We continue the study of process representation and equivalence, begun in Chapter 4. We start with the first-order model theory of process equivalences over labeled transition systems, including definiability and axiomatization over general and special model classes. Next, we move toward connections with the literature on process algebras, via generalizations of modal techniques in parts I, II. such as invariance and safety for bisimulation, and the use of extended modal formalisms. Except for the later sections on general safety, most results in this chapter come from van Benthem and Bergstra 1994.

10.1 DEFINITION OF PROCESS EQUIVALENCES

what is the logical complexity of process equivalence? Consider single translation models with simultations ≡ between pairs of states. Let **K** be all those moels where ≡ is one of the notions. We call a process euquivalence elementary (EC) of **K** is definable by a first order sentence, and EC_{Δ} if some infinite of sirst-order sentences does so. For instance, bisimulation in EC, as is immediate from its definition.

10.1.1 Finite Trace Equivalence

Proposition 10.1 Finite Trace Equivalence is EC_{Δ}

Proof. The definition had the first-order form

$$\forall xy\ (x \equiv y \rightarrow (\phi(x) \leftrightarrow \phi\ (y))),$$

where the ϕ are arbitrary successful path formulas' of the form

$$\exists x_1\ (R_{a1}\ xx_1 \wedge \ldots \exists x_n\ (R_{an}\ x_{n-1} x_n \wedge \surd(x_n))\ldots).$$

Proposition 10.2 *Finite Trace Equivalence is not EC.*

Proof. we refute Ec-ness, even with one atomic label a, let φ (≡) be any putative first-order definition, of quantifier depth N. Consider two models One has disjoint chains of length $2N$ ending with success, starting at states which are ≡ related (and this match is the only pair in ≡), the other has two such chains of lengths $2N$, $2N + 1$:

• → • → ··· → •√ 2^N
≡ |
• → • → ··· → •√ 2^N

• → • → ··· → •√ 2^N
≡ |
• → • → ··· → •→ • √ 2^N

An Ehrenfeucht game for linear orders (cf. Doets 1996) shows that these two models are indistinguishable by first-order sentences up to quantifier depth N. (One must match initial and terminal points in the above LTSs, maintaining a judicious invariant throughout with i more move to go: on both sides, keeping relative distances $<2^i-1$ equal between all points chosen so far). But this is a contradiction, as the relation ≡ is a finite trace equivalence in the first model, but not in the second, whereas the purpoted definition ϕ (≡) cannot see any difference between the two.

Proposition 10.3 *Complete Finite Trace Equivalence is not* EC_Δ.

Proof. Suppose that T (≡) defined this notion. In particular, then,

$$T, \{\phi(x) \leftrightarrow \phi(y) \mid \text{all successful path formulas } \phi\} \models x \equiv y.$$

By Compactness, some *finite* set of ϕ equivalence implies x ≡ y from T. But then complete finite trace equivalence holds when we have it up to some fixed finite depth: *quod non.*

10.1.2 Full Trace Equivalence

Proposition 10.4 *Full Trace Equivalence is not* ECΔ

Proof, Again, take one atomic transition only. Consider the LTS with one root from which finite branches fan out of arbitrary length, all ending in success. By a standard Compactness argument, this LTS has an elementary extension with at least one infinite branch, our first model M consists of two disjoint copies of the former structure (denoted in our language by unary predicates A,B)—and the second model M' of the same *A*-copy but now with the elementary extension in its *B*-part. Moreover, in both cases, the relation ≡ consists of just the pair connecting the roots in the two components. In a picture we have following two three -

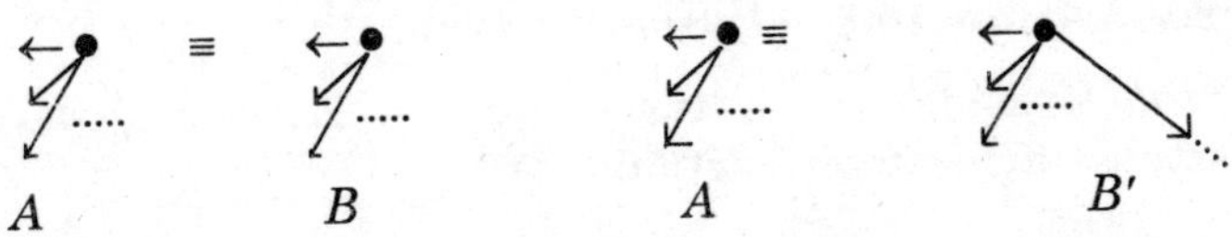

like structure:

Claim. M' *is an elementary extension of* **M**

Proof. By a simple inductive argument, in these models, each first-order formula is equivalent to a Boolean compound of formulas whose quantifiers are either completely *A* relativized of B-relativized. In particular, an atom $x \equiv y$ says that one of x,y is in *A* and the other *B*, and that both are roots. To prove the Claim, use the fact that both compon- ents of M' are elementary extensions of their counterparts in **M**.

To complete the main argument, it is clear that ≡ is a full trace enquivalence in M, but not in M': whence it cannot be first-order definable.

Proposition 10.5 *Complete Full Trace Equivalence is* EC$_\Delta$

Proof. On the LTS (N, >) with transitions (i,j) with $i > j$ and success only at the initial state O, identity of full trace sets coincides with real identity. Thus, ≡ must be equal to

=: i.e, the first order formula

$$\forall xy\ (x \equiv y \leftrightarrow x = y)$$

holds. Now take any elementary extension. It has at least one copy of the integers in its tail, while ≡ remains real identity. But all states in integer tails have the same trace set, and hence they share complete full trace equivalence. Thus, our class is not closed under elementary equivalence, whence it is not EC_Δ.

10.1.3 Bisimulation

As observed above, Bisimulation is EC by its definition. This works only if we finitely many atomic actions (which we shall assume henceforth). By contrast:

Proposition 10.6 *Maximal Bisimulation is not* EC_Δ

Proof. Consider the natural numbers N with predecessor as the single atomic action:

$$0 \leftarrow 1 \leftarrow 2 \leftarrow \ldots \leftarrow n \leftarrow \quad \ldots$$

The identity relation is the maximal bisimultation in this case (non-trival identifications eventually clash at zero). Now, take any proper elementary extension of the LTS N. It contains states with infinitely many predecessors (and successors) lying in copies of the integers, whose objects can be identified via a bisimultation. So the maximal bisimultation will not be real identity in the latter case. But, if the latter were definiable by a set of first order sentences $T(\equiv)$ then T would hold in both LTSs described: which is a contradiction as before.

10.1.4 Generated Graph Isomorphism

Similar reasoning establishes the following outcome.

Proposition 10.7 *Generated Graph isomorphism and Complete Ggi are not* EC_Δ.

These negative results do not exclude definition for non-

EC_Δ simultations in higher-order logics. For instance, Complete Tace Equivalence is definable L_{w1w} by an infinte cojunction of path equivalences for each finite length. Maximal Bisimultation is rather $\Delta\frac{1}{2}$ having a form

$$\forall xy\ (x \equiv y) \leftrightarrow \exists R\ (\text{"R is a bisimulation"} \wedge Rxy)),$$

Which reduces to a conjunction of a Σ_1^1 and Π_1^1 sentence.

10.2 AXIOMATIZATION OF PROCESS EQUIVALENCE

Process equivalences also generate systems of reasoning. When does the set **K** of models for a process equivalence have a *recursively enumerable* set of first-order consequences? (By a classical result of Craig's this implies recursive axiomatizability.)

Proposition 10.8 *The following process equivalences have a recursive axiomatiozation: Finite Trace Equivalence, Bisimulation, Generated Graph Isomorphism.*

Proof. (i) Finite Trace Equivalence was defined by an RE set of first-order sentences. Hence the latter is also an RE axiomatization for it's first-order consequences. The same reasoning applies a fortiori to Bisimulation, with its finite first-order definition,

(ii) To axiomatize the first-order consequences of Generated Graph Isomorphism, we rely on the preservation result for GGI. We proved (i) GGI preserves all 'restricted first order formulas' φ (x) constructed from atoms by Boolean operations and restricted existential quantifiers $\exists y\ (R_a xy, \wedge$ and (ii) in any countable recursively saturated model, the relation of agreeing on all restricted formulas is a generated graph isomorphism between states. Now, the relevant first-order theory is axiomatized by all first-order formulas

$\forall xy\ (x \equiv y) \rightarrow (\phi\ (x) \leftrightarrow \varphi\ (y))$. Where φ is a restricted first order formula.

These formulas all follow from GGI, by observations (i) Next, suppose some first ψ order does not follow from these axioms. Then there a countable model for the latter where ψ fails (by Completeness and Lowenheim Skolem), which has a countable *recursively saturated* elementary extension (ef. Keisler 1977). But then, as before, will be generated graph isomorephism in the latter model, whence the non-consequence ψ fails in an I.T.S. of the original class.

Proposition 10.9 *The first-order consequences of Maximal Bisimulation and Complete Trace Equivalence are not RE and not even airthmatically definable.*

Proof. We do Maximal Bisimulation only (CTE is similar). On the natural numbers with predecessor as an atomic action, maximal bisimulation coincided with identity. Consider a first-order language whose vocabulary includes predicates that allow one to express the Peano Axioms for zero, successor, predecessor, addition and multiplication (but without Induction). Call this theory PA*. Now, on LTS,s satisfying PA* where the binary relation coincides with the maximal bisimulation, the following formula defines the initial segment of the natural numbers (the reason is that all numbers in the 'integer tails' admit of non-trivial bisimulations):

$$\phi(x) = \forall y\ (x \equiv y \rightarrow x = y).$$

This implies the following effective reduction of standard truth for arithmetic sentences a in terms of their syntactically relativized versions $(\alpha)^{\phi}$:

$N \models \alpha$ iff

$PA^* \rightarrow (\alpha)^{\phi}$ holds in all LTSs where $\equiv$ is the maximal bisimulation.

Thus, the first order consequences of maximal Bisimulation are at least as complex as True Arithmetic—which is non arithmetical by Tarski's Theorem. (Under suitable encoding, this argument will work for non-arithmetical vocabularies too.)

Remark 10.10 (Concrete Axioms) Completed or maximal process equivalences satisfy the theory of their 'compatible notion', while adding certain 'induction principles'. e.g., both Complete Finite Trace Equivalence and Maximal Bisimulation satisfy the following principle:

$$\forall xy\ ((\forall a\ (R_a xz \rightarrow \exists u\ (R_a yu \wedge z \equiv u)) \wedge$$
$$\forall z\ (R_a yz \rightarrow \exists u\ (R_a xu \wedge z \equiv u))) \rightarrow x \equiv y).$$

10.3 INFINITARY THEORY OF TRANSITION SYSTEMS

Many computational notions have a natural formalization in infinitary first order logc.

10.3.1 Definability of Process Equivalences

Complete finite trace equivalence is easily defined by an infinite conjunction of successful path equivalences. Here are some negative results.

Proposition 10.11 *Full Trace Equivalence, Complete Full Trace Equivalence, Maximal Bisimulation, Generated Graph isomorphism and Complete Generated Graph Isomorphism are not* L_{w1w} *-definable.*

Proof. (I) Maximal Bisimulation. On *well-orders* with downward arrows for transitions, maximal bisimultaion is identity. But on non-well orders, any downward infinite chain yields a non-trival bisimulation. Suppose that maximal Bisimulation is L_{w1w} -definable. Then saying that some relations $<$ is a linear order and $\equiv$ is its maximal bisimulation while

$$\forall xy\ (x \equiv y \leftrightarrow x = y),$$

defines the well-orderings with their maximal bisimulation in L_{w1w}–This contradicts the non L_{w1w}– ness of well-order.

(ii) The other assertions follow as in earlier sections, using the Löwenheim-Skolem Theorem for our countably infinitary language.

10.3.2 Scott Isomorphism Theorem

A corollary of the invariance Theorem for bisimulation was that two finite LTSs satisfy the same modal formulas in states x,y iff there is a bisimulation ≡ between them with x ≡ y. This folklore fact may be extended to the infinitary language $L_{\omega 1\omega}$ via the following modifications of Scott's Theorem. The modal fragment is defined with infinite conjunctions and disjunctions.

Theorem 10.12 *For each countable LTS* ***M*** *with state a, there exists a modal* $L_{\omega 1\omega}$ *formula such that,* $\phi(x)$ *for each countable LTS* **N** *and state b, N, b* $\models \phi$ *iff there exists a bisimulation ≡ between* **M**, **N** *with a ≡ b.*

Corollary 10.13 *In countable LTSs M,N, states a,b, verify the same modal* $L_{\omega 1\omega}$*–.theory iff there exists a bisimulation connecting them,*

Proof. An easy adaptation of the usual argument suffices, via an infinitary description up to some countable ordianl. Cf. van Benthem and Bergstra 1994, or de Rijke 1995.

Here is another piece of folklore. Bisimulation occurs between any two models **M**, x, **N**, y, iff they have the same modal theories in the full infinitary set language $L_{\infty\omega}$.

10.3.3 Invariance under Bisimulation

Earlier preservation results have infinitary versions. Here is a key example.

Theorem 10.14 *The* $L_{\infty\omega}$ *formulas invariant for bisimulation are precisely the infinitary modal ones, constructed using arbitrary conjunctions and disjunctions.*

Proof. We adapt the proof sketch for the Invariance Theorem for the infinitary langauge $L_{\omega 1\omega}$ in van Benthem and Bergerra 1994,avoiding compactness or saturation. Of course, infinitary modal formulas (defined in the obvious way) are all invariant for bisimulation. Consider the converse. Let ϕ (x) be or any formula of $L_{\infty\omega}$ without a modal equivalent. We construct two models **M**, **N**. with a bisimulation *E* between them which has a link *aEb* such that **M** $\models \varphi$ (a), **N** $\models \neg\phi$ (b). This refutes invariance for bisimulation. The models are constructed from *good triples* A, Σ, Δ where A defines the relation E, Σ, the model M, and Δ the model **N**. but first, some auxillary definitions.

(i) *By extended modal formulas* over a set of variables X we mean all formulas of L∞w that are constructed using unary atoms Px ($x \in X$), Boolean operations (finite or infinite), and existential modal quantifiers by $\exists y$ (R$xy \wedge [y/u]\ \psi$) (where. x, $u \in X$). (One can find a more perspicuous normal form for such formulas, but we shall not need this.) If $|x|$ = 1, these are just ordinary infinitary modal formulas.

(ii) For Convenience, we assume that all formulas have negotiations pushed inside to atoms, leaving only operators. $\bigwedge$, V, $\forall$, $\exists$.

(iii) Let μ= max($\aleph_0$. [TC ($\neg\ \phi$) |), where TC ($\neg\ \phi$) is the transitive closure of the formula $\neg\ \phi$ which contains (amongst others) all its infinitary subformulas.

(iv) Choose two disjoint sets C,D of *new* individual constants of cardinality μ^+ (a regular cardinal), Henceforth, all *formulas* will be C– or D–substitution instances of subformulas of $\neg\varphi$. The total cardinality of this set is again μ^+. (In counting this size, recall that formulas of $L\infty\omega$ have only finitely many free variables.)

(v) Call two sets of formulas, Σ, Δ *modally inseparable* in *A* if there is no extended modal formula α over a set of variables *X* (of cardinality $< \mu^+$) with $\Sigma \models \alpha$ (c) and $\Delta \models \neg\alpha$(d) — for subjects c,d of C,D where corresponding pairs *c/x*, *d/x*, have the atom *cEd* in *A*.

(vi) A *good* triple A,Σ. Δ satisfies four conditions: A,Σ Δ have cardinality ,$< \mu^+$ *A* consists oof bisimulation atoms cEd, Σ consists of formulas with constants only from C, and likewise for Δ and *D* —while Σ, Δ are modally inseparable with respect to *A*. Note that the good triples form a set.

Next, we state some closure conditions on good triple. The first are familiar from infinitary 'consistency properties' describing consistent diagrams of models (cf. keisler 1971), whence we omit their detailed proofs. Let A, Σ , Δ be a good triple.

- adding to Σ all conjunctions of an infinitary conjunction in Σ aain gives a good triple, and the same holds for infinitary conjunctions in Δ (This addition does not affect modal separation, and it keeps the cardinality of Σ below μ^+).
- adding to Σ, all substitution instances of a universally quantified formula in Σ, with respect to all constants from C already occuring in Σ, again gives a good triple and the same holds for universal quantifiers in Δ.
- each infinitary disjunction in Σ has at least disjunct that can be added to Σ produce a good triple, and the same holds for Δ (If each disjunct leads to a modal separation for the extended triple, their disjunction will separate the original triple. Here, we need extended modal formulas, as the constants involved may be different. Also, some care is needed, by choosing disjoint sets of variables for each disjunct).
- each existentially quantified formula in Σ has a substitution instance with some individual constant c that is new to Σ and A which can be added to Σ form a good triple—and the same holds for Δ. (Notice that the new constant trigger new modal separations,since it has no available bisimulation atoms.)

The final observations guarantee *atomic harmony* and *zigzags* for the bisimulation E:

- if $cEd \in A$ and $Pc \in \Sigma$, then A, Σ, $\Delta \cup \{Pd\}$ is good. (if modal α separtes Σ and $\Delta \cup$ {Pd}, then $Px \wedge \alpha$ separtes the original Σ, Δ.) Vice versa for Δ.

- if cEd $\in$ A and $Rcc' \in \Sigma$, there is an atom d' new to A, Σ, Δ such that $A \cup \{cEd'\}$, Σ, $\Delta \cup \{Rdd'\}$ is a good triple — and vice versa. (If some modal α separtes Σ and $\Delta \cup \{Rdd'\}$, then $\Diamond_x\alpha$ epartes the original Σ, Δ.)

Finally, we construct our models. First, we enumerate all 'tasks' at hand, ensuring fair scheduling. Tasks are either C– (D–) formulas, to be verified in the models M(N), or bisimulation atoms plus R–successor atoms to be matched in the opposite model. The total number of tasks is μ^+ (by a simple calculation)—whence we can enumerate them in a sequence T_α ($a < \mu^+$) so that each task occurs cofinally often. We construct a corresponding sequence of good triples, starting with an initial triple.

{cEd}, $\{\phi(c)\}$, $\{\neg\phi(d)\}$.

The latter is good. Modal separation would imply modal definability for ϕ: *quod non*. At each stage α, we take the component-wise union of all previous triples, and add formulas according to the scheduled task (if relevant), via the above closure properties. The final result is a triple A* Σ^* Δ^*. This defines two obvious models M.N. (over domains consisting of those constants from C,D, respectively, which occur in Σ^* Δ^*) plus a binary relation E between them in the obvious way. An easy induction them shown that

- C–formulas are Σ they are true in M, and likewise for D–formulas and Δ
- E is a bisimulation between M and N.

This method of proof also works for the finitary first-order language.

10.3.4 Safety for Bisimulation

The main theorem of Chapter 5 has not found its counterpart yet. But the proof methods of Barwise and van Benthem 1996 provide strong evidence for the following

Conjecture 10.15 *A relational operation $O(R_1 .... R_n)$ definable*

in L∞ω is safe for bisimulation if and only if it can be defined using atomic relations Raxy and atomic tests (q)? for propositional atoms q in our models, using only the three operations;, V and ~, where the unions may now be infinitary.

10.4 SPECIAL TRANSITION SYSTEMS

On important special LTSs, axiomatization and definiablity must be reanalyzed.

10.4.1 Finite Models

Working within the universe of finite models may or may not decrease the complexity of our logical results. (In Finite Model Theory, many standard techniques fall away.)

Proposition 10.16 *Every earlier notion of process equivalence is EC_Δ.*

Proof. All definitions describe model classes closed under isomorphism.Every class of finite models, in a finite vocabulary, with this closure property is EC_Δ -definable, by the negotiations of all complete first-order descritions of its finite non-members.

Proposition 10.17 No Process equivalence becomes EC which was not EC in general.

Proof. Unlike compactness; Ehrenfeucht Games still work on finite models. E.g., the earlier argument for Finite Trace Equivalence goes through. Another typical case is Complete Finite Trace Equivalence, whose definability by any first-order sentence of quantifier depth N may now be refuted by comparing (i) a chain of immediate successors of length 2^N with ≡ equal to the identity relation, (ii) the same chain plus a disjoint 'large circle'. (1996has alternative model theoretic arguments, with detours via infinte integer models.)

Proposition 10.18 *A notion of process equivalence has a finite axiomatization if it is EC.*

Proof. From right to left, the defining first-order formula is an axiomatization. Conversely, let δ axiomatize ≡. Then, it holds in any model for this equivalence. Conversely, Suppose δ fails in some finite LTS M, fully described by the first order sentence α_M. Then δ does not imply ¬ αM on finite models, and so there is a finite model for $\delta \wedge \alpha_M$, which is isomorphic to M itself. Therefore δ holds in M.

Rosen 1995 proves the modal preservation theorem for bisimulation on finite LTSs (despite general failures of such results in Finite Model Theory; cf. Gurevich 1985).

10.4.2 Further Classes of Transition Systems

On *finitely branching models*, here is a typical new outcome (with finite trace equivalence' over arbitrary finite traces, whatever the status of their end-points):

Proposition 10.19 *Finite Trace Equivalence and Full Trace Equivalence are equivalent.*

Proof. FullTE implies FinTE. Vice versa, let x, y be finite trace equivalent. Let any infinite trace start at *x*. Consider the subgraph at *y* matching all its initial segments. Königs" Lemma gives an infinite branch at *y* matching the infinite trace at x.

Finally, consider LTSs whose transition relations are all well-founded.

Proposition 10.20 *Maximal Bisimulation is EC on well-founded. Models.*

Proof. Consider one atomic action. A good definition here has the first order definition of bisimulation plus the earlier 'Induction Principle'. Let C be any relation on a well-founded LTS (S, R_a) satisfying these two requirements which does not equal the maximal bisimulation ≡ As C is a bisimulation, it is contained in ≡. Now, by well-foundedness, take some minimal point *x* where a situation of the type $x \equiv y$, $\neg\, xCy$ occurs, with some *y* exemplifying this mismatch. Then, by minimality, it is easy to see that the condition triggering the induction principle is satisfied for all Ra-successors of x and y. (For instance, if $x \rightarrow^{a} z$, then z must have a ≡ matching $\xrightarrow{a}$ -successor u of y because ≡ is a bisimulation. By the minimality of x with respect to $\equiv / C$ mismatches, this implies that zCu. The proof for the converse is analogous.) Thus, the induction principle would imply that xCy after all: which yields a contradiction.

10.5 PROCESS ALGEBRA

Next, we link up with elaborate process theories in the computational literature. We shall be concerned with elementary operations, ignoring higher process operations such as recursion, or hiding of vocabulary.

10.5.1 Algebraic Operations and Term Models

To get the flavour of process algebra, here is *elementary process algebra* with finitely many atomic actions (a subset of CCS in Milner 1980), with signature

O	p	zero process
+	$P \times P \rightarrow P$	alternative composition ('choice')
a;	$P \rightarrow P$	action prefixing, for each atomic a ** A

EPA (A)

$$\begin{aligned} x + y &= y + x \\ (x+y) + z &= x + (y+z) \\ x + x &= x \\ x + 0 &= x \end{aligned}$$

The *initial algebra*, or *term model* for these axioms is calls A^{e}_{ω}. It turns out useful to introduce a first-order axiom system EPT with a relation of inclusion defined as usual:

$$x \subseteq y \Leftrightarrow x + y = y.$$

The theory EPT (A) adds the following principles to EPA (A):

$$0 \subseteq y$$
$$(x+y) \subseteq z \quad \Leftrightarrow \quad x \subseteq z \wedge y \subseteq z$$
$$a\,;\,x \subseteq (y+z) \subseteq z \quad \Leftrightarrow \quad a;x \subseteq y \vee a;\,z \subseteq z$$
$$a\,;\,x \subseteq a\,;\,y \quad \Leftrightarrow \quad x \subseteq y$$
$$a\,;\,x \subseteq b\,;\,y \quad \text{If a, b are distinct atomic actions}$$
$$\neg a\,;\,x \subseteq 0$$

Proposition 10.21 EPT (A) is sound and complete for validity of both ground equation and inequalities in A^e_ω.

10.5.2 The Finite Graph Model

For a more complex process logic, take the full first – order theory of the algebra A^e_ω. Equivalently, consider the model **G** of all finite graphs identified under bisimulation, with the following operations (which are well-defined over representatives):

O single success node
\+ fusion of graphs at the root
a; prefixing a single incoming a-arrow to the root

Its first order theory *Th* (**G**) may actually be formulated in various ways:

Proposition 10.22 *The following theories are effectively equivalent:*

(i) Th $((\mathbf{G}, 0, +, \{a; \mid a \in A\}))$

(ii) Th $((\mathbf{G}, \subseteq, \{a, \in A\}))$.

This theory contains a full lattice structure for the above inclusion ordering $\subseteq$. Moreover, it exemplifies special features not found in the general case, such as

(E) $\forall xy(\bigwedge_{a \in A} \forall z(x \xrightarrow{\cdot} z \leftrightarrow y \xrightarrow{\cdot} z) \rightarrow x = y)$
Extensionality

Indeed, *Th*(**G**) encodes a well-known mathematical structure which we will sketch. (The following technical digression may be skipped without loss of continuity.)

Theorem 10.23 *The first order theory of the Finite Graph Model under Bisimulation is effectively to True Arithmetic.*

Proof. Think of **G** as a labeled transition system of equivalence classes #**G** of all finite rooted graphs **G** under bisimulations connecting their roots. Its relations include identity = as well as transition relations $\overset{a}{\rightarrow}$ (for all a in some finite set A), defined via 'root prefixing' (this is well defined on equivalence classes, being invariant for bisimulatin). As will be shown shortly, the first-order theory *Th* (**G**) gives us the whole process algebra with the above $\subseteq$ + and all prefix operations a;. As usual, True Arithmetic is the complete first-order theory of the model (**N**,+,.). Now there are two directions to the above assertion:

From Graphs to Natural Numbers. Under any effective coding scheme, the following arithmetical predicates are recursive, and hence airthmetically first-order definable:

GRAPH (*n*) "n codes some finite graph"

BISIM (*m*,*n*) "m, n code bisimilar finite graphs"

a-TRANS (*m*,*n*) "m encodes a graph having an write -a transition from its root to the root of a generated subgraph encoded by n"

Now (.)* translates first-order formulas about these graphs into first-order arithmetic:

x = y BISIM (x,y)

x $\xrightarrow{a}$ y zu BISIM (x,z) BISIM (y,u) a-Trans (z,u)

¬, ∧ Boolean connective are translated homomorphically

$\exists x$ existential quantifiers become restricted numerical quantifiers over codes of graphs: $\exists x$ (GRAPH(x) ∧...)

Claim. For all finite graphs G_1 .....G_k *with numerical cods* g_1......g_k and *all first-order formulas*

$$G \models \phi[\# G_1,......\#G_k] \text{ iff } N \models (\phi)^* [g_1,...,g_k].$$

From Natural Numbers to Graphs. In the opposite direction, we need auxillary first-order predicates on (equivalence classes of finite graphs, encoding basic numerical operations. Each natural number n is identified with the (equivalence class of) finite linear order $\xrightarrow{a}$ over {....n}. Thus, numerical graph objects are defined by a –NUM (x) saying: "x is a graph with just a transitions, on which $\xrightarrow{a}$ is transitive irreflective and linear". Isomorphism of disjoint intervals on linear graphs amounts to there being a larger graph containing these intervals, with a second relation $\xrightarrow{b}$ serving as a bisimulation between them. More precisely, this involves the following first-order predicates:

BISIM (x,y,s) s has only $\xrightarrow{a}$ and $\xrightarrow{b}$ successors, and s $\xrightarrow{b}$ x, the $\xrightarrow{a}$-successors of as form a transitive, irreflexive linear ordering, and is a bisimulation between $\xrightarrow{a}$-successors of s and points in the closed $\xrightarrow{a}$-interval $[x,y]$ with respect to $\xrightarrow{a}$

EQUI(x,y,z,u) $\exists s$ (BISIM(x,y,s) $\wedge$BISIM (z,u,s))

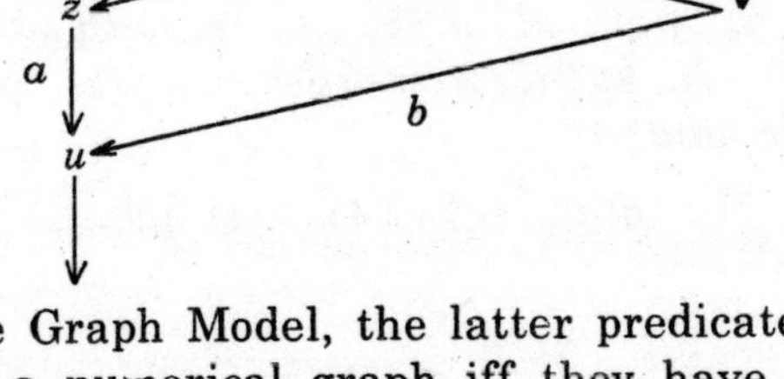

In the Finite Graph Model, the latter predicate holds of intervals on a numerical graph iff they have the same cardinality. Care is needed here, as objects in **G** are not graphs, but their equivalence classes under bisimulation. For suitably 'bounded' first-order formulas (cf. Chapter 4,) there is no real difference between the two kinds of object.

- One may describe *addition* by a first-order predicate SUM (x,y,z) which first distinguishes some marginal cases (e.g., "x = O" and "y = O" are trivial), and then states that x,y lie in some sequence on the linear order z, say > y, where the top interval [z,x] is equinumerous to the bottom interval on z starting from y.
- Multiplication TIMES (x,y,z) is encoded via a division of the linear order into y intervals, all of equal length (introduce a larger graph with suitable new $\xrightarrow{c}$ transitions marking the boundary points), stating that each interval is equinumerous with x while the subgraph of boundary points (identifiable via the new relation $\xrightarrow{c}$) is equinumerous with y. (some trivial cases are to be treated separately.)

Finally, we define the relevant first-order translation $(.)^s$. Without loss of generality, the arithmetical first-order language may be restricted to atoms x = y +z and x=y.z. These are translated via the above predicates SUM (x,y,z) and TIMES (x,y,z). Boolean connectives are treated homo morphically, and numeril existential quantifiers are restricted to the above predicate a NUM defining the numerical graph equivalence classes (cf. (1)). The relevant reduction is then straightforward from the above motivation:

Claim. *For all natural number n ....n, with matching graph (classe)s N.....N., and all first-order formulas , φ the following equivalence holds*:

$$\mathrm{N} \models \phi[n_1.., n_k] \text{ iff } \mathbf{G} \models (\phi)^s [N_1...,N_k].$$

10.5.3 From Algebras to Labeled Transition Systems

Any model M for the above process theories induces a LTS TS (M):

$$x \xrightarrow{a} y \Leftrightarrow \exists z x = a;\ y + z.$$

Several open questions of definability and axiomatizability arise. Are the two classes TS (MOD(EPA(A)), TS(MOD(EPT(A)) EC or EC_Δ? Our conjecture is negative. Both are Σ_1^1-definable in second – order logic, as their defining condition states the existence of predicates or functions verifying the finite list of EPA (EPT) axioms. By general logic, this implies recursive axiomatizability for their first-order theories. One would like explicit axiomatizations. Analyzing the signature (0, +, {a; | a A}) via the above stipulation, one finds the following first-order principles for TS (A_ω^e):

A_1 $\exists x \bigwedge_{a \in A} \neg \exists y x \xrightarrow{a} y$ End-Point

A_2 $\forall xy \exists z \bigwedge_{a \in A} \forall u(z \xrightarrow{a} u \leftrightarrow (x \xrightarrow{a} u \wedge y \xrightarrow{a} u))$ Sums

A_3 $\forall x \bigwedge_{a \in A} \exists y(\forall u(y \xrightarrow{a} z \leftrightarrow z = x \wedge$ Predecessors

$\bigwedge_{b \in A, b \text{ distinct from } a} \exists z y \xrightarrow{b} z).$

Proposition 10.24 MOD ({A, A,A,E}0 $\subseteq$TS (EPA)

Proof. A1, A2, A3, E follow immediately from EPT under the above stipulation. Conversely, given these principles, one can introduce operations of 'sum' and action prefixing with the right properties. For instance, Associativity follows because both possible ways of computing a 'sum' of three objects lead to points with the same successors, which must be identical by Extensionality.

Often, a process algebra is retrievable from its derived transition system:

Proposition 10.25 The following first-order theories are effectively equivalent for the model M = (G,O, +, {a;[a*a}):

(i) *Th* (M).
(ii) *Th* (TS(M)).

10.6 SAFETY FOR PROCESS CONSTRUCTIONS

In Process Algebra, operations are described by algebraic equations. Examples were *action prefix ax, choice* $x_1 + x_2$ or *product* $x_1 + x_2$. other typical operators deal with parallel execution of processes, such as the *merge* $x_1 || x_2$ and its directed variants. The equations governing these operations are reminiscent of an algebra of relations. But this time, only one distributive law holds:

$(x + y).\ z = (x.z) + (y.z)$ but not $x.\ (y+z) = (x.y) + (x.z)$.

From a modal point of view, this divergence with Chapters 3,5 may be explained as follows. Process algebra lies 'one level up'. It is not a calculus of binary *relations inside* labeled transition systems, but rather an external calculus of *constructions over* such systems. This shows clearly in the quite different constructions for the two distributive laws in the Finite Graph Model. Even so, the situation is not fully clear. In what follows, we sketch two ways of comparing dynamic logic and process algebra, one more 'internal', and the other more 'external'

10.6.1 Varieties of safety

Safety for bisimulation makes sense for process-algebraic operations O, too, when viewed as constructions over LTSs. In the literature, the latter are usually taken to satisfy the following minimal requirement of *Respect for Bisimulation*:

Whenever $M_1 \equiv_1 N_1$. $M_2 \equiv N_2, \ldots$, then O $(M_1, M_2, \ldots)$ admits of a bisimulation with respect to $O(N_1, N_2, \ldots)$

This condition is non-trivial; mathematical operations in general only require respect for *isomorphisms* between their values and arguments.Even so, Respect is very liberal. In addition to prefix, sum, product or merge, many other process operations pass this test. Here are two examples that make good sense as constructions on finite automata:

Process Negation: reverse all success/failure markings in an LTS *Process Iteration*: join all success nodes to all successors of the initial mode Respect for Bisimulation suggests a hierarchy of looser or stricter process operations. Usually, the bisimulation between the two labeled transition systems $O(M_1 M_2...)$ and $O(N_1 N_2...)$ is effectively constructed from the for the arguments $M_1 N_2$., Varying requirements on effectiveness with fine-structure our options. We will proceed by example, in order to motivate more concrete requirements.

10.6.2 Analysing Specific Constructions

Action Prefix. The operation **ax** taken a rooted LTSx, and gives it a new root y joined to the old only by one *a*-arrow—as happens in the following picture

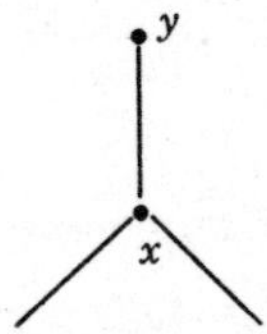

This definition may even be analysed inside LTSs – via a special relation AP (y,x) which holds between two states just when y heads a submodel of the required form with respect to the submodel headed by *x*. Here, x serves as a distinguished 'state parameter'. Thus, the new relations in the submodel generated by y. In the present case, these definitions look as follows:

$$R_a^{new}uv := R_a^{old}uv \vee (u = y \wedge v = x)$$

$$R_a^{new}uv := R_b^{old}uv \text{ for all other atomic actions } b.$$

Note that y does not occur as a successor of itself. *We make this assumption throughout.* Respect for bisimulation has a straightforward meaning for Action prefix. Any bisimulation between two models M, M' connecting x to x' remains a bisimulation when we add one link between y and y'. Let us call this the *Bisimulation Extension Property*

(BEP). It may be analyzed in terms of safety after all for, what matters is only how the R_a^{new} , lie inside the new LTS ax. As the generated submodel of x does not change in the construction, we need only specify the unary predicate S_a of being an R_a-sucessor of y, for each action a. BEP says this predicate is *invariant* for bisimulations with distinguished parameter x, Thus S_a, has a syntactic normal form described with just safe operations and resetting to x. The above definition indeed has this format: $S_a(\upsilon) = RES_x(x, v)$. Essentially

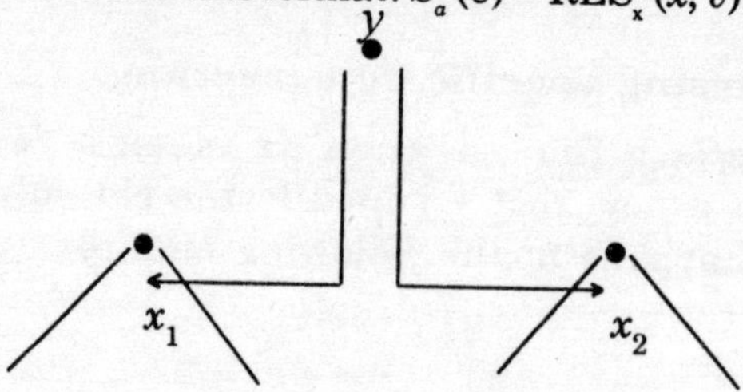

this same analysis works for our next process operation.

Binary Choice. Consider the following defining picture for $y = x_1 + x_2$

Again, Respect holds in a strict sense. The bisimulation for the sum in the union of those for the arguments, plus one new link (y, y'). The preceding analysis gives us a similar defining format, now with both $RES_{x'}$ and RES_{x2} allowed in defining R_a^{new} via S_a. As a check, we have indeed that

$$R_a^{new}uv \ := R_a^{old}uv \vee (u = y \wedge (R_a x_1 v \vee R_a x_2 v)).$$

The second conjunct here has the right normal form, viz.

$$(RES_{x1}; R_a) \cup (RES_{x2}; R_a).$$

Negation and Iteration. Similar consideration apply to other process operations. We state some outcomes without proof. Negation leaves a graph 'the same' except for reversing success markings. This yields a different item in the LTS–representation of machine diagrams (or the Finite Graph

Model). But the *original* bisimulation serves for the new LTS, as it leaves success marks √ invariant. This shows in the new relations:

$$R_a^{new}uv := \quad R_a^{old}uv$$

$$\surd^{new} \quad v := \sim ((\surd)?) \text{ with the safe strong negation } \sim$$

$$P^{new}v \quad := P^{old}v \text{ for all other atomic propostion P.}$$

For iteration, the same analysis applies (with the slight complication that the root may now also occur as the end-point of a new transition). Here is the resulting definition:

$$R_a^{new}uv \quad := R_a^{old}uv \vee ((\surd)?;\ RES_x\ ;\ a).$$

Product. Our final example is more complex. In a sequential product $y = x_1 . x_2$, the new relations R_a^{new} consist of R_a^{old} plus all new pairs (u,v) with u a success node in the generated graph for the argument x_1, and v some R_a successor of x_2:

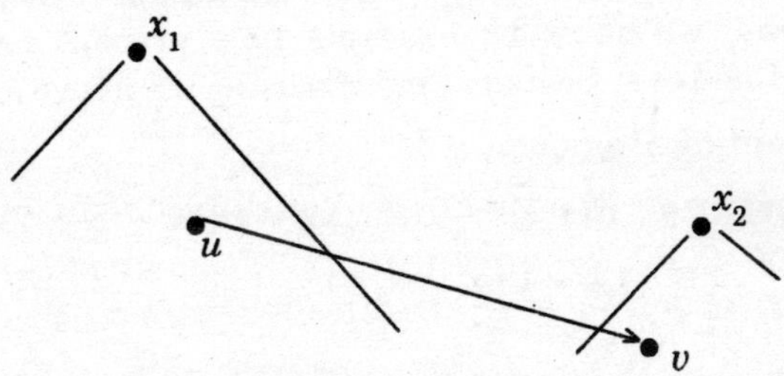

Here, the previous format of definition fails. It cannot enforce that success modes must lie inside the *submodel generated by* x_1. We lack Respect in the earlier sense. We need predicates D_x defining submodels generated by x. Semantically, we want safety only for bisimulations that leave the latter in place. Still, this can be handled by 'propositional parametrization.' This shows in the actual definitions for this case:

$$R_a^{new} := R_a^{old} \cup (D_{x1})?;\ RES_{x2};\ R_a^{old}$$

10.6.3 Respect for Sequence Extensions

With further process operations, such as *direct products* x * y or *merges* x || y, states themselves change to *ordered pairs* of old states. One cannot just specify new relations. To overcome this, Hollenberg 1995b considerably extends the previous analysis of Bisimulation Extension. Consider a rich first order langauge whose vocabulary includes unary predicates S_i for argument domains, binary transition relations $R_{(a,i)}$ (encoding R_a over S_i) unary predicates P_i (encoding P over S_i), constants s_i, for roots of the arguments and s for the new root, plus a ternary sequence concatenation predicate C. This language is a powerful format for defining process operations which covers most cases in the algebric literature. Here are its preferred first-order models. For ant finite family of LTSs $(M_i)_i$ representing n arguments, the *sequence* model M = Pc $(M_i)_i$ has a universe of all finite sequences up to length n from the S_i plus a new set C (of distinguished nodes), closed under concatenation. Instead of reciting formal definitions, we show by example how process operations can be defined over Sequence models using the above formalism:

sequential Product

$$\rho_\alpha (x,y) := R(a,1)xy \vee R_{(a,2)}xy \vee (\surd 1x \wedge R(a,2)s_{2y})$$

$$\delta_\surd(x) := \surd_2 x \vee (\surd_1 x \vee \surd_2 s_2)$$

$$s := s_1$$

Free Merge

$$\rho_\alpha (x,y) := \exists x_1 x_2 y_1 y_2 \, (Cx, x_1, x_2 \wedge Cy, y_1 y_2 \wedge) \, (R\,(_{a,1})\, x_1 y_2 \wedge x_2 = y_2) \wedge (x_1 = y_1 \wedge R_{(a,2)} x_2 y_2))$$

$$\delta_\surd (x) := \exists x_1 y_1 \, Cx, x_1 x_2 \wedge \surd_1 x_1 \wedge \surd_2 x_2)$$

$$s := s_1 s_2.$$

Separate bisimulations for the argument domains S_i may be lifted canonically to their *sequence extension* in the product model. We say that a first-order definition for an operation O (as illustrated in the preceding examples) *respects sequence extensions* if each sequence extension is a bisimulation for its LTS-value O (S_1, S_2) in product models. Clearly this condition will hold if the definition has a suitable modal format. Hollenberg proposes 'safe/invariant' definitions, which are sufficient (though not necessary) to enforce respect—and which covers all ACP-style process operations (baeten and Weijland 1990). His main result is a modal characterization of safe/invariant process operations as precisely those definable in a suitable extended modal fragment of the above full first-order language. This outcome suggest a natural *Safety Hierarchy* for process operations—though this time, for LTS constructions.

10.7 APPENDIX I: MODAL LOGIC OF CONSTRUCTIONS

There are other modal viewpoints on process operations. The above LTS constructions resemble modal ones. Choice is 'disjoint rooting' (Chapter 4), and sequential product 'glueing' for modal models (cf. Blok 1979, Marx 1995). Also, modal merge products have been studied. (Goldblatt 1988 has a category theoretic vista). A main concern has been *preservation*: what truth values for modal formulas in a compound arise from those in components? There is no explicit modal calculus of model constructions as such. We briefly explore the latter, as another promising interface with process algebra.

10.7.1 A Modal Calculus

Take ordinary kripke models or LTSs M, identifying processes x with nodes via their generated submodels as before. We introduce two new modalities {a} and +, corresponding to action Prefix and Choice, on top of the standard modal propositional language with standard modalities <a>, [a] over these models:

M, $x \models \langle a \rangle \phi$ iff there exists some R_a-successor y or x with M, $y \models \phi$

- M, $x \models \{a\}\ \phi$ iff there exists some y which is a unique R_a-successor of x, such that x has no other R_b-links to y, with M, y $\models \phi$
- M, $x \models \phi + \psi$ iff there exist states y, z with M, $y \models \phi$ and M, z $\models \psi$ such that (for all atomic actions a) the R_a-successors of x are just those of y and z.

10.7.2 Frame Correspondences

The new modal operators satisfy principles, whose semantic content may be gauged by frame correspondence. We start with three valid modal distribution laws:

$$\{a\}\ (\phi \lor \psi) \quad \leftrightarrow \quad (a)\ \phi \lor \{a\}\ \psi$$

$$(\phi_1 \lor \phi_2) + \psi \quad \leftrightarrow \quad (\phi_1 + \psi) \lor (\phi_2 + \psi)$$

$$\phi + (\psi_1 \lor \psi_2) \quad \leftrightarrow \quad (\phi + \psi_1) \lor (\phi + \psi).$$

The next principle expresses that successors for Action Prefix are unique:

$$\{a\}\ \phi \land \{a\} \lor \psi \rightarrow \{a\}\ (\phi \land \psi).$$

Finally, here are principles regulating the interaction between the new modalities $\{a\}$, + and the standard one (a), $[a]$, which approximate the intended interpretation for their associated accessibility relations Ax, y and Cx, yz:

$\{a\}\ \phi \rightarrow (a)\ \phi$	$\forall xy\ Axy \rightarrow R_a xy$
$\{a\} \rightarrow \neg(b)$ (all other b)	$\forall xy$ A$xy \rightarrow \neg\ \exists z\ R_b xz$
$\{a\} \land (a)\ \phi \rightarrow [a]\ \phi$	$\forall xyzu(Axy \land R_a xz \land\ R_a xu) \rightarrow z{=}u)$
$[a]\phi + [a]\phi \rightarrow [a]\phi$	$\forall xyzu(Cx,\ yz \land R_a xu) \rightarrow (R_a yu \lor R_a zu))$
$[a]\phi +\ \rightarrow [a]\phi$	$\forall xyzu(Cx,\ yz \land R_a yu) \rightarrow R_a xu$
$+\ (a)\phi \rightarrow (a)\phi$	$\forall xyzu(Cx,\ yz \land R_a zu) \rightarrow R_a xu$
$\phi + \psi \rightarrow \psi + \phi$	$\forall xyz\ Cx,\ yz \rightarrow Cx,\ zy$
$\phi \rightarrow \phi + \phi$	$\forall x\ Cx,\ xx$

The last lines state algebric commutativity and idempotence x+y = y+x, x+x = x. by contrast, a modal counterpart φ+ (ψ +χ) $\leftrightarrow$ (ϕ +ψ) + χ to Associativity requires the existence of enough 'union' states (Chapter 8) which need not be valid in all models.

10.7.3 Extended Modal Logic

The preceding principles express only half of the desired behaviour. For Action Prefix, we lack the converse fact that, if there is some unique R successor, R-inaccessible for all other b, which satisfies ϕ, then {a} ϕ holds. Expressing this fact requires a stronger modal language, say, with a difference operator' D:

$$((a)\ \phi \wedge \neg(a)\ D\varphi \wedge \bigwedge_{b \neq a} \neg(b)\ ) \rightarrow \{a\}\varphi.$$

A corresponding converse statement for + will involve backward versions of $\{a\}$, $[a]$.

10.7.4. First - Order Translation

Our modal language admits of translation into a standard first-order one (Chapter 3):

- ST ({a} ϕ) : =
  $\exists y\ (R_a xy) \wedge ST(\phi)(y) \wedge \neg\ \exists z\ (R_a xz \wedge z \neq y) \wedge \bigwedge_{b \neq a} \neg \exists z\ R_b xz)$
- ST (ϕ + ψ) : =

$$\exists yz(\forall u \bigwedge_a (R_a xu \leftrightarrow (R_a yu \bigvee R_a zu))\ ST(\phi)(y) \wedge ST(\psi)(z)).$$

The modal logic inherits RE ness of first order logic but ST does no guarantee *decidability*. (Transcriptions for modal formulas may be outside of the Guarded Fragment. The sub language with {a} is guarded, and hence decidable. Also, the modal language of {a} only ends up in a *three-variable fragment* of first-order predicate logic, while + needs a *four*-variable fragment.

10.8 APPENDIX II: CONCURRENT DYNAMIC LOGIC

Here is yet a different modal process theory. *Concurrent* PDL (CPDL) has the following syntax.

formulas $p \mid \neg\phi \mid (\phi \wedge \phi) \,/\, (\pi)\phi \mid [\pi]\phi$
programs $a \mid \pi^* \,/\, (\pi;\pi) \,/\, (\pi \cup \pi) \,/\, (\pi \cap \pi) \,/\, (\phi)?$

The new operation $\pi_1 \cup \pi_2$ performs π_1 and π_2 concurrently. I.e., several states can be reached by a number of independent processes triggered by a program. Thus, the reachability relation R_π of a program π connects a states to the *set* of all *states* reached by these internal processes after successful execution. To model indeterminism, we also allow different output sets here. Here is the truth definition supporting this system (Peleg 1987). Note that the two modalities are no longer duals:

M, $s \models (\pi)\,\phi$ iff there exists T with s$R_\pi T$ and for all t $\in$ T, M, t $\models \phi$

M,$s \models \phi$ iff for all T, if s$R_\pi T$, then for all t$\in$T, M,t $\models \phi$.

Here are the intended operations. Program disjunction is union, as in standard dynamic logic. Program *intersection* corresponds to the following set-theoretic operation #:

$$R \# S := \lambda x, Y. \exists Y_1, Y_2\ xRY_1 \wedge xSY_2 \wedge Y = Y_1 \cup Y_2.$$

Sequential product now gets a more complicated description, via this operation Θ:

$$R \Theta S := \lambda x, Y.\ \exists Z\ xRZ \wedge \exists f\colon Z \rightarrow pow(S)$$
$$\forall z \in Z\ zS\ f(z) \wedge Y = \{f(z) \mid z \in Z\}.$$

For a complete axiomatization, cf. Goldblatt 1992. We merely generalize bisimulaion.

Definition 10.26 (Concurrent bisimulation) A binary relation ≡ between states in models M, N is a *concurrent bisimulation* if

(i) if S ≡ r, then s, r verify the same propositional atoms

(ii) if s ≡ r and sRZ, then there exists *U* with rRU and for all u U, there exists a $z \in Z$ with $z \equiv u$

(iii) vice versa in the opposite direction.

This definition is motivated as follows (van benthem, van Eijck and Stebletsova 1994).

Proposition 10.27 *All CPDL formulas are invariant for concurrent bisimulation. All CPDL operations are safe for concurrent bisimulations.*

10.9 NOTES

Process Algebra. Key references are Milner 1980, Bergstra and klop 1984, hennessy and Milner 1985. A text book is Baeten and Weyland 1900. Cf. also the survey chapter Stirling 1989. An elegant extension with process iteration is in Fokkink 1994, Bergstra, Bethke and Ponse 1994. Being based on bisimultation equivalence over graphs on trees, rather than flat strings, process calculi often throw interesting new light on regular algebra and other traditional theories. An example is the decidability of strong (bisimultation0 equivalence for context-free grammars (Baeten, Bergstra and Klop 1992).

Silence. Many process theories have 'silent steps' $\xrightarrow{\tau}$ for unobservable transitions. These arise by hiding certain transitions in an LTS under one relation. Structures then have the form (S,A, → $\xrightarrow{\tau}$). A binary relation ** is a weak bisimulation between transition systems with silent steps if the following conditions hold, whenever x ≡ y: (i) atomic markings agree on x and y, (ii) if $x \xrightarrow{a} x'$ then there exists some finite sequence of transitions on the other side of the from

$$y = y_1 \xrightarrow{\tau} \ldots\ldots \xrightarrow{\tau} y_n \xrightarrow{a} y_{n+1} \xrightarrow{\tau} \ldots\ldots \xrightarrow{\tau} y_{n+k} = y'$$

such that x‘ ≡ y‘; and vice versa, (iii) if x $\xrightarrow{\tau}$ x‘, there exists a finite sequence of transitions on the other side of the form

$$y = y_1 \xrightarrow{\tau} \ldots\ldots \xrightarrow{\tau} y_n = y'$$

Such that x‘ ≡ y‘ ; and vice versa. De Nicola and Vaandrager 1900, van Benthem, van Eijck and stebletsova 1994 give variations. It is easy to show by previous methods that weak bisimulation is non-EC_Δ on all LTSs, but EC on so-called Δ-saturated ones. Invariance results make sense here, too. But they are delicate, due to an asymmetry in the above definition. A restricted existential quantifier for a $\xrightarrow{a}$ step on one side need not match with one such quantifier on the other, because of τ-prefixes and suffixes Quantification must be over successors in compound relation τ; *a;* τ*. In $L_{w1w,}$ we conjecture a preservation theorem for invariance under weak bisimulation (Chapter 4).

Process Algebra , Set Theory and Modal Logic. Analogies between Modal logic and Process Algebra remain elusive. This chapter had by no means settled all. Hollenberg 1996b takes a big leap forward by moving to a modal logic of sequences. Along a quite different route, Janin 1996 links up definability of program constructions in *μ-propositional calculus* with invariance for bisimulation using tree automata techniques. Another route would run via a third party, viz. Set Theory. Process operations look like Δ_0–definable set-theoretic operations, and Milner's process algebra has inspired the non-well founded set theory of Aczel 1988. Equivalence classes of graphs may be identified with (non-well-founded)sets, which simplifies analysis of the finite graph model (it becomes a non-well-founded analogue of the natural numbers). Thus, some of the theories mentioned here become fragments of set theory. This is the promising research program in Barwise and Moss 1996, d' Agostino 1996.

Alternative Process Theories. One main point of this

chapter is that first-order process theories may be attractive alternatives to existing ones. Here are two examples. (1) The first order theory of *trace models* over branches *in infinite trees* is decidable (by an effective reduction to Rabin's Theroem). This should be contrasted with the high complexity found for the finite graph model. (2) The first-order theory of unwound infinite trace models is effectively axiomatizable, using Ehrenfeucht style compression arguments as in Doets 1987, or Backofen, Rogers and Vijay –Shanker 1995.

Acknowledgement

The work reported here on first-order theories of labeled transition systems and their connections with equational theories in process algebra is mostly due to joint research with *jan Bergstra* (programming Group, University of Amsterdam and Department of Applied Logic, University of utrecht). This is part of a current effort in the Netherlands interfacing the research programs of Dynamic Logic and Process Algebra. Cf. the recent bridge publications van Benthem, van Eijck and Stebletsova 1994, van Benthem and Bergstra 1994 and Ponse 1994 as well as the state of the art collections van Eijck and Visser, eds, 1994, and Ponse, de Rijke and Venema, eds., 1995.

Chapter-13

The Phenomenon of Meaning

Chapter 13

I. HUMAN THOUGHT AS A FABRIC OF MEANING AND A CONTEXT FOR PHENOMENA OF MEANING

In contrast with sense-awareness, e.g. visual experience, thought is meaningful awareness: it is a disclosure of meaning, plan, intelligibility in the world or affairs of life. Its logical quality is measured under the following values:

Clarity: how clearly meaning is grasped and communicated in speech and writing;
Precision: sensitivity to what exactly this or that judgment or statement would commit one to: a skill in finding words that communicate what one wishes to say, no more, no less;
Relevance: how systematic our thinking is, maintaining a proper connection with the topic or conclusion under discussion;
Consistency: sensitivity to compatibilities and incompatibilities of meanings: this ensures that in the sequence of thought incompatible judgments are not made. i.e. Judgements or assertions which, in virtue of their meaning, cannot all be true;
Cogency: the capacity to reason in perfect logical sequence. i.e. to so structure a sequence of thought that acceptance of the evidence compels acceptance of the conclusion.

These are key terms in the logical evaluation of thought, just as dimensions, lines proportion, symmetry are key terms in an architectural description of a building. They represent values that characterize the judicial mind—trained, clear and accurate in its ideas and use of words, relevant and cogent in its reasoning, searching in its testing of the reasoning of others; it is characterized by discipline and accuracy, by clarity and fluency, by a sensitivity to what words mean and what the evidence given really proves.

When one looks at human thought analytically, one can notice that its building blocks, ideas or concepts, have much in common with their linguistic counterparts, words. Both the idea and the word can bring into human consciousness something other than itself; they have the power to disclose, to signify, to mean something else; each is a sign. A word like Peter brings an individual before our consciousness; the thoughts of a mechanic bring before him the plan of the motor-car he is repairing—indeed if he is obsessional in his thinking he may not be able to disengage himself, mentally, from the car until it is repaired. Physical entities may be used like words as conventional signs: due to conventional agreement, a barber's pole brings shaves, shampoos and haircuts to our mind; a green light brings to mind a conceptual traffic rule. There are also physical entities which have a natural power to signify something else, e.g. smoke is a natural sign of fire, a good complexion is a natural sign of health, a photograph is a natural sign of the person photographed.

But among all these signs, the idea or concept has a unique feature. Each of the others is an entity in its own right and can be known entitatively before that which it signifies is also brought into consciousness. In technical terms the word or physical entity, like a traffic light, is an instrumental sign (an entity *used* to convey something else to the mind). But while my ideas disclose, e.g. physical objects, to me the peculiarity about them is that they cannot be known at all in separation from what they signify. There is an immediate apprehension of what is meant, represented or signified by the idea without the idea itself being known as an entity in itself. Thus the concept or idea is *essentially* a disclosure, a disclosure of meaning. It makes known without its existence as an idea being adverted to. except by reflection. It is a *medium in quo objectum directe cognoscitur*. Such a sign is called a formal sign because formally or essentially it is simply a representation: it has no other nature or form than its signification or meaning. The only formal signs are those within consciousness— concepts, judgments and reasonings. Signs extrinsic to the knowing process have only instrumental signification.

While it is important to become sensitive to the variety of vehicles which carry meaning—thought, language and to a limited extent physical entities—logic is not at all concerned with the vehicles as such, with the psychic reality of thought or the linguistic reality of statements. The facts and phenomena it studies appear only when meaning is achieved, and the same logical phenomena—e.g. the same implication—may appear both psychically in my thought and linguistically in my script. Thus thought and language are contexts for logical work rather than a subject matter of the science.

II. LANGUAGE AS A FABRIC OF MEANING AND A CONTEXT FOR LOGICAL PHENOMENA

In language the mind succeeds in putting into public and human circulation its own thinking. Language is a system of conventional signs designed and learnt for the purpose of externating and transporting thought. Some speak in an associationist way of the link between words and the ideas or judgments they signify, saying that the mind attaches to sounds and marks the meanings it conceives within itself and structures these sounds and marks into propositions and arguments. For others it is incorrect to be separating word and thought in this way and thus better to speak of verbal thought, with the word as a unit of verbal thought. All are agreed that language succeeds in embodying thought without being a facsimile of it, and that it is a fabric of meaning and a context therefore for logical phenomena. Indeed it is the context where early logical observations and discoveries were made.

Medieval logicians spoke of Logic as being concerned with discourse, i.e. with our talking and thinking rather than with the natural world. This expresses the fact that the two contexts in which logical entities and phenomena *may* be discovered or produced are thought and language. This is an important consideration for Metalogic but the work of the Formal Logician is done in and through the medium of language.

Most of the following observations will deal with words. statements and arguments rather than with their mental counterparts—ideas, judgments and reasonings. However. they will be in some way valid for the latter, although language must not be looked on as a facsimile of the mental. The observations will proceed systematically from atomic units of meaning to the more complex.

III. THE STRUCTURING OF MEANING

The incessant flow of ink. and of sound waves into our lives is sufficient evidence of a human drive to communicate meaning and of skill in doing so. A basic exercise in observing this skill consists in noting the variety of words we use and how various are the shapes of symbolized meaning.

Some words name a single individual or a single group, e.g. 'Socrates', 'this man', 'this football team'; they are called *singular names.* A *common name* is one that can be used distributively of many things—it is a class name which can be applied to each member of the class taken separately. e.g. man, soldier, team. A singular name may be a uniquely descriptive one, serving both to identify the individual and to describe it in some aspect, e.g. 'the President of Ireland', 'the discoverer of penicillin', 'the capital of Ireland'. Or it may be a proper name with which we identify but do not describe. Of course proper names acquire a private meaning for acquaintances of, e.g. John Smith, but this is not a conventional general meaning (technically called connotation). In the course of time a proper name may acquire a fixed invariable meaning and so be transformed into a common or general name. We speak of an individual as being a Don Quixote, a Nero, a Solomon, a Quisling, Captain Boycott, General Shrapnel, the Earl of Sandwich and Mr Joseph Aloysius Hansom have also enriched conventional language with their names.

'The angles of a triangle are equal to two right angles,' is an imperfect statement: it is not clear from the wording whether 'angles' is meant to be understood distributively or collectively. Some words are invented especially to signify a group or collectivity, e.g. 'jury', 'team', 'army'. A *collective term* is singular if it names a single group, e.g. 'this jury', 'the Irish army'; it is general if it can be used distributively of many groups, e.g. 'fleet', 'audience'. A singular collective name may', be a proper name, e.g. 'the National Library', 'the Rockies'. or a uniquely descriptive name, e.g. 'the congregation here present'. Collective statements are not as vulnerable to criticism as statements about a class of things distributively; the former are not refuted by a small number of adverse particular instances.

Abstraction—focusing aspects of reality and mentally isolating them—is both a human need and a human capacity. It gives rise in language to words which name natures, qualities or actions considered in isolation, e.g. 'humanity', 'height', 'navigation'. Such words contrast with *concrete names* which signify either the full individual or a nature, quality, action in its real context, e.g. 'Socrates', 'man', 'white'; and 'running' in 'he was running'. Abstract names are plentiful in Western languages: they are easily formed from adjectives (e.g. 'height', 'devotion'. 'whiteness') and verbs (e.g. 'attention', 'walking' in 'walking is a fine exercise').

The words 'as such', 'ut sic', 'qua tale' qualifying a noun make its meaning abstract, e.g. in the sentence. 'A judge as such has not the power to make law' the force of the words, as such, is to make one consider the person precisely and exclusively in his role as judge. It is only in the mind however that a person can be precisely and exclusively an official. Since abstract names refer to attributes considered in isolation from their subjects, there is not a range of subjects to which they are applicable—as there is for instance in the case of the concrete term 'man', which can be applied to Europeans, Americans, Japanese, etc. Thus the meaning of an abstract name has a reference value ('whiteness' refers to the quality of being white) but not extension.

Being *positive or negative* is a prominent feature of meaning, and indeed the phenomenon of negation is of great importance in logic. Many words signify the absence of a quality, e.g. 'colourless', 'unfit'; where the quality should normally be present the negative word signifying its absence is called a *privative* term, e.g. 'deafness'. A positive name of course signifies the presence of a quality; it may also be abstract (e.g. 'greed') or concrete (e.g. 'hot').

Logic is interested in the opposition between paired names, one positive the other negative. Thus 'hot' and 'non-hot' are contradictories; 'hot' and 'cold' are contraries. The former are exact opposites they are mutually exclusive and collectively exhaustive, i.e. their opposition is such that in failing to come under one, any object with a temperature must come under the other. Contraries are not opposed in this exact way and so do not collectively exhaust all possibilities.

One can make the contradictory of any term by simply prefixing 'non' to it. Such terms are thoroughly negative, indefinite or indeterminate in range since they are applicable to anything that has not a certain quality. Some of them can create obscurity: 'Institutions for the care of the non-sick' presumably does not mean 'institutions for the care of the healthy'—but the difference is not apparent.

A distinction between *relative and absolute names* develops out of the systematic quality that meaning can have. A relative name signifies a thing or quality in relation to something else, e.g. 'Father'; an absolute name signifies a thing or quality simply in itself, e.g. 'man'. A relative term is paired with a correlative, e.g. 'equal', 'greater', 'father' have as correlatives 'equal', 'less'. 'child'. Is 'mountain' a relative term or an absolute one?—'A mountain is so only by its elevation above the plain, and yet in calling it a mountain we have in mind many features besides this relation.'

The words of vernacular languages are subject, through

constant social use, to development and change. Few are *univocal,* i.e. used always in the same sense *(una voce). Equivocal* terms are used in two or more equal and independent meanings *(aequa voce),* e.g. 'vice', 'bit': equivocation is based on the clever use of such terms. Most vernacular words are *analogical.* i.e. in the course of time they develop a variety of senses which are partly but not wholly the same. Scientists try to have a system of technical terms that are fixed in meaning: in philosophy the question is discussed as to whether a language applicable univocally to both God and creatures is in principle impossible.

Of cardinal importance to logic is the distinction between *first-order* and *second-order language,* or between *object-language* and *metalanguage.* Thus when I say: '"cat" is the subject of that sentence.' I am talking about the language used and have to employ a new level of words invented after *(meta)* the primitive object-words. Medieval logicians made the same point in distinguishing *terms of the first intention* and *terms of the second* intention. Mental activity was imaged as a stretching towards *(intendere, intentio)* the object and grasping *(apprehendere, apprehensio)* of it. Awareness of the world in which we live was called the primary or first intention of the mind; our reflective awareness of our own thinking—psychic or verbal—was called the second intention of the mind. By extension of usage, everything discovered in the first intention was itself called a first intention. Similarly terms of the second intention referred to such features. distinctions and properties as are discovered in the second intention of the mind. These terms (e.g. 'abstract', 'specific', 'contradiction', 'predication', 'implication') obviously constitute a meta language.

Logic has been described as a science of second intentions: it is not concerned with the natural world; it is developed in and through reflective awareness and it operates with a second-order language.

This fact is emphasized by the concern logic has for *syncategorematic words.* These words are so-called because they can never function as subjects or predicates *(categorein*, to predicate): they go with *(syn)* the categorematic words and link them together as subject and predicate, or modify them as subject and predicate or express an operation of thought. Examples are: 'all, some, and, is, not, or, if, if and only if, if ... then, not . . - both, both ...and, either...or, Nowadays they are often called functors, logical constants, logical operators. They are the formative elements in discourse: one can change the other (categorematic) words of a statement without changing its form: e.g. 'All *men* are *spiritual'* has the same form as 'All *animals* are *mortal'*. The categorematic words give content or matter to the two statements, but it is the words 'all' and 'are' which structure and form them.

Logic is 'very concerned with the formative elements in symbolized meaning. Thus in the argument: 'If all men are mortal and if Socrates is a man, then Socrates is mortal,' the logician is not concerned with men or mortality but simply with the truth of the words, 'if... and if... then'. What is the force of these words? Am I entitled to use them, i.e. is the argument in fact valid? These are formal questions and can be answered without investigating the particular content of the statements and their material truth.

IV. A DUALISM WITHIN MEANING: SENSE AND REFERENCE

(It is the function of definitions and classifications to give a systematic presentation of sense and reference.)

Taking a simple word like 'man', one notes that it signifies the possession of certain attributes. This constitutes the sense or connotation of the word. The process of formulating this is called definition, and the formula is the familiar dictionary meaning of 'man'. However, the word has also a reference value: it is applicable to anything that realizes the definition. The range of sub-classes and individuals to which it is applicable constitute its reference value, extension or denotation. Thus the total signification of the word 'man' is complex—a blend of sense and reference.

Some words have reference merely, e.g. a proper name: it identifies an individual without connoting any attribute present. There are words also which have sense but no individual reference, e.g. abstract words. Most categorematic words have the two dimensions of meaning—sense and reference.

An expert in any subject will not only be able to define its technical terms accurately; he will also have a wide, personal experience of their range of reference. The technical operations which formulate sense (connotation) and reference (extension, denotation) are respectively definition and classification or division. They are basic to systematic thinking; thus definitions and classifications appear in the elementary section of pedagogical presentations—inverting the order of real enquiry where they are reached laboriously.

Indeed frequently definitions are only approximate and are called 'definition' only by a polite fiction. For the purpose of a definition is not merely to ascribe a fixed meaning for a term but to do so by revealing the nature of the thing signified, i.e. to verbalize an adequate insight into reality. To quote Aristotle (in *Posterior Analytics,* p. 101^{b}) 'a definition is a phrase signifying a thing's essence'. Of course there are definitions which are concerned wholly with artificial symbols—with correct usage and not at all with any *object* apart from the symbols; these simply express volition and are not true or false in an objective sense They are called merely *nominal definitions,* as opposed to the other *real definitions.*

It is important to evaluate the kind of information which a formula proposed as a definition gives. Is it merely nominal? If real, but approximate only, it may give a concrete picture with or without metaphor. If the description is literal and enables us to identify, e.g. a disease, the definition is called distinctive—this type is valuable in medicine: it enables the physician to diagnose and prescribe with confidence even though the nature of the disease is not properly known. The description of charity in I Corinthians 13 : 4 is a distinctive 'definition' of it. Some approximate definitions give the origin of the *definiendum,* or the way in which it can be produced really or ideally, e.g. 'An eclipse of the moon is a deprivation of light from the moon caused by the interposition of the earth between the moon and the sun'; 'A sphere is a solid figure formed by the revolution of a semicircle about its diameter. which remains fixed.' Others present samples and vary greatly in value according to the sampling that is done, e.g. 'The *Ilad,* the *Odyssey',* the *Aeniad, Paradise Lost* are Epic poems.' Others again signify purpose, e.g. 'A clock is a mechanical device for showing time.'

The classic technique of defining is *per genus et differentiam,* i.e. to detect the class of things to which the *definiendum* belongs and what differentiates it from the co-ordinate sub-classes. 'Man is a rational animal' is a familiar classic definition. It would be impossible to justify the claim that, this type of definition is the only genuine type. The technique, however, is extremely useful and helps to implement the following basic rules:

I. *The definition should be convertible with the word to be defined*—neither wider nor narrower in reference value. It is too narrow, e.g. to conceive a politician as a member of parliament; too wide to conceive him as a person interested in public affairs.

2. *The definition should not use or include the term to be defined.* If it does so explicitly the definition is said to be *idem per idem;* if it does so implicitly (by using an expression which can be defined only in terms of the *definiendum)* it is said to be circular. However, the writer who defines an archdeacon as one who exercises the archdeaconal functions may not be defining badly so much as conveying, humorously that no one knows what an archdeacon does.

3. *The definition should not be expressed in obscure or figurative language,* e.g. architecture is frozen music; memory is the tablet of the mind. A definition is not obscure simply because

it presupposes an educated audience.

4. A definition should not be negative unless the definiendum is purely negative. 'Alien' is negative and can *be* defined reasonably as 'a person who is not a citizen'. The schoolboy was less successful when he defined vitamins as 'things which make you sick, if you haven't got them'.

As one organizes the words of ordinary life or of any special discipline, it becomes clear that there is not an infinite regress towards simpler terms, and that there are primitive terms which are undefined and indefinable. Very general terms like 'existing', 'thing', 'good', 'unity', are so wide in reference value that it is technically impossible to formulate their sense. Terms which express elementary sense-experience or the primary sensible qualities we experience are also indefinable, e.g. sensation, pain. hardness, odour, sound, colour, shape. At the other extreme—complexity—the full reality of an individual object is not definable humanly; indeed in the Aristotelian and Thomistic philosophies it is regarded as, in principle, not completely conceptualizable. Today every discipline seeks to so organize its body of knowledge that primitive indefinable terms are evident and that all processes of definition are brought back to them.

Reference value is organized in the processes of division and classification, and it appears as a hierarchical series of genera and species. In logical division one begins with a term which names a very wide class (the *summum genus* of the series) and by processes of division and sub-division analyses it into subclasses and these again into more subordinate classes until the lowest level of classes is reached (the *infimae species)* whose members are simply individuals. Classification, on the other hand, begins with the individuals, sorting them into classes, these classes being then grouped under a smaller number of wider classes—in other words it constructs the hierarchical series upwards, rather than downwards from the *summum genus.*

The rules for a correct or good logical division are as follows:

1. *Each separate division or sub-division should have a single basis* (the basis being some attribute of the genus which is realized in different ways by the species). Thus in dividing the term 'building' one may use, at choice, as basis: (a) the function of buildings (there are, e.g. homes, schools, churches, businesses; or (b) architectural style (e.g. Colonial, Georgian, Byzantine, contemporary); or (c) structural material (brick, stone, frame, metal). But it is faulty to oscillate from one basis to another; thus the division of buildings into homes, schools, Georgian, contemporary, metal, stone is faulty: it is a cross division, failing to maintain a single basis *(fundamentum divisionis),* and, consequently, to separate the constituent species (the *membra dividentia,* so called because the species are pictured as sharing the genus between them).

2. *The division should be carried out exhaustively according to the basis chosen.* Every sub-class must be listed so that the extension of the subclasses taken together is equal to the extension of the wide class. This rule is of practical importance. If an income-tax law is being introduced, the legislators will have to divide wealth into various forms and legislate on what is to be regarded as income. If their division is not complete, people whom they intend to tax may not come under the law.

3. *Successive sub-divisions should be gradual,* i.e. each basis should be continuous with the basis of the preceding subdivision, and immediately so. *Ne fiat saltus in divisione.* If one divides quantity into continuous and discrete and then subdivides continuous quantity into triangles, quadrilaterals, etc., there is a jump in the division. A graduated process would subdivide continuous quantity into plane and solid, and then subdivide plane figures into rectilinear and curve linear before proceeding to the further sub-division of rectilinear figures into triangles, quadrilaterals, etc. In practice the work of defining and that of classifying interact. Both contribute to a total grasp of meaning and to expert knowledge in any subject-matter.

There is an interesting relationship between the sense and reference values of a word. Class names with richer sense have less reference value. Take the class names: square, rectangle, parallelogram, quadrilateral. Each name connotes a greater number of characteristics than the names which succeed it, and it has less extension than they. It is quite clear that a term with greater connotation has less extension for the connotation of a term determines its range of application. This point is sometimes expressed as follows: connotation and denotation vary inversely. However it is not accurate to speak so mathematically in this context. Connotation is not a calculable quantity and thus there cannot be a mathematical proportion between the variations in question.

Further, the actual number of individuals existing is not of logical interest. We must distinguish the range of species over which a term extends from the range of individuals to which it is applicable. We could speak of the former (with Joseph) as the extension of the term, the latter as its denotation. Joseph says *(Introduction to Logic,* ch. 6). 'It is plain that by the extension of a term we should not mean indifferently species and individuals: to be specified in divers ways is not the same as to be found in many instances.' Logic is more concerned with extension than with denotation. even when the term, denotation, is used to cover the indefinite number of possible instances, rather than an actual number.

V. MORE COMPLEX MEANING: PROPOSITIONAL *MEANING*

A word is an atom of meaning: a sentence is a molecular structure—it is a set of words which we can use to say something. *Proposition* is the technical word used for that which is said, the content of meaning or *lekton* (a term of the early Stoic logicians). The same proposition can be expressed in different sentences (e.g. in German. French, etc.) and the same sentence can express different propositions (e.g. 'I was born in Dublin as uttered by various people). The science of logic is concerned with the proposition not the sentence. Observations about sentences fall outside it, as to whether they are grammatical, ungrammatical, spoken, written, etc.

Since propositions are not sentences but the *lekton* or meaning conveyed in sentences, it follows that the elements of propositions are not words and the form of the proposition is not simply the verbal structure. Humanly however one comes to understand *propositions* better the more one understands the varying structures of se*ntences* which express them. Indeed in modern logic a great deal of time has been spent in creating a special artificial language and in studying the sentences which are constructed in this logical language.

For our purpose it is sufficient to note that even in a vernacular language such as English there is a great variety of structure in ordinary familiar sentences. For example:

S is P, S is not P: simple subject-predicate forms in which the link word is a part of the verb to *be,* present tense, indicative mood: the statement is categorical or unqualified in tone.
S must be P, S cannot be P, S may be P, S need not be P: here one has not a categorical statement but a modal one expressing the mode or manner in which *P* is asserted or denied of *S*.
a is b and c is d; a is b because c is d....: these types of statements are compound conjoining simple statements *with* the word *and* or with words like *because, although,* etc., which contain the meaning of *and* but add some further nuance of meaning to it.
If a is b, then c is d: this is a conditional statement; the important, structural words are 'if... then'.
Either a is b or c is d: this is the type of statement in which we express alternatives.

VI. THE COMPLEXITY OF SIGNIFICATION IN PREDICATIVE SENTENCES: SOME ELEMENTARY FEATURES

The verbal structure of 'Some men are self- sufficient' consists of a subject-term, a predicate-term, a copula ('are') and a sign of quantity ('some', which indicates that the statement is not universal but limited in range).

The subject-term. The subject-term designates the object about which we are making the predication. This object is called the supposit of predication. Thus in the sentence: 'men are mortal', 'men' is the subject-term, but the statement is not about the term but about the real men signified by the term. The supposit of predication then is the real men.

It is the function of a subject-term to designate the supposit of predication. This may be done by means of a term like 'this' or 'that' accompanied by a gesture (e.g. '*this* is a hospital') or by means of a term which classifies the supposit (e.g. '*hospitals* are necessary') or which connotes some of its attributes (e.g. '*the older patients* are difficult'). In the first case the supposit is presented at the level of perception without any formal conceptualization of it; in the other cases terms that could be used as predicates are used in the subject position as explanatory and descriptive features of the supposit.

In some cases it may be quite difficult to determine the supposit, e.g. in impersonal statements such as: 'it is raining'.

A subject-term may be related to the supposit of predication in either of two ways: (1) It may be the supposit, as in the sentence: 'man is a three-lettered word'. Here the term is employed non-significatively, materially: the statement is about the term itself and the supposition is said to be material. (2) The term may be employed as subject because of its signification; it may be used significatively. In this case it signifies the supposit. If the supposit is a mental entity signified by the term, the supposition is said to be mental (e.g. in 'Man is abstract not pictorial' we are talking about the idea, man); if it is extra-mental the supposition is said to be real (e.g. 'Man is mortal').

The supposition of terms arises from the fact that reference has direction, i.e. a vector quality. As used in the vernacular the same term may refer to a real entity or to the idea of that entity or it may refer to itself as a word, In Logic terms which are not identical in supposition are really distinct terms: accordingly, instead of speaking of the word. man, as being self-referring and being used in material supposition, it speaks of a new, second-order word, 'man' (spelling it with inverted commas). It is not relevant to logic to go further and differentiate in its language between terms used in real supposition and those used in mental supposition. However. it is an important rule that terms which are not identical in supposition cannot be used in reasoning as identical terms.

The predicate-term. The predicate-term signifies that which is attributed to the subject (or denied of it in a negative sentence). Predicates give various kinds of information about their subjects and these are called *predicables.* Porphyry's list of predicables is the traditional one; it is based on Aristotle's and is only slightly different from the original. Worked out systematically it is as follows: If one takes a singular term. e.g. Socrates as subject, a predicate may express the essence of Socrates fully and thus give his *species* ('rational animal') or it may express the essence partially, giving either the *genus* of Socrates ('animal') or the attribute which differentiates his species from others in the same genus ('rational' is the *differentia* of the species, man); if it does not express anything essential. it may give a *property'* of Socrates deducibic from the type of being he is (e.g. 'free', 'risible') or an attribute that is purely individual, an *accident* (e.g. 'snub-nosed').

Thus *species, genus, diffrentia, property. accident* are Porphyry's list of Predicables. The original classification by Aristotle was made having in view a subject term that was general (e.g. 'man') not singular (e.g. 'Socrates'). Accordingly the first predicable was not species but definition—the predicate 'rational animal' gives the species of Socrates, but the definition of 'man'.

The copula. The fact of predication is signified by the copula. Of course the linguistic symbol of predication is fixed by convention. Vernacular languages, however, display a remarkable bias for the verb of existence (e.g. *S* is *P, S* is not P). The question arises: has every predicative sentence an existential import or is there any appropriateness in using the verb *to be* as copula? It is clear that when I assert 'Mount Olympus is the abode of the gods' or 'Jove is the king of the gods' or 'Cerberus is a fierce three-headed dog guarding the gates of Hades', I do not mean to assert that Mount Olympus or love or Cerberus are real, physically. But they figure in Greek mythology and my sentences make a truth-claim, claim to conform to fact in some way. Accordingly some would speak of a predicative proposition as having existential validity for some universe of discourse—whether that be the physical world, or the world of Greek mythology, etc.

However, these considerations are extra-logical. They are bound up with vernacular language, and they concern the supposition of terms (mental or real) rather than the force of predication. A study of predication should not be confused with a study of the verb of existence. Indeed Aristotle signified predication by the words 'belongs to' *('B* belongs to all *A'* instead of 'All *A* is *B')*. In modern logical notation the verb of existence does not appear: e.g. *F* is a symbol used for any predicate, *a* is a symbol used for any subject and the expression *Fa* (read as *F* of *a)* signifies that the property *F* belongs to the individual *a*.

Quantity and quality in predicative sentences. The final elementary features of signification in predicative sentences are *quantity* and *quality*. The latter refers simply to their affirmative or negative character. The former concerns range of reference. In 'All *S* is *P*' and 'Some *S* is *P*, the words 'all' and 'some' are signs of quantity; 'all' indicates that the subject-term is to be taken in the whole range of its extension, that the statement is universal; 'some' indicates that it is to be taken in part only of its extension, that the statement is particular. The former is called an *A* proposition, the latter an *I* proposition, and traditionally they are symbolized *SaP* and

SiP (*a* and *i* being vowels from the latin word *affirmo*). In the negative propositions 'No *S* is *P*' and 'Some *S* is not *P*', 'no' is now the sign of universal quantity and 'some' again signifies that the statement is particular. These negative statements are respectively *E* and *0* and are symbolized *SeP* and *SoP* (Using the vowels of the Latin word, *nego*)

Thus on the combined basis of quantity and quality simple predications are classified as *A, E, I* and *0* propositions.

A proposition without any sign of quantity is called an indesignate (or indefinite) proposition and, logically, its signification is defective. However, in the vernacular, certain words or phrases which grammatically are part of the predicate, function as signs of quantity, e.g. 'Never', 'nowhere', 'under no circumstances', 'in no case', 'always', 'everywhere', 'not always', 'not everywhere', 'occasionally', 'once', 'somewhere'. A proposition with 'the' prefixed to the subject-term often functions as a universal, e.g. 'The horse is a quadruped'. The indesignate form may be used deliberately to express a group tendency (rather than a universal truth), e.g. 'country children are more impressionable than city children'.

It is often difficult to say how far a writer or speaker wishes to commit himself by a statement of the form 'All *S* is not *P*'. Is he conceding that 'Some *S* is *P*' but stressing the fact that 'Some *S* is not *P*'? Or is he simply going as far as stating 'Some *S* is not *P*' without excluding either the possibility that 'No *S* is *P*' or the possibility that 'Some *S* is *P*'? Where the latter two possibilities are left entirely open, commitment is minimized. It is this minimum commitment that is imposed by the words of the statement, not anything stronger whatever be the intention of the speaker.

Where the subject-term of a modal proposition has a sign of quantity, the proposition is said to have *dictum* as well as (mode) dictum here Connotes the presence of a quantity or range in the statement. There are eight kinds of modal propositions which have dictum: necessity and impossibility may be asserted in universal or particular statements ('All *S* must be *P*', 'Some *S* must be *P*'; 'No *S* can be *P*', 'Some *S* cannot be *P*'); *so* also may possibility both in its positive and negative senses ('All *S* can *be P*,' ' Some *S can be P*; 'No *S* need be *P*, 'Some *S* need not be *P*').

VII. VALUE AS A PHENOMENON WITHIN MEANING

A meaningful statement either possesses or lacks the value of truth. A simple inspection of meaning is sometimes sufficient to show that a statement is true, e.g. '*A* is either *b* or non-b'. Such a statement is called a tautology or an analytic proposition: the act of seeing its truth and the act of grasping its meaning coincide. It is also called an *a priori* proposition, one that can be known to be true prior to, and independently of, experiencing actual instances of it. At the other extreme, there are statements which are self-contradictory, i.e. their meaning is such that it could never be verified. If the incompatibilities within meaning are present at the level of the basic form of a statement, then it is called a logical or formal contradictory, e.g. '*A* is both *b* and non-*b*'.

Most meaningful statements are contingent, i.e. their truth value cannot be read off from their meaning; they are known to be true in and through experiencing the facts signified or, indirectly, through the evidence of other facts. Experience, not simply meaning, is the criterion of their truth—they are empirically true or empirically false.

VIII. SIMPLE RELATIONSHIPS BETWEEN PREDICATIVE PROPOSITIONS

The above diagram sets out the relationships between *A*, *E*, *I* and *0* propositions which have the same subject- and predicate-terms. It is traditionally called the Square of Opposition although the relationships it displays are not all ones of opposition or conflict.

Contradictory opposition exists between propositions which differ both in quantity and quality—between a universal affirmative *(A)* and a particular negative *(0)*, and between a universal negative (*E*) and a particular affirmative (*I*). Contradictories are an exact negation of each other, mutually

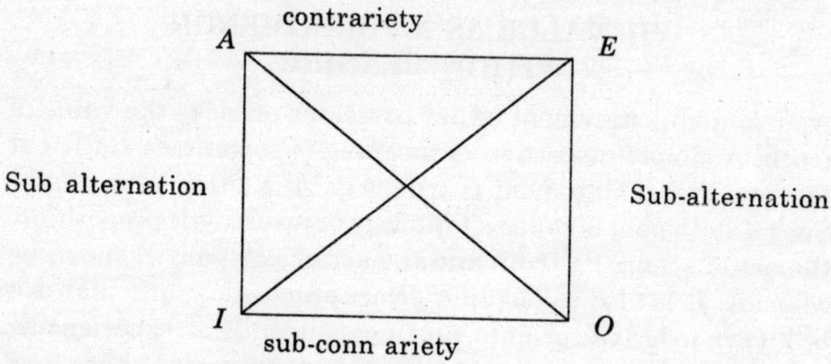

exclusive and collectively exhausting all possibilities; thus one must be true, the other false.

A and *E* are contraries; indeed they are extreme contraries, for contrary opposition exists wherever the conflict is greater than contradiction (thus some propositions have many contraries). Contraries cannot both be true but they may both be false. Note that *I* and *O* propositions have not contraries: to contradict the I one must make a universal statement in the opposite direction *(E)* and there is no stronger statement remaining in that direction.

The relationship between *I* and *O* is not one of opposition although the technical name, sub-contrariety, suggests conflict. Both can be true at the same time, but both cannot be false.

Finally, the relationship between *A* and *I* and between *E* and *O* is one of sub-alternation. This is subordination not conflict: the particular affirmative is a sub-alternate of the universal affirmative, and the particular negative is a subalternate of the universal negative.

In some vernacular propositions quantity is signified by an adverb rather than by 'all', 'no', 'some', e.g. 'Men are always unhappy'. One can work out the full set of relationships between such propositions: e.g.

Since, as we have seen, there are eight types of quantified modal propositions, the whole set of relationships between them is diagrammed in an octagon. The contradictory relationships may be worked out as follows:

Relationships of incompatibility can, of course, exist between all types of proposition, not merely between the predicative type. Every proposition has a contradictory—an exact minimal negation of its meaning—and any proposition which is stronger than this is a contrary. Formulating the contradictory of a statement is a good way of testing our grasp of its meaning.

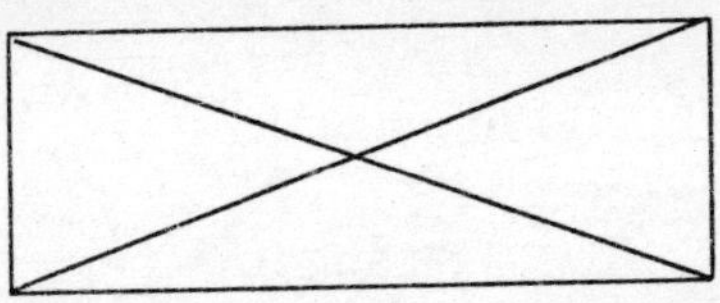

The minimal negation of *'A* is *b* and *c* and *d'* is that *'A* is either not *b* or not C or not *d'*. This kind of negation is implicit in a plea of not guilty and it puts the onus on the prosecution of proving every part of the indictment. The contradiction of'

MODEL PROPOSITIONS WITH DICTUM AND MODE

All S must be P Some S must P	Asserts the mode necessity.	Denies (some S need not beP) that mode (No S need be P)
All S can be P Some S can be P	Asserts the mode. Possibility.	Denies (Some S cannot be P) that mode (No S can be P)
No S need be P Some S need not be P	Negative Possibility, Possibility of not for being P, is stated	Negative (Some s cannot beP) Possibility of (All S mustbeP) is denied
No S can be P Some S cannot be P	Impossibility stated	Impossibility (Some S can beP) denied (All S can beP)

If a is *b*. c is *d'* is 'Even if a is *b*. c need not bed': 'If a is *b*, c is not d' is a contrary. To contradict *'A* is either *b* or c' it is sufficient to assert that *'A* may be neither *b* nor c'. Finally, the contradictory of 'A cannot be b and c' is '*A* can be *b* and *c*': '*A* is both *b* and *c*' is a contrary.

Some predicative propositions seem to have double quantification, e.g. 'Some men are never satisfied'. 'No man is always polite', 'Every man is sometimes selfish'. Here the adverbs do not function as quantifiers: they are part of the predicate and do not determine the range of the statement. The contradictories are accordingly: 'There is not any man-who-is-never-satisfied'. 'Some men are always polite (the-sort-who-are-always-polite)', 'Some men are not the-sort-who-are-sometimes selfish'.

Chapter-14

The Phenomenon of Implication

Chapter-14

1. INFERENCE AND IMPLICATION

The words 'infer', 'inferring', inference' refer to the mental act of drawing and asserting a conclusion and since this is a personal act the mind may be gravitated towards the concluding assertion by a variety of forces. Certainly in real life reasoning is not simply structured in full and conscious conformity with logical rules of evidence. The word, implication, does not refer at all to the context of personal reasoning. It denotes a relationship between propositions such that the meaning of one proposition (the conclusion) is folded up (implied: plex', a fold) in the meaning of another proposition or in the combined meaning of other propositions (the evidence). The implication is objective: it is *there* whether or not any person is subjectively conscious of the fact. Thus 'All S is *P*' implies that 'Some S is *P*'; ideally, of course, my inference that 'Some S is *P*' should be governed by a perception of the implication. On the other hand, 'Some S is *P*' does not imply that 'All S is *P*'; notwithstanding.the lack of implication, I may in real life make that kind of inference. We apply logical principles when in this or that context of personal inference we seek to discover whether the mental inference was governed by objective implications.

Synonyms for implication are 'consequence' (this gives a dynamic image of meaning: the conclusion follows on, and from, the evidence) and 'logical necessitation' (there is a compulsion, based on meaning, to accept the conclusion once the evidence is accepted).

II. IMPLICATIONS WITHIN THE SQUARE OF OPPOSITION

In virtue of their meanings, contradictories cannot both be true and cannot both be false; contraries cannot both be true but may both be false; sub-contraries cannot both be false and may both be true; if a universal is true the corresponding particular is true, if a particular is false the corresponding universal must also be false. Accordingly, the following is a table of inferences we can make on the basis of the square of opposition:

If A is true, E is false, O is false, I is true.
If *E* is true. *A* is false, *I* is false, *0* is true.

(Since the *A* and *E* propositions are of universal range, a complete set of inferences can be made when they are given as true.)

If *E* is true, *A* is false, I is false, *0* is true.

(Since the *A* and *E* propositions are of universal range. a complete set of inferences can be made when they are given as true.)

If I is true, E is false, A and O may or may not be true.
If O is true, A is false, E and I may or may not be true.

(Since *I* and *0* are of minimal range, the truth or falsity of any proposition other than the contradictory is simply not implied.)

If *A* is false, *0* is true. *I* and F may or may not be true.
If *E* is false, I is true, *0* and *A* may or may not be true.

(Since *A* and E are of universal range to know simply that they are false gives us minimal information.)

If I is false, *A* is false, E and *0* are true.
If *0* is false, E is false. *A* and *I* are true.

(Since I and *0* are of minimal range, to know they are false gives complete information about the whole set of propositions.)

The universal (e.g. *A)* implies the particular (I), the particular (e.g. I) is implied by the universal *(A)*. The former implication is sometimes called superimplication, the latter subimplication.

III. Simple operations on predicative propositions which disclose implications: conversion, obversion, contraposition and inversion

Conversion is an operation in which we transpose the subject and predicate terms symbolized as S and *P*. Thus S becomes the predicate of the new derived proposition and *P* its subject. What is the converse of *SaP?* It will have the form P S, and it must be an implication of the original, i.e. be logically necessitated by the meaning of *SaP*. Is the converse *PaS* or *PiS?* An example would seem to counter indicate the former: 'All French men are Europeans does not seem to imply that a 'All Europeans are Frenchmen'.

At this point one must examine the relationship of evidence and conclusion: if we have not information about all S in the evidence we cannot say that a conclusion about all S is logically necessitated: similarly for the term *P*. This leads to the question: what information have we, quantitatively, about P in the propositions *SaP, SeP, Sip, Sop?* A sign of quantity tells us whether S is used in the whole range of its extension or not, i.e. to use a technical phrase, whether S is or is not distributed; thus the symbols *a* and e tell us that a universal affirmation or denial is being made about S, the symbols i and o that the affirmation or denial is particular. But there is no sign of quantity for *P*. Do the forms of the. propositions disclose anything about the extension of *P?* The answer is important for the validation of operations such as conversion.

For the purpose of drawing implications from the meaning of a proposition, it is clear that a term must be treated as undistributed if it is not known to be distributed. Taking the two affirmative propositions, *A* and I, the *A* does not signify whether 'All S's are all the *P's'* or whether 'All S's are only some of the *P's'*, and the *I* does not signify whether 'Some S's are all the Ps' or 'Some S's are some of the Ps'. Thus for the purpose of inference *P* must be treated as undistributed in affirmative propositions.

In negative propositions, on the other hand, whether we are talking about the whole range of S or about some S only, we are excluding them from the class *P*. Thus we are talking about *P* in its class extension and *P* is accordingly distributed.

The rule for inference therefore is that a negative proposition distributes its predicate, an affirmative proposition does not. On this basis the valid converse *of SaP* (where *P* is undistributed) is not *PaS* (where *P* is distributed) but *P is* (where *P* remains undistributed). The converse of *SeP* is *PeS;* of *SiP* is *PiS.* There is no valid converse of *SoP:* the only feasible claimant, *PoS,* distributes S which in the original evidence is undistributed.

Obversion is an operation in which we introduce a double negation into a proposition, substituting for the predicate *(P),* its logical contradictory *(P)* and balancing this by changing the quality of a proposition (an *A* to an *E,* an *I* to an *o* or vice versa). The original proposition is called the obvertend, the implied one is called the obverse. Thus the obverse of *SaP* is *SeP;* of *SeP* is *SaP:* of *SiP* is *SoP;* and of *SoP* is *SIP.*

When a single predicative proposition is the evidence, conversion and obversion are the basic operations on it which disclose implications. The other operations, contraposition and inversion, are a combination of conversion and obversion.

Contraposition alternately obverts and converts so as to derive a new proposition which has for its subject the contradictory of the original predicate *(P):*

	(I)	(2)	(3)
	Ohverse	Converse of Ohveroo	Obverting (2)
SaP	SeP	*PeS*	*PaS*
SeP	*SaP*	*PiSPoS*	
SiP	*SoP*	None, and thus the not a contrapositive	*I* proposition has
SoP	*SiP*	*PiS*	*PoS*

Thus there are two contrapositives of A, E and 0 propositives. Some writers call (2) a partial contrapositive and (3) a full contrapositive.

In inversion the derived proposition has as its subject *the contradictory* of the original subject, i.e. the inverse has the form S P or S P. Actually only A and E propositions have inverses. To get the inverse of A you obvert first; with E you convert first:

Sap, *Sep* *PcS*, *PaS*, *SiP* *SoP*
Sep, *PeS*, *Pas*, *SiP*, *SoP*

If you begin converting with the *A* proposition or obverting with the E, the sequence of conversions and obversions leads to an *0* propositions which cannot be converted, as is the case with the I and *0* propositions no matter how the sequence is structured.

If one is converting, obverting, contraposing or inverting vernacular propositions it is often necessary to put them into a more appropriate shape where (1) subject and predicate are clearly indicated, (2) the copula is part of the verb *to be* in present tense, indicative mood, and where (3) there is a sign of quantity before the subject term. If the meaning of the original proposition is not clear enough to formulate in this way, then it will not be possible to convert it. etc. It is not a matter of the new form being better than the original but of its being convenient for the operations of conversion, etc. Thus one would not want to improve on 'No news is good news' or 'Men think' but to convert these propositions one must translate them into something like 'In every instance the absence of news is good news', and 'All men are such-that-they-think'. It is not a happy phrase to describe this as putting propositions into logical form, the suggestion here being that the new propositions are an improvement on the originals.

IV. THE CRUX OF INVERSION

The inverse of *SaP* is *SoP* in which the predicate is distributed while it is not distributed in the original proposition. A rule of inference seems to be violated, and yet each separate step of conversion and obversion is valid.

The inverse of *SeP* does not involve this particular formal difficulty but in it a difficulty arises which has essentially the same solution.

By analysing an example of each kind of inversion we shall see that an assumption is made in inversion, and that the process is valid or not according as that assumption is or is not verified.

Inverting an A proposition

*Given:*All future acts are known to God *(SaP),* the successive stages are:
No future act is unknown to God *(SeP)*
Nothing unknown to God is a future act (PeS)
Everything unknown to God is a non-future act *(PaS)*
Some non-future acts are unknown to God *(SiP)*
Some non-future acts are not known to God *(SoP)*
(Notice by contrast that given: All Frenchmen are Europeans, the inverse: Some non-Frenchmen are not Europeans, is also a *true* proposition.)
Solution: There is an assumption that the new term *P*, developed in this process, can be used in real supposition, i.e. that there are or can be non-P's. Thus there is an auxiliary statement understood along with the original S *a P,* namely that there are non-P's. i.e. there are some things which are not P's—an *0* proposition with *P* distributed. It follows then of course that these things which are not P's are things which are not S's.

Thus the reasoning in the example can be presented fully as follows:

Granted that all future acts are known to *God, then if* there are things unknown to him, these things must be non-future acts.

Inverting an E proposition

SeP, PeS, PaS, SiP

Granted: No great poet (is one who) has actually written a flawless epic poem.
Inverse: Some non-great poets (are ones who) have actually written flawless epic poems.
Solution: It is assumed that the term *P* (poets who have produced flawless epic poems) admits of being used in real supposition, i.e. that there are such poets. The inverse that it is non-great poets who are such, follows on this assumption. Without this assumption you could not pass validly from the original negative statement *(SeP)* which does not involve the existence of *P,* to the positive assertion *SiP* which does involve the existence of *P.*

As a general conclusion one can *say*: Only those *A* propositions have a valid inverse in which the term *P* has designation (i.e. in which there are non-P's); and only those *E* propositions have a valid inverse in which the term *P* has designation (i.e. in which there are P's). Thus the operation, inversion, is not absolutely self-guaranteeing—it will not develop a true conclusion from an original truth under all conditions. The solution to the crux of inversion lies in formulating the conditions under which it is valid. The governing rule is that we are not entitled to use a term in real supposition in a conclusion, if the evidence does not use it in real supposition. And the requisite conditions are that in the case of the *A* and E propositions respectively, *P* and *P* be *given* in real supposition. *b*

V. OTHER SIMPLE IMPLICATIONS

Immediate inference by added determinants consists in adding the same qualification to the subject and the predicate of the original proposition, e.g. 'A statue is a work of art' implies that 'A beautiful statue is a beautiful work of art' This kind of inference is valid provided the qualification has an identical meaning when applied to both subject and predicate. 'A cottage is a building' does not imply 'a huge cottage is a huge building'—'huge' is a relative qualification.

Immediate inference by omitted determinants is an inference in which from a proposition affirming of a given subject an attribute qualified by a determinant, we infer a proposition affirming of the same subject the attribute without qualification. Thus 'God is an infinite spirit' implies 'God is a spirit'. An inference of this kind is not valid if the determinant negatives the attribute: 'this is a bad shilling' does not imply 'this is a shilling'.

Immediate inference by complex conception consists in employing both the subject and the predicate of the original as parts of a more complex conception: A horse is a quadruped' implies 'The head of a horse is the head of a quadruped'. Similar errors may occur here as in the other types mentioned.

Immediate inference by converse relation consists in inferring correlations. Thus the proposition 'A is older than B' implies that 'B is younger than *A'*,

Finally *immediate inference by modal consequence* consists in inferring that a thing *can* be so from the fact that it *is* so; or in inferring from the *necessity of* it being so that it *can* be so, and also that it *is* so; or in inferring that it *is not* so from the fact that it *cannot* be so.

VI. COMPLEX IMPLICATIONS: THE SIMPLE CATEGORICAL SYLLOGISM

In syllogistic reasoning two propositions (called premisses) are so combined as to imply a third proposition (the conclusion). The syllogism is named after the type of propositions which constitute it; accordingly where premisses and conclusion are simple categorical propositions the syllogism is called a simple categorical one. Aristotle analysed it fully and in studying his presentation of its mechanism one is experiencing a Formal Logician at work.

All things which reproduce their kind are living
All viruses are things which reproduce their kind

Therefore all viruses are living

This is an argument in biology, but one can abstract from the biological content and focus the general structure. Two terms ('virus' and 'living') are linked up in the conclusion through being alternately linked in the premisses with a third term ('things which reproduce their kind'). Aristotle saw that by using variables for these terms (*S* for the subject of the conclusion. *P* for the predicate of the conclusion, and *M* for the common middle term) he could isolate and completely analyse the basic structure of this kind of argument. Just as the chemist in his laboratory physically isolates chemical entities, so too the logician by his use of variables succeeds in isolating structures of meaning. The chemist and logician work in two different worlds but there is a basic identity about their needs and about the movements of their intelligence.

Substituting variables the biological argument becomes

All *M is P*	*(MaP)*
All *S* is *M*	*(SaM)*
Therefore all S is *P*	(Therefore SaP)

To present the argument in a completely formal way, eliminating any suggestion of personal belief in the constituent propositions and focusing simply the fact of implication, one can use the format

If all *M* is *P*	(If *MaP*)
and if all *S* is *M*	(and if *SaM*)
then all *S* is *P*	(then *SaP*)

What is asserted here is simply and solely a logical fact, the truth of the words 'If and if ... then.' The syllogism then is simply a single continuous implicative statement.

From this point a complete treatment of the categorical syllogism almost writes itself. There are four possible Figures according to the position of M in the premisses:

First Figure	*Second Figure*	*Third Figure*	*Fourth Figure*
MP	*PM*	*MP*	*PM*
SM	*SM*	*MS*	*MS*
S-P	*SP*	*SP*	*S-P*

The premiss in which *P* appears is called the major premiss and by convention is written first. *P* is called the major term and *S* the minor term. The premiss in which *S* appears is called the minor premiss. In the First Figure *S* and *P* occupy their natural positions: *S* is subject in the conclusion and in its premiss, *P* is predicate in both the conclusion and its premiss. Reasoning which embodies this First Figure format is very natural and fluent. In the Fourth Figure on the other hand *S* occupies the predicate position in the minor premiss and *P the* subject position in the major. It is not easy to experience the cogency of valid reasoning when it is in this form. Aristotle regarded the First Figure as the perfect form. Actually, the Fourth Figure is not frequently used.

Since simple categorical propositions are of four kinds, *A, E, I* and *0,* categorical syllogisms may consist of various combinations of these. The same combinations are not valid in every figure. In the First Figure the following sequences (for major premiss, minor premiss, conclusion) are valid: *AAA, EAE:, AII, E IO* are valid; all other possible sequences would violate some rule governing the syllogism. There is a medieval latin mnemonic for memorizing the valid combinations (or *moods)* of each Figure through the sequence of vowels in each word:

> Barbara, Celarent, Darii, Ferioque prioris. Cesare, Camestres, Festino, Baroco secundae. Tertia Darapti, Disamis, Datisi, Felapton, Bocardo, Ferison, habet. Quarta insuper addit Bramantip, Camenes, Dimaris, Fesapo, Fresison.

This mnemonic is quite dispensable as the general rules of the syllogism are simple and their application to each figure is not difficult. However, it contains a code also for reducing all syllogistic reasoning to a first figure format.

The general rules of the simple categorical syllogism refer to structure, quantity and quality:

Rules of structure

(1) A syllogism must contain three and only three propositions.

(2) It must contain three and only three terms.

Since the implied relationship between *S* and *P* is rooted in their separate relationships to a common term, it follows that a syllogism is defective if it fails to have a term common to both premisses. This is the logical flow or fallacy of *Quaternio Terminorum—having* a set of four terms instead of three. Sophistical arguments sometimes commit this fallacy, e.g.:

Every rare thing is a dear thing
But a-horse-for-a-penny is rare

Therefore a-horse-for-a-penny is dear

Rules of quality

(1) From two negative premisses there can be no conclusion.

(2) If one premiss is negative, the conclusion must be negative; and if the conclusion is negative one premiss must be negative.

Information that neither *S* nor *P* is linked with *M* does not imply any particular interrelationship between them; again information that one is positively linked with the common term and the other is not can at most imply a negative interrelationship.

Rules of quantity

(I) The Middle Term must be distributed in one at least of the premisses.

(2) No term may be distributed in the conclusion

unless it has been distributed in its premiss.

If the reference in both premisses is to some *M* merely, then the *M's* to which *S* is related need not necessarily be any of the *M's* to which *P* is related, so that there is not effectively any common term. Distribution of *M* in one premiss ensures a common area of reference. Violation of this rule is called the fallacy of Undistributed Middle. With regard to the quantity of *S* and *P*, quite clearly one cannot draw a valid conclusion about 'all *S*' or 'all *P*' if one has information about only some *S* or some *P* in the relevant premiss. Violations of this rule are called an Illicit Process of the Minor Term (*S*) or an Illicit Process of the Major Term (*P*).

Every detective is armed.
But No criminal is a detective

Therefore No criminal is armed

Here an Illicit Process of the Major Term is committed-*P* is distributed in the negative conclusion but is undistributed in the major premiss where it is the predicate of an affirmative proposition.

Corollaries

(1) From two particular premisses there can be no conclusion.

Proof: Both premisses cannot be negative. The remaining possibilities are that only one premiss is negative or that neither premiss is negative.

If one of the premisses is negative, the conclusion must be negative and *P*, consequently, be distributed in it. Since the premisses are particular none of the subject terms are distributed, and of the predicates only the predicate of the negative premiss is distributed. Thus there is not provision for the distribution of *P* along with *M;* there must be then either an Illicit Process of the Major Term or an Undistributed Middle.

If both premisses are affirmative (as well as particular)

there is not any term distributed in them. Consequently there is the fallacy of Undistributed Middle.

(2) If one premiss is particular, the conclusion must be particular.

Proof: If both premisses are affirmative only one term can be distributed, the subject of the universal premiss. For validity it must be *M*. Accordingly *S* is undistributed in its premiss and may not be distributed in the conclusion.

If one premiss is negative an additional term is distributed, the predicate of the negative premiss. But since the conclusion must now be negative and distribute *P*, the extra term distributed in the premisses must be *P*. Thus S is still undistributed in its premiss and may not be distributed in the conclusion.

These general rules and corollaries enable us to eliminate some of the 16 possible combinations of *A E I O* in the premisses:

AA	*AE*	*AI*	*AO*
EA	~~*EE*~~,	*EI*	~~*EO*~~
IA	*IE*	~~*II*~~	~~*IO*~~
OA	~~*OE*~~	~~*OI*~~	~~*OO*~~

Special rules may be worked out for each figure determining the moods that are valid in each. In the First Figure (I) the minor premiss must be affirmative and (2) the major premiss must be universal. If the minor premiss were negative, the major premiss would have to be affirmative (with *P* undistributed in it) and the conclusion would be negative (distributing P) involving an illicit process of the major term. The major premiss must be universal to distribute its subject, *M* (Thus *AAA, EAE, AII, EIO* are the only valid First Figure moods.)

In the Second Figure, (I) one premiss must be negative (to distribute *M*) and (2) the major premiss must be universal (to distribute *P* and so avoid an illicit process of the major term.) Thus *EAE, AEE, EO, AOO* are the valid moods of the Second

Figure which is sometimes called the figure of exclusions because its conclusions are negative.

In the Third Figure (I) the minor premiss must be affirmative for the same reason as in the First Figure. Consequently, (2) the conclusion must be particular as S is predicate of the affirmative minor premiss and so undistributed in it. *AAI, lAl. All, EAO, OAO, EIO* are the valid moods of this figure, called the figure of examples because its conclusions are particular, being used either to contradict or prepare the way for a universal.

The rules of the artificial Fourth Figure are only listed for the sake of completeness: (1) If the major premiss is affirmative, the minor must be universal; (2) If the minor premiss is affirmative, the conclusion must be particular: and (3) If either premiss is negative, the major premiss must be universal. Thus *AAl. AEE, IAI, EAO, ElO* are the valid Fourth Figure moods.

Nineteen valid moods are listed in all. Of these, fifteen are called fundamental moods. The other four are called strengthened moods; two of them are from the Third Figure *AAI* (Darapti) and *EAO* (Felapton) and two from the Fourth Figure *AAI* (Bramantip) and *EAO* (Fesapo)—in each case the two premisses need not be universal in order to imply the conclusion. Finally, the number of valid moods can be brought from nineteen to twenty-four, as in five of the moods the conclusion is universal so that there is room for five more weakened moods in which the conclusions are particular.

(Note: In translating vernacular arguments into the *S, P, M* symbolism, it is important to remember that although singular propositions are not universal they are symbolized as *A* (affirmative) or *E* (negative). This convention is based on the fact that there is a sufficient identity of behaviour within the syllogistic context to warrant this extended use of the symbols. Thus the classic syllogism, All men are mortal, but Socrates is a man; therefore Socrates is mortal' is symbolized *'MaP,* but *SaM;* therefore *SaP.')*

VII. SOME EXERCISES ON THE RULES OF THE SIMPLE CATEGORICAL SYLLOGISM

Procedure in doing the exercises:

(I) Work out your answer roughly. if necessary by testing the problem in the separate figures; but have as your aim to find a reason from the *general 'rules* of the syllogism.
(2) Formulate your final answer fully but concisely.

Samples of formulated answers:
First Exercise: Why do not the premisses *IE* yield a valid conclusion in any figure while the premisses *El* yield a valid conclusion in every figure?

The premisses *lE* yielding a negative conclusion (with *P* distributed in it) involve an illicit process of the major term *(P* being undistributed in the major premiss whether in subject or predicate position).

The premisses EI provide for the distribution of two terms *(M* and P) in the major premiss. If the conclusion is particular no other term need be distributed in the premisses for validity.

Second Exercise: Prove that when the minor term is predicate in its premiss the conclusion cannot be *A*.
The symbol *A* connotes a proposition that is affirmative and universal. If the conclusion were *A,* both premisses would have to be affirmative. *S* being the predicate of an affirmative premiss would be undistributed and so it would have to be undistributed in the conclusion that is to say, the conclusion would have to be particular.

Third Exercise: If the major term be predicate in the major premiss, what do we know about the minor premiss?
The minor premiss must be affirmative. If it were negative the conclusion being negative would distribute *P*. Further the major premiss would have to be affirmative leaving *P* undistributed in it (as predicate). Thus there would be an illicit process of the major term.

Fourth Exercise: Why can an *0* proposition occur as a major premiss only in Fig. 3 and as a minor premiss only in Fig. 2? An *0* premiss gives rise to a negative conclusion in whi^h *P* is distributed. Consequently *P* must be distributed in its premiss, i.e. be predicate of the *0* major premiss. This rules Out Figs 2 and 4 where *P* is subject in its premiss. In Fig. I, *M* is not distributed in the major (being subject of *0)* and cannot be distributed in the minor premiss (which is affirmative and has *M* for predicate).

An *0* minor premiss also gives rise to a negative conclusion in which *P* is distributed. It involves the major premiss being affirmative. In Figs I and 3 where *P* is predicate in its premiss this means that an illicit process of the major term cannot be avoided. In the 4th Figure, *M* is undistributed in both minor premiss (which is *0* and has *M* for subject) and in the major premiss (which has to be affirmative and has M for predicate).

Fifih Exercise: Prove that an *A* proposition can be proved only in Fig. I.
None of the other figures can prove a conclusion that is both affirmative and universal. Fig. 2 proves only negative conclusions (one of the premisses must be negative to distribute *M* once). In Figs 3 and 4, *5* is predicate in its premiss. If the conclusion is universal it will have to be distributed in its premiss which must then be negative. But a negative premiss cannot give rise to an affirmative conclusion.

Sixth Exercise: Prove that if the middle term is distributed in both premisses the conclusion must be particular.
If both premisses are affirmative only two terms can be distributed in them (the terms occupying the subject positions). Actually *M* is distributed in each. Thus *S* is not distributed in its premiss. Consequently the conclusion must be particular.

If one premiss is negative an extra term is distributed but this must be *P* which is now distributed in the negative conclusion. Once again *S* is not distributed in its premiss and consequently the conclusion must be particular. No conclusion follows from two negative premisses.

VIII. IS THERE ANY REAL INFERENCE IN THE SIMPLE CATEGORICAL SYLLOGISM?

Even in Aristotle's time it was urged that a simple categorical syllogism begs the question, i.e. assumes the conclusion in the very course of the proof. The English logician, John Stuart Mill, formulated the objection very clearly: It must be granted that in every syllogism, considered as an argument to prove the conclusion, there is a *petitli principli,* When we say, *All men are mortal, Socrates is a man, therefore Socrates is moral,* it is unanswerably urged by the adversaries of the syllogistic theory, that the proposition, *Socrates is mortal,* is presupposed in the more general assumption, *All men are mortal,* that we cannot be assured of the mortality of all men, unless we are already certain of the mortality of every individual man.' *(A System of Logic,* Bk II, ch. 3, § 2)

Throughout history, logicians who are radical or extreme empiricists in their philosophy (believing that human knowledge is exclusively an organic sense knowledge) classify universal propositions as numerative. *SaP* means simply that every instance of *S* is *P:* it is either a valid shorthand expression if our experience is comprehensive or it is an excessive generalization if our experience is incomplete. In our reasoning therefore a universal proposition functions either as shorthand for complete numeration of instances or as an acceptable practical guide when our experience is extensive. In the latter case the real evidence present is not the universal proposition but such experience as we have and which has induced us to formulate the universal as a practical guide. Mill puts the point very forcibly: 'All inference is from particulars to particulars. General propositions are merely registers of such inferences already made, and short formulae for making more: The major premiss of the syllogism, consequently, is a formula of this description; and the conclusion is not an inference drawn *from* the formula, but an inference drawn *covvding to* the formula: the real logical antecedent or premiss being the particular facts from which the general proposition was collected by induction.' *(A System of Logic,* Bk II. ch. 3, § 4)

Concerning. e.g. the syllogism 'All men are mortal. Socrates is a man, therefore Socrates is mortal' it is also objected that to know the minor premiss is true, one must know that Socrates has all the attributes of man including mortality. Inevitably again (it is contended) the conclusion must be known or assumed in the course of an alleged proof.

Sir W. D. Ross summarizes Aristotle's contribution to an answering of these objections:

> Aristotle is not unaware of the objection that has been brought against the syllogism, that it involves a *peittio principii.* If I argue 'All *B* is *A,* All *C* is *B,* Therefore all *C* is *A* , it may be objected that I have no right to say All *B* is *A* unless I already know *C* (which is a *B)* to be A and that I have no right to say All *C* is *B* unless I already know *C* to be *A* (which is implied in its being B). These objections rest on erroneous assumptions. (I) The first rests on the assumption that the only way of knowing that All B is A is to examine all the instances of *B.* As against this Aristotle is aware that in dealing with certain types of subject-matter (e.g. in mathematics) a universal truth may be ascertained by the consideration of even a single instance that the generic universal is different from the enumerative. (2) The second objection rests on the assumption that, to know that All C is *B,* you must know it to have all the attributes involved in being *B.* This objection he implicitly meets by his distinction of property from essence. Among the attributes necessarily involved in being *B* he distinguishes a certain set of fundamental attributes which is necessary and sufficient to mark *B* off from everything else; and he regards its other necessary attributes as flowing from these and demonstrable from them. To know that *C* is *B* it is enough to know that it has the essential attributes of B the genus and the differentiae; it is not necessary to know that it has the properties of *B.* Thus each premise may be known independently of the

conclusion. And even both may be known without the conclusion being known. The drawing of the conclusion involves the 'conjoint contemplation' of the premises, and if they are not thus viewed in relation to one another, we may be ignorant of the conclusion, and may even believe its opposite without thereby explicitly breaking the law of contradiction. The advance from premises to conclusion is a genuine movement of thought, the explication of what was implicit, the actualising of knowledge which was only potential. *(Aristotle,* ch. II: Logic, Published by Methuen, pp. 37-8)

Thus the fundamental position of Aristotle and of all moderate empiricists is that human thinking is not simply a sense knowledge: we possess and often display a capacity for insight into what is so universally and what is so by necessity, and the most valuable universal propositions that we have mean, primarily, that *S is essentially* P the quantitative meaning, *every instance of S is P,* being subordinate. Of course where a universal proposition is purely numerative (e.g. 'All the days of last week were wet') we cannot reasonably adduce it as proof of any instance (e.g. 'Wednesday of last week was wet').

IX. SYLLOGISMS OTHER THAN THE SIMPLE CATEGORICAL TYPE

Abbreviated forms. Concrete reasoning is rarely formulated fully; perhaps indeed in argument we differ most in what we do not say. Often a syllogism is abbreviated by the omission of a premiss or of the conclusion; such an abbreviated syllogism is called an enthymemea part of it is en (in) thumos (the mind) and according as the major premiss, minor premiss or conclusion is tacit, it is said to be of the first, second or third order. An example is the statement: 'That war was long and bitter, for it was a civil War.' Fully formulated the argument is 'All civil wars are long and bitter, that war was a civil war, therefore that war was long and bitter.' This example illustrates an Interesting fact: we Often know a proposition is true (e.g. an historical fact) before we are able to discover the premisses which will prove and therefore explain it. For Aristotle one is able to explain a proposition when one can show the general principle from which it can be deduced. Thus we often construct a syllogism not to prove the conclusion is a true proposition but to show why it is true, to demonstrate or explain it.

Sometimes a reason is annexed to one or both premisses in support of it Such a premiss can be expanded into a syllogism; thus there are really two or more syllogisms telescoped into one. The abbreviated syllogism is called an *epicheirema* (so called, perhaps, in Aristotle's logic because it was a weapon in Greek debate). An example is 'Every *M* is *P* because it is *N*, every *S* is *M*, therefore every *S* is *P*.' The major premiss can be expanded into the distinct syllogism 'Every *N* is *P*, every *M* is *N*, therefore every *M* is *P*.' This is a single Epicheirema; in a Double Epicheirema a reason is annexed to both premisses.

A polysyllogism is any chain of syllogisms. It is called a Sorites (from the Greek *soros*, a heap) if the intermediate conclusions are suppressed. There are two kinds of Sorites, the Aristotelian and Goclenian (named after Rodolfus Goclenius, Professor at Marburg at the end of the sixteenth century). In the former one advances to terms of greater extension and each conclusion becomes the minor premiss of the following syllogism. An example is '*A* is *B*, *B* is *C*, *C* is *D*, *D* is'; this expands into three syllogisms; 'B is *C*, *A* is *B*, therefore *A* is *C*; *C* is D *A* is *C*, therefore *A* is *D*: *D* is *E*, *A* is *D*, therefore *A* is *E*.' The special rules for an Aristotelian Sorites are (I) only the last premiss may be negative: and (2) only the first premiss may be particular.

In a Goclenian Sorites the terms are of decreasing extension, i.e. are regressive in extension, and each conclusion becomes the major premiss of the following syllogism. An example is '*D* is *E*, *C* is *D*, *B* is *C*. *A* is *B*, therefore *A* is E'; this expands into '*D* is E, *C* is *D*, therefore *C* is *E*; *C* is *E*, *B* is *C*, therefore *B* is *E*; *B* is *E*, *A* is *B*, therefore *A* is E'. The special rules for a Goclenian Sorites are (I) only the first premiss may be negative; and (2) only the last premiss may be particular.

The modal syllogism. It includes one or more modal propositions, e.g. 'All *M* must be *P*, all *S* may be *M*, therefore all *S* may be *P*.' Here, although the major premiss affirms necessity, the conclusion follows the weaker mode of the minor premiss.

Compound syllogisms. There are as many varieties of compound syllogisms as there are varieties and combinations of compound propositions, e.g. compound categorical, conditional, alternative, disjunctive syllogisms.

Examples of *compound categorical syllogisms* are '*A* is both *b* and c, *D* is *A*, therefore *D* is both *b* and C: 'An eternal being is immortal, only God is eternal, therefore only God is immortal.' This latter syllogisms is invalid: its conclusion consists of two statements, 'God is immortal' and 'No one else is immortal'; in the latter statement *P* is distributed although it is not distributed in the major premiss.

The purely *conditional (or hypothetical) syllogism* consists exclusively of conditional propositions, e.g. 'If *A* is *B*, *C* is *D*, and if *E* is *F*, *A* is *B*, therefore if *E* is *F*. *C* is *D*.' If one of the premisses is categorical, the syllogism is called a *mixed conditional (or hypothetical) syllogism.* It has two very important valid forms:

If A is *B*, *C is D*
A is *B*
Therefore *C* is *D*

This is called the *modus ponendo ponens,* i.e. in positing the antecedent one posits, by implication, its consequence

If A is B, C is D
C is not *D*
Therefore *A* is not *B*

This is called the *modus tollendo tollens,* i.e. in denying the consequent one is committed to denying the antecedent which implies it.

The following two forms, however, are invalid, i.e. the conclusion is not really implied:

If A is *B, C* is *D*
A is not *B*

Therefore C is not *D*

The fallacy of denying the antecedent is committed here. We have not evidence that *A* being *B* is the only condition under which *C* is *D;* accordingly we are not entitled to argue that since *A* is not *B* then C is not *D;* nor would we be entitled to argue that since *C is D* then it must be a fact that *A* is B this is the fallacy of affirming the consequent:

If A is *B, C* is *D*
C is *D*

Therefore *A* is *B*

An example of the valid *alternative syllogism* is 'A is either *b* or *c, A* is not *b,* therefore *A* is *c'.* There are two valid forms of the *disjunctive syllogism:* 'A is either *b* or non-b, *A* is b, therefore *A* is not non-b' and 'A is either *b* or non-b, *A is* not *b.* therefore *A* is non-b'. The valid *conjunctive syllogism reads* 'A is not both b and *c, A* is *b,* therefore *A* is not C'.

The *dilemma* is a syllogism having as major premiss a conditional proposition and as minor premiss an alternative or disjunctive proposition. The conditional premiss must contain at least two antecedents or two consequents.

If A is B,C is D; and if E is F, G is H
But Either *A* is B or E is *F*

Therefore Either *C* is *D* or G is *H*

The antecedents are called the horns of the dilemma as they face us with a choice between unpleasant consequences. (The figure is taken from bullfighting.) The choice may be between two, three, four or many consequences, so the analysis of dilemma covers also trilemma, tetralemma, polylemma.

The rules for a valid dilemmia are:

(I) The antecedents must involve the consequences attributed to them.

(2) The disjunction in the minor premiss must be complete, i.e. there must not be a third possibility.

To escape from a dilemma one may

(a) *grasp one of the horns,* i.e. deny that an antecedent really entails the consequence attributed to it. One could perhaps grasp both horns in the following dilemma:

> If you take wine, you will gradually becomes intemperate; if you don't take wine, you will become dull and anaemic.
> But you must either take wine or not take it.
>
> ---
>
> Therefore you will either become intemperate or become dull and anaemic.

(b) *Escape through the horns,* i.e. assert that there is a further possibility which the minor premiss does not visualize. One could escape through the horns of the following:

> If you advise a person to do what he intends to do, your advice is superfluous; and if you advise him to do what he intends not to do, your advice is useless.
> But you advise a person to do either what he intends to do or what he intends not to do.
>
> ---
>
> Therefore your advice is either superfluous or useless.

Quite clearly the possibility of a person being undecided is not listed.

(c) *Rebut the dilemma get* another bull to attack it by formulating a second dilemma in which one formulates the same facts from a different (and more pleasant) point of view:

> If you go through the field you will meet the bull, and if you go down the lane you will meet the farmer.

But you must either go through the field or down the lane.

Therefore you will meet the bull or meet the farmer.

One rebuts this dilemma as follows:

If I go through the field I will not meet the farmer, and if I go down the lane I will not meet the bull.
But I must either go through the field or down the lane.

Therefore I will either not meet the farmer or not meet the bull.

X. VALIDITY AND TRUTH IN ARGUMENT

An argument is an implicative statement: it claims that the evidence it brings implies the conclusion it draws. And it claims that the evidence is factually true. Thus there are two kinds of truth claim in an argument a claim that the physical facts referred to are as they are said to be (natural truth) and a claim that the logical fact of implication is present in the argument as it is said to be by. e.g. the word, *therefore* (logical truth). Validity is really a synonym for logical truth the truth of words such as 'therefore', 'then', 'as a consequence'; The 'truth' with which it is contrasted is natural truth, not truth in its general sense of conformity to fact of any kind.

When one detects that an argument is invalid one does not thereby learn anything about the truth or falsity of the conclusion. One simply sees that there is no logical sequence or necessitation from evidence to conclusion: implication is not present as it is claimed to be, so that there is a logical falsity about the argument. But the natural facts asserted may or may not be so: some or all of the propositions in the argument may be materially true. It is a mistake, therefore, to infer that because an argument is invalid, its conclusion is a false proposition.

When an argument is seen to be valid we have this guarantee: if its premisses are true propositions, the conclusion is a true proposition also. It is a fascinating fact that we can have such a guarantee about natural truth from the logical form of the argument. i.e. from the presence of implication which is a phenomenon of meaning. When premisses are false propositions, is a valid conclusion from them false also? An example shows that since we are not dealing with facts in the evidence, the presence of implication ensures *consistency of meaning* solely the conclusion may be true: 'All Roman Emperors were Presidents of U.S.A.: Lincoln was a Roman Emperor, therefore Lincoln was a President of U.S.A. In this consistent argument the premisses are false but the conclusion states a fact.

XI. RULES OF INFERENCE

All men are mortal
But the Greeks are men

Therefore the Greeks are mortal

Here we see very easily that the conclusion is implied by the premisses. But what precisely causes the implication? We could answer that there is a principle or canon governing this argument, namely that what is stated or denied about any class in its entire extension (e.g. mankind) is also stated or denied for each member and each species of that class (e.g. the Greeks). (In Aristotelian logic this particular canon is technically called the *Dictum de Omni et Nullo.)*

The rules that govern valid argumentation, giving rise to implications, constitute a very important topic in modern logic. This topic covers every form of argument, not merely the syllogism.

XII. HOW TO ANALYSE AN ARGUMENT

(One should be concerned to observe the argument fully before passing to value judgments about its validity or the truth of the statements in it.)

I. What is the question at issue?

2. What conclusion or conclusions are drawn in the course of the argument?

3. What evidence is presented for each conclusion? Is there any assumption made? What is the nature of the reasoning?

4. With regard to each conclusion and its evidence, note the presence of any or all of the following features in the language

(a) Ambiguity in any word or phrase. If the statements are quite clear note that fact.

(b) Metaphorical words and phrases. i.e. note the presence of picturesque, colourful language.

(c) Emotive words. i.e. words that are emotionally toned.

(d) Intimidating words and phrases.

(e) Prestige words or associations.

(f) Repetition.

5. Is the reasoning for each conclusion *valid* reasoning? If there is a flaw, point it out.

6. With regard to each of the statements constituting the evidence, a further and separate question is: is it true?